Faster Than Light

Faster Than Light

THE ATARI ST AND THE 16-BIT REVOLUTION

Jamie Lendino

Steel Gear Press
Audubon, NJ

Steel Gear Press
PO Box 459
Audubon, NJ 08106

Printed and bound in the United States of America.

Edited by Matthew Murray.

Atari is a brand name owned by Atari Interactive, a subsidiary of the French publisher Atari, SA. Atari, SA doesn't sponsor, authorize, or endorse this book.

While every precaution has been taken in the preparation of this book, the publisher and author assume no responsibility for errors or omissions, or for damages resulting from the use of the information contained herein.

Library of Congress Control Number: 2019906387
ISBN: 978-1-7323552-1-7

To my wonderful wife Allison and my incredible daughter Siena

Contents

Introduction 9

1 Beginnings 15
2 Software 35
3 Mainstream 67
4 Gaming 85
5 Mega 111
6 Arcade 141
7 Studio 157
8 Enhanced 185
9 Thirty-Two 207
10 Falcon 231
11 Emulation 249
12 Mods 255
13 Collecting 267
14 Community 277
15 Forever 283

Acknowledgements 287
Bibliography 289
Notes 297
Index 307
About the Author 323

Introduction

For the first decades of its life, the computer was a room-filling monstrosity found only in dusty, dimly lit backrooms at universities, in research labs, and on military bases. You wouldn't think of stepping foot near one without a thorough knowledge of electronics and programming, or at least punch cards. But with the advent of the personal computer, that all changed. For the first time, *anyone* could buy a complete computer system, set it up on a regular desk, and run software, as tens of millions of people had discovered by the early 1980s.

But it was what happened *next* that was just as significant in revolutionizing personal computing. The Apple Macintosh, the Atari ST, and the Commodore Amiga featured GUIs you could control intuitively with a mouse, based on innovations first developed at the Stanford Research Institute and Xerox's Palo Alto Research Center (PARC). Command lines gave way to pointing devices, windows, menus, icons, check boxes, and radio buttons. The three new machines, released within 18 months of each other, also featured built-in support for mass storage and enhanced word processing and desktop publishing. In addition, they included improved graphics and sound capabilities that forever changed the trajectory of visual art, music production, and computer gaming.

The Atari ST, Atari Corporation's underdog entry in the 16-bit computer wars, was named for the platform's internal architecture: Sixteen/Thirty-Two, for its 16-bit external bus and 32-bit internal data path. The machine contained a powerful Motorola 68000 processor, and it was the first Atari computer to come with a mouse and a graphical user interface, the latter derived from Digital Research's GEM running on top of Atari's own operating system. And unlike the company's excellent 8-bit line, which used 5.25-inch floppy disks, the ST used new 3.5-inch disks, with their higher storage capacity and tidier, more rigid packaging. From music production to gaming, the ST delivered in a way no 8-bit computer could.

As much as the ST was a next-generation platform, it was also a cost-cutting move meant to save Atari. Although the ST was more powerful than the 800, as well it should have been with six years between release dates, it lacked the earlier computer's advanced coprocessors for graphics and sound production, leaving the (admittedly fast) CPU to do most of the work. The ST was similar to but not quite as powerful as the Amiga, which arrived a few months after the ST and did have hardware coprocessors. Both the ST and the Amiga came out in 1985, one year after the Macintosh, and yet neither machine featured the Macintosh's raw ease of use. It's easy to see why some dismiss the ST's influence as a result.

If the cost cutting worked to Atari's disadvantage in some areas, it also landed the ST platform in a real sweet spot in the market, with pricing that undercut both the Mac and the upcoming Amiga. Thanks to that and some shrewd design choices, the ST became a compelling platform. It delivered more advanced gaming in many genres, including simulations and role-playing games. It displayed color graphics, something the Mac couldn't do for another several years. And thanks in part to favorable exchange rates, the ST also found a serious following in business markets in parts of Europe for its computer-aided design (CAD) and desktop publishing capabilities.

Perhaps most significantly, the ST kick-started a revolution in music recording with its built-in Musical Instrument Digital Interface (MIDI) ports, a then-new innovation that let synthesizers, drum machines, and other audio gear talk to each other. MIDI is still in wide use today in recording studios around the world. The ST was the only computer to include MIDI ports. "We might all be using PCs and Macs these days," a 2008 story on the pro audio site MusicRadar wrote, "but back in the 80s, the Atari ST was the machine that every computer musician wanted to own."[1]

Why You Should Read This Book

Even with the above advantages and fervent fan bases, the ST never quite reached critical mass in mainstream popularity. We'll address that dichotomy in this book. But more importantly, we'll celebrate all of what the ST had and still has to offer. The ST was an amazing music machine, a phenomenal game system, and a do-it-all general computing platform anyone could use. There's a lot of wonderful stuff to cover.

Throughout the book, I'll also tell a little bit of my own ST story, which centered around gaming, getting online, using it as a main home computer, and ultimately setting it up as the center of my first home music studio. I owned one of the first machines, the one with the dreaded "drop" chip-seating problem (I can't wait to get to that part), and one without the OS in ROM at first. Nonetheless, moving from the 8-bit 800 to the 16-bit 520ST felt like a tremendous upgrade. I owned my 520ST from late 1985 through the year 2000, though I also got a 286 PC in 1989. In the late 1990s, I picked up a Mega 4 and a 1040ST. And, of course, I kept my two Atari 800s throughout, one of which ran a BBS for three years even as I tinkered with the 520ST on another desk. I'll never lose the sense of wonder I had for these machines and the incredible software that ran on them.

Ultimately, though, my own experience with the ST will play second fiddle to the main narrative: the history of the platform within the context of the tech industry. We'll go through its entire production run, including the TT and Falcon, until the last system rolled off of Atari's assembly line in 1993, as well as the time afterward when many ST fans (musicians and otherwise) stayed with the platform. Along the way, we'll touch on some tangential developments, such as the evolution of CRPGs, the Atari Lynx handheld, and the aforementioned rise of computer-based music recording, but always from within the "world" of the Atari ST. Finally, we'll take a close look at the thriving global community of enthusiasts that exists today, and talk about how to collect, maintain, and mod these wonderful computers to keep them humming for many more years to come.

You *Can* Go Home Again

In a world of downloadable software on Steam, iOS, Google Play, and other places in the cloud, the art of the physical box containing a new piece of software has been lost. That said, high-quality scans of just about everything that came out for the ST have been made available online. I've found it's not enough to just download a ROM or boot an old floppy disk. To get the most out of each ST program, it's worth seeking out scans of the manual, quick reference cards, maps, the box copy (front and back), and any other information about what was in the package, assuming you don't have the money for a complete-in-box version (though if you do, more power to you).

Several famous examples many 1980s computer gamers know are the titles in the Ultima series. Each came with a beautiful cloth map, often two different manuals, a reference card, and some kind of trinket related to the game. The same goes for classic Infocom text adventures; often you needed whatever clues were included in the box and documentation in order to solve the game. To this day I wish more software came with this sort of thing and miss the days when it was commonplace.

Our nostalgia for these machines, combined with their historical significance, also tends to color what's most desirable about them. Some readers may believe I should have included this or that program, for example. I wanted to strike a balance between the best software and games the ST offered and an emphasis on ST exclusives, firsts, and significant developments. A lot of people see the ST as merely a gaming platform, but there's a lot more to it—and that's the story I want to tell. A second edition sometime down the road is always a possibility, and I welcome any and all feedback for and against additional game coverage.

By the same token, there's not going to be as much wistful longing for, say, a certain spreadsheet or now-outdated CAD program that wouldn't be of much use today. I will cover the most significant productivity programs on the ST, and there were many that were excellent, given the machine's status as the first low-cost way to get a computer with a real GUI. But I won't be as exhaustive covering, say, the spreadsheet market as I will hardware, gaming, and music software developments.

In fact, it was because of the ST's nature as a computer chameleon, with its unique feature set that catered to musicians, gamers, students, programmers, and business users alike, that the platform meant different things to different people. Music fans may wish the entire book focused on recording, nostalgic gamers may care more about emulators and collecting, and so on. This is especially true with regard to different countries. For example, the ST was much more of a general business computer in Germany than it was in the US. And Sega game conversions were largely confined to Europe, thanks to the best-selling, UK-only

Power Pack (among others) that bundled many Sega games with each ST. Rest assured that in some capacity, we'll get to it all.

Conventions

In this book, you'll come across plenty of release dates. Even for such a well-covered and popular computer platform just 35 years ago, accurate release dates are difficult to come by today. Often, multiple sources, even direct from the time period, will conflict with one other. Muddying the issue was the often long period between a product's initial announcement, when the first ads and coverage appeared in magazines or on television, when the product hit store shelves, and when the first publications reviewed it (which happened sometimes before retail availability, and sometimes after). And that's to say nothing of the differences between what happened in the US and overseas. If a hard date is known, I'll list it, but if there's some uncertainty, I'll place the topic within the time frame it took place but not specify one day or another. And in the case of games, I'll put the best-known release date for the Atari ST version of the game, not the original. That's why you'll see 1987 listed for Gauntlet, instead of 1985 when Atari Games first distributed the arcade coin-op machine.

For all release dates, I cross-referenced trusted sources, such as Michael Current's "History of Tramiel Technology" FAQ, Curt Vendel's Atari Museum, and Atarimania, along with interviews, newspaper and magazine articles, and print advertisements from the period in order to come up with the narrative order. For our purposes, it usually doesn't matter if a piece of software came just before or just after, say, a new Atari ST peripheral, or an unrelated game from a different vendor. Product development cycles were too long, and tech news sources too diffuse, for there to be any real call-and-answer pattern between companies except in broad narrative arcs, especially on the same software platform. Larger, overarching competition between platforms, such as the ST, the Amiga, and the Mac, were more significant and will be discussed throughout when relevant.

As is always the case when writing about vintage computer hardware, tense is a...tense subject. People designed and released Atari ST hardware and software products in the 1980s, but they still exist now and people still use them today. Most of the time, I'll use the past tense, because I'll be talking about things that happened in the 1980s and

1990s. Toward the end of the book, I'll switch to the present tense for new hardware mods and software created long after the ST left production, because, wonderfully, that whole scene is happening now.

With that, let's turn to the birth of an incredible hardware platform, one that in many ways showed us the future of personal computing. That future would be graphical. It would require a mouse. It would feature sharp color graphics, professional document production, and support for CAD and engineering. It would revolutionize music studios around the world. It would play sophisticated video games. And it would be inexpensive enough for anyone to own. The Atari ST was all of this and more.

1 | Beginnings

Pong put Atari on the map, and the 2600 made it a household name. But by the end of 1983, Atari was in deep trouble. There were many reasons for this, including saturation of game consoles in people's homes and a glut of poorly programmed cartridges that flooded retailers. A few high-profile bombs, such as Atari's dreadful 2600 conversion of Pac-Man, helped. But the biggest contributing factor was the rise of inexpensive personal computers. Thanks to their full keyboards, sharp color graphics, and fast floppy-disk-based storage, personal computers could play more sophisticated games than consoles *and* let you type out letters, run a small business, or print birthday cards for your grandmother.

Consumers began to buy personal computers in droves. The Apple II, the Atari's own 400 and 800 line, the Commodore VIC-20, and the C64 racked up millions of sales in the US. In the UK, the diminutive ZX Spectrum led a different field of innovative computers like the BBC Micro and the Amstrad CPC. Although IBM remained focused on the business sector at first, Big Blue soon introduced the PCjr to compete in the exploding home market. Atari and Apple, meanwhile, lowered prices and freshened their lineups to compete with crushing competition from a surging Commodore.

Right around the same time, a new generation of computers was just beginning to take shape. In 1983, Apple introduced the Lisa, an obscenely expensive business machine with a mouse-controlled GUI. In October, Microsoft announced it was developing its own GUI for IBM-compatible PCs called Windows. And three months later, Apple introduced the Macintosh in an Orwellian Super Bowl commercial, casting IBM as Big Brother. The Mac was a compact 16-bit computer that booted into its own mouse-driven graphical OS. It was still pricey, but much less so than the Lisa that preceded it. Even without color graphics, it looked like the future.

As Atari circled the drain, the tech industry was evolving. The action was no longer in game consoles, such as the Atari 2600 and ColecoVision, but in personal computers, and all of the existing 8-bit machines were engaged in a price war that Commodore was winning. The time was right for a new kind of computer for the masses, one based around a 16-bit processor and a GUI, but that also came in at a price much lower than anything from IBM or Apple. The question was whether Atari, in the state it was in, could pull it off.

First Prototypes

A big part of the problem at Atari was simple hubris. Before the crash, Atari had already looked into doing a 16-bit computer system, though none of the research amounted to anything. Engineers at Atari's Sunnyvale Research Lab went as far as designing two prototypes around the 68000 CPU, the chip that would ultimately end up in the ST. The first, dubbed Sierra, utilized a new "Silver & Gold" GPU and a more powerful AMY sound chip that were together dubbed Rainbow. A diagram of a Sierra prototype case showed a desktop computer more like the Apple II than the Atari 800, albeit with two 3.5-inch disk drives in the front above the keyboard. Several prototypes of another design called Gaza were built, according to Atari historian Curt Vendel. Each utilized two MC68000 processors in tandem running CP/M-68K[1]. Sources differ on what each prototype contained, but the sum total was management decided the machines conflicted with Atari's stated purpose as an entertainment company and pulled the plug on them.

A third 68000-powered design had the most potential, although it arose in a somewhat roundabout fashion. Before the crash, Atari had already lost some star talent because of the company's indifference to a next-generation computer—notably Jay Miner, the brilliant electronics engineer behind the blockbuster 2600 game console and the 400 and 800 home computers. After their release, Miner soon became disgruntled with the mismanagement pervasive at the company. The final straw was when Miner and his coworker, another famed Atari engineer named Joe Decuir, pitched management on a 16-bit game machine. "They talked to Atari management about building a more powerful machine and Atari management nixed it," said engineer Ron Nicholson, a friend of Decuir's.[2] "They wanted to keep on milking the 800. So even though they had beat the innovator's dilemma by jumping from the [2600] to the 800, they couldn't do it twice in a row."[3] Miner said executives also didn't live up to an earlier agreement over the 2600 and 8-bit computers. "They decided not to pay the bonus they promised me and the engineers," he said. "So I quit, as did nearly all of the engineers and programmers."[4]

He wasn't out of work for long. Larry Kaplan, a former Atari colleague who cofounded the wildly successful Activision, approached Miner in 1982 about starting up a new company to make a next-generation platform. Miner, whose interest lay first and foremost in engineering, was all too happy to accept the offer. The new company, originally named Hi-Toro and later Amiga Corporation, let Miner, Decuir, and Nicholson design their dream game system. It was code-named Lorraine and also based around Motorola's 16-bit 68000 processor. Similar to its Atari forebears, Lorraine would have multiple custom graphics and sound chips that freed up the 68000 to do other work and allowed for much more powerful software to be written for the machine. Miner's earlier designs led to powerful personal computers and consoles that could play games or run other software with sophisticated graphics and sound. This latest model would be his first 16-bit hardware and his best effort yet.

The team needed to raise money to build Lorraine, though, and it wanted to do so in a way that kept the nature of the project under wraps. To this end, the new Amiga Corporation manufactured and sold a variety of joysticks and cartridges for the 2600 and ColecoVision; the team then used the proceeds to fund Lorraine development. Nonetheless, the company soon began to run out of money. Cue Atari to the (temporary) rescue: Despite its various management foibles that led to Miner and some other high-level employees leaving, the company remained interested enough in Miner's work that it contributed $500,000 to his Lorraine project. The contract ensured Atari would get first dibs on Miner's new system and sell it exclusively as a game console for one year. After that, the company could repackage the system in some way as a home computer as well. Atari dubbed the latter future machine the 1850XLD and codenamed the project

Mickey.[5] A 256KB expansion card for the system was code-named (what else?) Minnie.

Tramiel Technology

Jack Tramiel, a Holocaust survivor and later Polish-American entrepreneur, first moved to the United States when he was 18. In 1954, at age 25, he founded the Commodore Portable Typewriter Company selling typewriters and, later, calculators. Commodore lost both markets to the Japanese but later found success with its PET 2001 personal computer launched in 1977, the VIC-20 in 1981, and especially, the C64 in 1982. As a result, Commodore and Atari soon became formidable and rabid competitors for the same customers. Both remained neck-and-neck for a time, though with the one-two punch of the VIC-20 and the C64 at aggressive prices, Commodore began to pull away from Atari in 1982 and 1983. Tramiel was becoming more known more for his ruthless cost cutting and focus on the bottom line than for his role in helping to launch the computer industry.

Soon, a rift developed between Tramiel and his longtime Canadian business partner Irving Gould, Commodore's chairman since 1966.[6] Tramiel and Gould were the two largest shareholders at Commodore, but they sparred over what Tramiel's sons Leonard and Sam could do at the company.[7] With no resolution in sight, Tramiel quit Commodore in the middle of January 1984 after a boardroom showdown with Gould.

Tramiel wanted to quickly move on and build a new computer, so he soon began to meet with current and former Commodore employees from around the world. Among them was Shiraz Shivji, Commodore's director of engineering, with whom Tramiel discussed starting a new company. Shivji said many people still at Commodore were loyal to Tramiel, and they could form the core of a new team. Tramiel soon started up Tramel Technology, Ltd. (without the "i" in Tramiel, to help people pronounce it). His goal for the new firm, aside from being able to give his sons top executive positions, was to build and sell a cutting-edge 16-bit home computer that would prevent his mortal enemy, the Japanese, from beating the US.[8]

Tramiel's talent drain from Commodore began to affect that company's plans. Among the projects brewing at Commodore were the unreleased 900, also known as the Z-8000 and a planned successor to that company's PET line. The 900 was one of at least three different

16-bit computer prototypes Commodore engineers created around 1984. This one was based on the Zilog Z8000 CPU and running an OS similar to UNIX; one iteration of the machine ("rcv 2") even featured the 68000. Key engineers from the project, including Shivji, left Commodore for Tramiel's latest venture.[9]

By the end of May, Tramiel had rented out a room in an apartment complex in Sunnyvale to begin work on the machine.[10] In that apartment complex room, Shivji drew out a block diagram on a piece of paper. Before this point, the ST didn't exist. Just seven months later, after a frenzy of designing, programming, and testing, Atari would be ready to show five working prototypes off at the Winter 1985 Consumer Electronics Show.

Atari Corporation

By the first half of 1984, Atari was losing $1 million per day, mostly thanks to its poorly performing consumer division. Warner Communications, which had purchased Atari from cofounder Nolan Bushnell in 1976, was now looking for a way out. Jack Tramiel needed to get his new computer built, which meant securing a supply chain, manufacturing, and distribution.

The stars aligned. Warner's Steve Ross rang up Jack Tramiel in April 1984 and entered into talks.[11] Within two months of that first call, Tramiel made a $30 million offer to Warner, with $25 million coming from Tramiel and $5 million from Shivji and other former Commodore employees. On July 2, 1984, Tramiel officially acquired Atari's computer and console division from Warner Communications and opened Atari Corporation. Warner ended up keeping Atari's coin-op division, which Ross didn't mind. Managing it was a much easier lift than rescuing the consumer division. Tramiel and his team quickly went to work interviewing the remaining 900 (now ex-) Atari employees, and in the end only rehired a few hundred. More Commodore employees left for the newly reformed Atari, some 35 when all was said and done, spanning managers, engineers, technicians, and executives.[12] And Tramiel became the CEO of Atari Corporation—a stunning 180 from chairing Atari's fiercest competitor just six months prior.

Tramiel soon moved to trim the balance sheet. The "new" company bought out its $10 million contract with Alan Alda that had promised new television commercials through 1988. "It is the philosophy of the company to promote products, not people," James Copland, Atari's vice president of marketing, told *InfoWorld*.[13] Atari pushed ABC to sell as much of its $6 million 1984 Olympics ad buy as was possible.[14] It also canned the 600XL, shelved the new 7800 console and began consolidating its offices after the acquisition.

It wasn't until several weeks later that Leonard Tramiel discovered the existence of the $500,000 payment and the contract with Amiga, which had promised delivery of a new chip design by June 30, 1984, a deadline that came and went. Amiga execs demoed a prototype at a Chicago trade show in June. They tried to line up other suitors, fearing they wouldn't be able to meet the deadline. But Sony, HP, Philips, Apple, and Silicon Graphics all weren't interested in the Amiga because it wasn't IBM PC–compatible.[15] Steve Jobs of Apple criticized Lorraine, saying, "there was too much hardware in the machine."[16] Commodore execs, reeling from management turnover and the loss of so many key employees to Atari, were nonetheless interested and decided to just buy Amiga outright and return Jack Tramiel's money with interest.

Commodore also decided to retaliate after all of Atari's employee poaching. It sued four of its ex-employees, including Shivji, and accused Atari of stealing trade secrets. On August 13, Atari countersued for $100 million for fraud,[17] saying Commodore's purchase of Amiga violated Atari's contract with Amiga,[18] and that the chips Miner's team designed are Atari's.[19] The next day, on August 14, Commodore announced the purchase of Amiga Corporation for $24 million. After this, the company canned the 900 design.[20] Then Atari and Commodore both went ahead and kept working on their new computers while the lawyers battled it out. The two companies settled several years later, long after the release of the ST and the Amiga.

"The problem was that the Amiga was not quite ready and would need a lot of money to fully acquire," Shivji said in a 2015 interview in Imagine Publishing's *The Atari Book Second Edition*. "We decided to pass, but that put enormous pressure on our own development team. Commodore, on the other hand, did not have an internally developed 32-bit graphics oriented machine or the confidence to develop anything internally, so they ended up buying the Amiga for $25-$30 million and spent a further $20 million or so on it, releasing it a little after the launch of the ST."[21]

Despite how far along the project was, Commodore didn't officially unveil the finished Amiga 1000 until July 1985. The delay gave Atari a head start on finishing its own new machine, even if the timeline was tight. The end result of all of this was within the span of just a few years, Miner's Lorraine design, originally intended for Atari, became the Amiga. Meanwhile, the CEO of Commodore quit, purchased Atari, and released the ST. It was exactly backward from how it was all planned.

ST Architecture and Design

As Tramiel launched Atari Corporation, work continued on the new ST, and ambitions were running high. The team was considering three CPUs for its new computer—not just the 16-bit 68000 employed in earlier prototypes, but a couple of 32-bit chips as well. "We were hot on the 32016 and 32032," said Shivji, now Atari's VP of research and development and widely considered the father of the ST. "We had a bunch of meetings with National Semiconductor regarding the availability of the chip, and when it was obvious that we could not have the number of chips that we wanted and the pricing was not right, then the decision was made to go with the 68000."[22] Shivji said that they had also built their own prototype based on the 32032 and were "quite disappointed."[23]

In the end, Shivji designed the ST around the 68000 CPU, the same chip at the center of the Amiga and the original 1984 Macintosh. Motorola developed the 68000 in 1977 and introduced it in 1979, but it took a while for it to become inexpensive enough to be suitable for personal computers. The 68000 offered 16 data bits, 24 address bits with a 16MB address range, an easy-to-learn assembler syntax, 14 different kinds of addressing, and 17 32-bit–wide registers.[24] The 68000 also handled all of the graphics processing.

Not all of the ST's components would represent an upgrade. Unlike Atari's earlier computers, the ST lacked hardware sprites and scrolling. The Atari 8-bit lineup could do these tasks in hardware without soaking up CPU cycles or memory, aside from calling the routines in the first place. Although the ST's CPU and memory were a leap beyond anything found in the 8-bit realm, you'd have to tap into some of that power to scroll the viewable area or animate in-game elements. With the right programming chops, this would prove sufficient, as we'll see later.

For sound, Atari had planned to employ its new AMY chip, which first surfaced in Atari's internal Sierra prototype and appeared in the 65XEM prototype shown at the Winter 1985 Consumer Electronics

Show. Tramiel found the AMY too expensive—it was later shelved—so for the ST Atari decided to go with an off-the-shelf solution. The team settled on Yamaha's YM2149, a slight variant of the extremely popular General Instrument AY-3-8910 first developed in 1978 that found its way into arcade machines (notably five of them in Gyruss), pinball machines, the ZX Spectrum home computer, the Apple II's Mockingboard upgrade, and the Intellivision and Vectrex game consoles. The YM2149 was also similar to the Texas Instruments SN76489, the sound chip found in the ColecoVision, the Texas Instruments TI-99/4A computer, the BBC Micro, and IBM's PCjr.

The YM2149 featured three independently programmable tone generators that produced square waves. It also contained a programmable noise generator, a software-controlled analog output, a mixer for the three channels and noise, 15 logarithmically raised volume levels, programmable ADSR envelopes (for attack, delay, sustain, and release) that made it a genuine synthesizer, two bidirectional 8-bit data ports, and 16 registers.[25] The YM2149 was powerful, but it wasn't a straight upgrade from Atari's custom, ahead-of-its-time POKEY chip used in the 8-bit line. The most obvious difference was losing a voice of polyphony, from four in the 8-bit to just three on the ST. Nonetheless, the YM2149 was enough to create some surprisingly complex compositions.

In a shrewd move, Atari engineers complemented the Yamaha chip with a pair of MIDI ports. The MIDI In port let you connect a synthesizer keyboard or other electronic instrument to use as an input controller. The MIDI Out port let the ST control an external instrument, including its various channels (up to 16), the notes played, the "patch" triggered for each channel (such as for a flute or oboe), the tempo, whether a piano's sustain pedal is pressed, and more.

Including MIDI ports with the ST ended up proving a crucial, and incredibly forward-looking, decision. "Since we felt that the Yamaha chip in the ST was not as strong as we would have liked, we thought that we should put in an interface for external music access," Shivji said in a 2015 interview. "We found that we could do it rather inexpensively using a Motorola serial chip and a connector for the MIDI port. The total cost for this was 75 cents. The biggest problem was finding the space for connectors in the back. Musicians found [the ST] a great and inexpensive MIDI instrument."[26]

Numerous other chips made up the rest of the ST system. A group of four ICs, called GLU, MMU, DMA, and Shifter, helped keep the

ST's price down by each performing hundreds of overlapping functions.[27] The Generalized Logic Unit (GLU) chip handled interrupts, as well as HSYNC, VSYNC, BLANK, and DE (Display Enable) to control the monitor or sync the ST with a video camera. GLU held the system together, as its acronym suggests, by decoding the address range and working the peripheral ICs. The Shifter, the ST's graphics processor, converted data in video RAM into impulses on the computer monitor in all three graphics modes.[28] The DMA chip handled communication between the ST's memory and the hard drive port, moving information at up to 1MBps.[29] The MMU worked with Shifter to produce the video signal and addressed memory via DMA.

The rest of the ST's chips performed lesser, but still crucial, functions. The Western Digital 1772 disk controller supported single- and double-density disks as well as hard drives, and handled all read and write operations.[30] The MC68901 Multi-Function Peripheral chip controlled the parallel interface,[31] while the aforementioned MC6850 ACIA controlled the serial and MIDI interfaces.[32] Besides MIDI, each ST contained plenty of other ports for maximum expandability: RGB monitor, cartridge, parallel, serial, high-density floppy drive, joystick, and mouse (which doubled as a second joystick port).

Along with the hardware architecture, there was the design of the computer itself. Ira Velinsky, Atari's director of industrial design and another poach from Commodore, designed the ST enclosure and its peripherals. Velinsky had previously designed the slick Commodore SX-64 portable and the Plus/4 system.[33] Velinsky's enclosure design featured new industrial styling in a wedge shape, fashioned in a futuristic-looking light gray color with white keys. There would still be a separate monitor, so it wouldn't look much like the Mac, but both the monitor and the mouse would match the main system's' styling and color scheme.

The ST's hardware design, although not perfect, enabled the machine to take its owners—and Atari Corporation—into the next generation of personal computing. "The idea was an advanced computer," Shivji said, "16/32-bit, good graphics, good sound, MIDI, the whole thing—but with the latest in software technology."[34]

GEM

With the ST's internal and external hardware beginning to come together, next up was the operating system and graphical user interface.

Atari began to seriously evaluate the possibilities. First, Microsoft approached Jack Tramiel with its new Windows operating system, but it wouldn't be ready for two years, which was much too long. Atari could also develop its own OS and GUI, but the Tramiels weren't confident they had the necessary software engineering talent on board.

There was a third option. "We went down to Digital Research," said John Feagans, a software engineer and ex-Commodore employee. "GEM wasn't called 'GEM' at that time. It was called 'Crystal.' They showed it to us working on an Apple Lisa. Well, actually, it was all smoke and mirrors. There was hardly anything of use in that demo because they had devoted their entire programming effort to putting it on the IBM PC,"[35] which would soon become known as GEMDOS. The demo on the Lisa was running on top of CP/M-68K. This made it the only version of the aging CP/M OS available for the 68000 and therefore a natural fit for the ST's development. Tramiel now had to choose between GEM or Atari rolling its own OS for the ST.

"Basically [at Atari Corporation] we had a bunch of programmers we knew nothing about," Leonard Tramiel said. "We did not know—we could not know—that we had the talent in-house to design and write our own OS. With GEM we had something that was already laid out and planned based on a previously existing product," he said, referring to the PC version of GEM.[36] The GEM desktop, like the Lisa in 1983 and Macintosh in 1984, adopted many of the same graphical interface conventions developed by Alan Kay at PARC in the early 1970s.

Leonard oversaw two teams of people working on the ST's operating system. The first team was from Atari and handled the main OS. It was originally dubbed Project Jason, in a nod to the original designer Jason Loveman, and soon to be known as TOS (for The Operating System,[37] Tramiel Operating System, or Total Operating System, depending on your source). The second team handled the GUI. In September 1984, Atari sent its software engineers to Digital Research in Monterey to begin porting GEM to the 68000 for real—a genuine nightmare of a task, because the original code was in 8086 assembly for the PC. "The killer," said OS programmer Dave Staugas in 1988, "was that Digital Research would give me this 8086 code and say, 'Translate this,' and then a week later they'd say, 'Oh, there was a lot of bugs in that, here's the new one.' I never really had a spec. The latest code was the spec."[38]

Buying Time

Market analysts were beginning to wonder about the new Atari. By this point, the company had 300 employees remaining. Tramiel cut the price of its existing 64KB 800XL computer twice. First, from $239 to $179, and then on November 13, 1984, ahead of the holiday rush, again to just $119 to undercut the Commodore 64, the runaway success of a computer from Tramiel's former company and now archrival.[39] The Commodore machine was selling for $200. Although analysts believed Atari had several new home computers under development, "there [was] concern over whether Atari will continue to manufacture the computer or whether Tramiel [was] liquidating his inventory."[40]

Fortunately, that isn't what was happening. Atari was hard at work on the ST design and building a lineup of demonstration machines. Sam Tramiel told *InfoWorld* in December 1984 that although Atari designed the chips for its next-generation ST, they would be manufactured elsewhere, and that, similar to the 8-bit line, the machines themselves would be built in Japan rather than Taiwan and Ireland. He also confirmed in the same interview GEM would be part of Atari's proprietary new operating system for the ST, and Atari and Digital Research were working together "very closely."[41]

In the end, the negative press about Atari Corporation didn't matter much. The company pulled it off.

Winter 1985 CES

Miraculously, Atari had five computers ready to ship to CES right after New Year's Day. At the Winter 1985 Consumer Electronics Show the following week, the $599 520ST shocked and wowed attendees, none of whom had been expecting to see Atari back so quickly with a brand-new 16-bit computer. On the show floor, the company presented its new products underneath a new banner that read, "Atari Personal Computers" followed by an equally new slogan: "Power Without the Price."[42] The light-gray Atari 520ST, with its vibrant graphical user interface, struck a sleek and modern counterpoint to prior 8-bit machines. (The 130ST, also announced at the show at a lower $399 price with 128KB RAM, would never see retail.)

Figure 1.1: The machine that started it all, the 520ST brought a GUI, upgraded gaming, and low-cost music recording to the masses. Credit: Felix Winkelnkemper

Technology pundits had already nicknamed the rumored ST computer "Jackintosh," because it used the same 68000 processor as the Mac and had a similar graphical interface. One writer went as far as saying GEM "emulates the display and interaction capabilities of the Mac,"[43] while vastly undercutting the Mac's $1,500 price. Kept under wraps was one minor detail: On these demo machines, GEM was still running on top of CP/M-68K.[44] Atari's engineers had yet to complete the operating system.

"The industry was becoming very stagnant, everybody was trying to get fat," said Jack Tramiel. "My technique is to lower the prices of existing products. My pricing is based on cost, and I always want to be in a market with a product below $1,000."[45] That was the Tramiel way: Repackage another competitor's product—this time around, the Macintosh—into something that costs less. The $1,000 total price would include the 520ST, the monitor, and a floppy drive. The trick now would be picking up enough venture capital—Atari was said to be looking for $50 million—and sign some distribution deals, complete with up-front money and guaranteed purchases, to deliver the kind of sales volume Atari would need to hit those price points for the ST.[46]

Tramiel would also need to convince third-party software developers to write programs for a platform no one could buy yet, and no one would buy if there was no software available for it—the classic chicken-and-egg problem for any new computer. Fortunately, because the ST, Amiga, and Mac all used the same main processor, it would be at least superficially possible to port software between the three platforms, which would help grow the available libraries more quickly.[47]

Shivji was elated, as he later told *Start* magazine:

> [We] were able to show the product at CES with real chips, with real PCBs, with real monitors, with real plastic. Five months previous to that there was nothing that existed. You're talking about tooling for plastic, you're talking about getting an enormous software task done. And when we went to CES, 85 percent of the machine was done. We had windows, we had all kinds of stuff. People were looking for the VAX that was running all this stuff.[48]

The company said the ST would include TOS in ROM, which meant the machine would boot quickly and also leave all of its RAM available for software, and that the system would also include either Atari Logo or ST BASIC in ROM as well, much the same way the 800XL and 130XE included BASIC in ROM.[49] Atari wisely demonstrated the ST's MIDI capabilities at the show. To do this, company representatives hooked up one of the STs to Casio's new CZ-101 synthesizer, a compact product that quickly became iconic for its wide adoption and use in schools as well as studios.[50]

Peripherals

Not all of the peripherals Atari announced at CES made it into production, so let's start with the ones that did. First up, the most important. Unlike with the 8-bit lineup, where Atari offered regular television connectivity but inexplicably never offered a dedicated computer monitor, the company initially made two 12-inch models available for the ST: The SM124 ($199.95 at launch), in high-resolution monochrome, and the SC1224 ($399.95 at launch), in low- to medium-resolution color. Later, the ST would gain an internal RF modulator for connecting to a television set (with the "m" model designator), but that feature wasn't offered on the initial machines.

The SM124 could display 640-by-400 resolution, which was twice as much as a color Atari ST display and significantly sharper for rendering both text and geometric images. On the right side, just behind the front panel, were two dials for brightness and contrast, and a volume dial that doubled as a power switch. It contained an internal mono speaker. The SC1224 displayed RGB color at either 320-by-200 or 640-

by-200 resolution. Like the SM124, the SC1224 contained three hardware dials just behind the front panel on the right side that controlled brightness, contrast, and volume, with the volume knob doubling as a power switch. The back panel contained recessed controls for horizontal position, vertical size, vertical linearity, vertical hold, and horizontal hold. This model also contained an internal mono speaker. Ultimately, Atari would sell three different versions of the SC1224, with tubes sourced from JVC, GoldStar, and Samsung and visibly different enclosure designs between the variants.

Out of the box, and as with many computers then, the ST didn't come with built-in storage or an integrated floppy drive. The SF354 was the Atari ST's original 3.5-inch external disk drive, made for use with the Atari 520ST. It transferred data at 250Kbps per second and used single-sided, double-density disks. It operated with a distinctive "whirr" sound. Atari also announced a hard drive for the ST, although this first iteration was never released.

Atari's new printer lineup for the ST spanned three models, each of which would connect to the ST's parallel interface: the SMM804, the STC504, and the SDM124. The ST504 was to be a color thermal dot-matrix printer, similar to those from Okidata and other manufacturers, that could print at 50 characters per second. The SDM124 was shown as a letter-quality daisy wheel printer, a successor to the popular (and super-loud) 1027 on the 8-bits, that could print at 12 characters per second. Neither the ST504 nor the SDM124 were ever released. The Atari printer that did see a retail release is the SMM804, a workhorse dot matrix model rated at 80 characters per second and up to 1,280 dots per line. The printer was both Epson- and Atari 825–compatible, and as an *Antic* story in December 1986 put it, "unlike other printers, [the SMM804] didn't waste a sheet of paper while setting up to start printing at the top of the next page." Despite the January 1985 announcement, the SMM804 didn't ship until the middle of 1986.[51] It listed for $219.95 and sold for $200 at retail.

Atari also unveiled revamped 65XE and 130XE 8-bit computers, styled in a similar light-gray-and-white idiom as the ST, along with new printers, drives, a modem, and a monitor to go with the latest iteration of the popular platform. Some of those products also never saw the light of day. Such was a typical Atari launch both before and after the Tramiel acquisition. We loved the company anyway.

Reception

Overall initial reaction to the ST launch was cautious optimism. *Compute!* magazine wrote up the Winter CES in its April 1985 issue, saying "Jack Tramiel and dozens of ex-Commodorians ... unveiled six new computers, seven printers, three disk drives, and four monitors."[52] (The total counted all of the 8-bit products Atari unveiled as well.) The magazine wrote the new ST machines could "basically be understood as color Macintoshes with a choice of input devices (keyboard, joystick, or mouse) and several more features." It went on:

> For $599, the 520ST offers 512K RAM, a built-in hard disk interface (for $399 you can get an extra 15 megabyte hard disk for storage, the equivalent of about 90 Commodore 1541 disks), three screen graphics modes (640 X 400 pixels in hires), a three-voice sound generator with a MIDI interface for communication with external electronic instruments such as synthesizers, and a GEM operating system, which controls graphics features such as icons, windows, and drop-down menus.

It was hard to argue with the value proposition, and Atari had the machines on display to prove it.

All told, the Winter 1985 CES was a tremendous success for Atari, and put its new computers and its existing 8-bit lineup right back in the center of the action. The launch was widely covered in the press, including in major national and regional newspapers as well as in computer magazines. Anticipation soon began to build for the ST's eventual release. Now the problem was finishing everything in time.

Completion

Once CES was over, Atari returned to reality: It still didn't have an OS for the ST, and time was running out. Thankfully, Digital Research's GEMDOS was almost finished, so Atari had to decide quickly between sticking with CP/M-68K or moving to the new one. In hindsight, going with the new GEMDOS was the obvious, forward-looking choice, but CP/M still carried plenty of weight and had a large installed base, so the choice was trickier than it seems now. "That was an extremely difficult decision to make," Leonard Tramiel said. "CP/M-68K had been around several years; it was a well-known, well-understood, relatively well-accepted existing operating system. GEMDOS was a completely brand-new, untried, untested, incomplete operating system. However, it also offered significantly higher performance and gave the full hierarchical file system that CP/M-68K simply did not have."[53]

In February, Atari pulled the trigger on GEMDOS.[54] It's worth noting GEMDOS was modeled on the increasingly popular MS-DOS, which helped its case for the ST. As an article in *STart* magazine put it, "there is nearly a one-to-one correspondence between GEMDOS operating system calls and those of MS-DOS, and the mechanism for storing files on disk is identical—which is why ST disk drives can read IBM disks."[55] Mike Schmal, an ST system engineer, said GEMDOS gave the ST a connection to the PC world and meant programmers developing software for the machine would feel as if they're already in the same universe as on the PC. In effect, GEMDOS became the file system for TOS.

Unfortunately, the finalized OS didn't happen quite fast enough. Atari didn't have enough time to press the OS into ROM chips, so the first run of machines would have to boot the OS from a floppy disk. This was how other computers worked, including Atari's own 8-bit line as well as the Macintosh. But it postponed what would have been an early, key advantage for the ST, and also meant not all of the 512KB of memory would be available for programs.

Launch

Finishing the ST meant not just finalizing the operating system and software and tooling up manufacturing, but also getting some machines into the hands of developers early enough so software packages would be ready on launch day. In a move reminiscent of what happens with crowdfunded projects today, Atari sent the first 5,000 to 10,000 systems not to stores, but to fulfill orders from Atari user groups in the US as a thank you for their continued support. Left unstated: These enthusiasts would make a useful source of feedback for finalizing the still-buggy OS.

"We've found that [Atari] users are not only fanatics but extremely loyal and dedicated people," James L. Copland, Atari's VP of marketing, had said in a June 1985 interview with *InfoWorld*. "They deserve to have this machine first."[56] There was no word on what developers thought of Atari's initial software development kit, which included an ST computer and cost a whopping $4,500, in 1985 dollars no less.

Atari also needed to finalize its retail strategy. Convincing retailers to take on the ST was arguably Tramiel's hardest obstacle to overcome, given his reputation as a relentless cost cutter and wheeler-dealer at Commodore, and Atari's own reputation for software piracy and, well, collapse. If you look at interviews from the period, Jack Tramiel was clearly pitching the ST as a lower-cost alternative to the Mac. But mass-market retailers, including K-Mart and Toys "R" Us, passed on the machine, after being burned and stuck with excess inventory thanks to Atari's 2600 Pac-Man cartridge and other high-profile flops. Atari was left scrambling to find smaller computer retailers across the US to distribute its new computer.

In the end, Atari lined up some 500 stores for the launch—a formidable number even despite the lack of top-tier outlets.[57] There were also the inevitable delays in getting the ST to retail shelves—April and May release dates came and went, and dealers were reportedly left in the dark for weeks. Finally, it all came together. By June 1985, Atari began shipping 520ST systems to retail distributors.[58] There were two main packages available in the US: a 520ST, an STM1 mouse, an SF354 3.5-inch floppy disk drive, and a monochrome SM124 monitor cost $799, and an equivalent package with a color SC1224 monitor cost $999. The ST arrived in the UK shortly thereafter, with both the 520ST and a lower-cost, 260ST variant with half the RAM.

The Competition

Industry analysts remained cautiously optimistic about the ST's prospects after its launch. The ST's archnemesis was the Amiga, which was also getting a lot of press coverage and was often mentioned in the same breath as the ST. Both Atari and Commodore battled hard in the 8-bit era, and their histories dovetailed so closely, that it was hard to mention one machine without the other. In a nutshell, the Amiga 1000 had better graphics, hardware support for digital sampling, and the ability to run several programs simultaneously, but cost twice as much as the ST and didn't begin to hit stores until several months later.

Figure 1.2: This early, aggressive ad ran in computer magazines right around the time of the 520ST's retail launch.

A fall 1985 episode of the popular PBS show *Computer Chronicles* pitted the two machines against each other.[59] "Because of the Atari name and the image in the past, [the 520ST] is looking more towards a home game entertainment market rather than a business crossover," Tim Bajarin, VP of microcomputer research at Creative Strategies, said, "whereas though Commodore has had a strong background in the same area, the Amiga…has the possibility of crossing over [to the small business market] we're just beginning to see emerge." In comparison with the PC and Mac markets, though, Bajarin went on to say that software dealers had a "wait-and-see attitude, that [while] both machines had potential, they are looking at [Atari and Commodore]'s financial positions which had been somewhat rocky over the past year, and they're waiting to see what will happen after the first of the year."

Both Apple and IBM were more trusted on the high end. The Macintosh, with its compact form factor and built-in monochrome monitor, was compelling, and it had a head start on a software library. But a color business model, the Macintosh II, wouldn't arrive until 1987. Although the Mac II had more CPU horsepower and graphics resolution than the ST, it cost thousands of dollars extra and still couldn't game as well. The DOS-based PC, well into its run with the more powerful and more expensive Intel 80286 processor in the AT, also cost several thousand dollars and often lacked a color graphics card. It definitely lacked sound, having nothing but the PC speaker to rely on. The PCjr was already failing. Microsoft Windows also arrived in 1985, but it was a crippled program out of the gate that couldn't display overlapped windows in the UI, and it ate too much memory to run most existing DOS software on top of it.

In retrospect, Apple's IIGS, which launched in September 1986, should have been a tough competitor. The IIGS even started at the same $999 as the 1040ST did, albeit without a color monitor and disk drive—by the time you added those, you were once again approaching the cost of a Macintosh. The IIGS was based around a slower 2.8MHz MOS 65C816 processor and came with 256KB of memory instead of the 1040ST's 1MB. The IIGS offered similar 640-by-200 and 320-by-200 color graphics modes. But it beat the ST in internal expandability, with its seven card slots. Its Ensoniq sound chip, with eight stereo audio channels and wavetable synthesis, ran rings around the Yamaha chip in the ST. And although the IIGS never built up as impressive a software library as the ST did, crucially, you could also run regular Apple II software on it. The ST couldn't run programs written for the Atari 8-bit lineup. In the end, though, the IIGS cost too much and couldn't match the ST's speed and gaming prowess. Inexplicably, later on, Apple even *raised* the IIGS's price, further dooming the machine's ability to capture market share.

To further complicate the situation, 8-bit home computers were still selling well on the extreme low end. These machines included the Commodore 64 at the top, the refreshed Atari 65XE and 130XE (now matching the new ST in design) supplanting the XL line, and Tandy's newer Color Computer all providing strong, if dated, competition for consumer dollars. In practical terms, none of these machines offered more than 128KB of memory, an 80-column display, or a mouse-driven graphical interface, at least without thinly supported add-in cards or external hardware. Commodore unveiled GEOS for the Commodore 64, which did make the machine look more like a Mac despite the machine's "limited computing power," with one popular computer column in the *Washington Post* noting, "Commodore needs all the help it can get to rekindle interest in its older machine" while the Amiga remained unavailable at retail.[60]

In the end, no other computer would ever gain the ability to boot the OS from ROM (which the ST couldn't do at launch, but would soon be able to do). None had built-in MIDI ports. And most important, none had a color GUI for such a low price. There was no software available yet—ST computers came with two programming languages and not much else—but that would soon change.

Some computer enthusiasts around for the ST's time in the spotlight will forever debate the merits of Atari Corporation's approach versus Jay Miner's with the Amiga. Thanks to a few key exchanges between just a few key eccentric players at the beginning, most notably Miner, Warner and Atari management, and Jack Tramiel, it set in motion a series of events that resulted in the machines we know today.

"The teamwork [on the ST project] was outstanding," Shivji said in a recent interview. "Even today, most of the members of the team look very fondly at that time as the best years of their lives. The total hardware development was done in the space of five months. I have not seen such an accelerated development for such a complex product in that amount of time."[61] Tramiel, for his part, added one other feature to the machine in addition to his ruthless attention to power and cost: He ensured the ST's ROM set included the Hebrew alphabet, in a nod to his Jewish heritage.[62]

When all was said and done, no other personal computer offered the 520ST's brilliant combination of sheer power, graphics and music prowess, ease of use, and overall value at launch, just as Atari's new "Power Without the Price" slogan had promised. Only one year had passed since Jack Tramiel bought Atari's consumer division, and it was just a bit longer since Shiraz Shivji scribbled that first block diagram on a piece of paper.

2 | Software

Using an Atari ST in 1985 for the first time was like standing on the edge of a new frontier. If you were already familiar with an older computer, as I was with the Atari 800, the ST seemed even more radical. Here's how the manual, specifically the 1985 version for the 520ST in America, introduced the computer:

> The Atari 520ST System combines advanced technology and graphic sensibility in an easy-to-understand and simple-to-use working environment. No more obscure commands to memorize and no more complicated procedures to follow. Computer operations are represented by icons on the screen—you simply choose what you want, point to the icon, and click!

The manual went on to sing the praises of the 520ST's 524,000 bytes of Random Access Memory (capitalization Atari's), and explained that it had the "capacity for the most complex word processing tasks or the most detailed spreadsheet procedures." Educational software programs took on "new potential when they are written to take advantage of the graphics and speed of the ST Computer." Not a word about games, though there was a passing mention to "even [connect] a music synthesizer," the two categories of software the ST became most famous for.

> When you use your ST Computer, you are interacting with the entire computer system. Your input goes through the keyboard and the mouse; the computer's output comes through the

monitor and disk drive; computation occurs inside the key-board unit, and information is stored on disks…The ST Computer is the center of the ST System. Attaching peripheral devices (like disk drives, monitors, and printers) lets your computer perform a variety of functions.

I love the simplicity of this. Granted, this idea is what made all personal computers so appealing back then: You were in control of the machine. Here's how you gave it input, and here's how it generated output. When the concept was presented in this fashion, it made you feel as if you can do anything with the computer. In 1985, it was still true, even if programming on the ST was a bit more complicated than on an 8-bit model with a text-based OS.

Before we get to what it was like to use the ST for the first time, let's look in more detail at how the computer was designed. The front panel held a 94-key keyboard with sculpted white keys, broken up into four main sections: the QWERTY section, a cluster of cursor keys, a numeric pad, and a row of slanted function keys across the top. The separate cursor key panel and numeric keypad approximated the standard PC layout and instantly separated this computer from Atari's 8-bit lineup. One noticeable omission: the Atari 800's "Fuji" key, which toggled inverse video mode, was nowhere to be found.

Around back, on the left side, you'd find a small, protruding Reset button; a power switch and AC input; and a pair of MIDI In and MIDI Out ports. On the right half of the back panel, there was a monitor input, a standard Centronics printer port, a standard RS-232C modem port (no more separate 850 interface!), and a round, proprietary floppy drive connector that supported two drives. There was also an ASCI hard drive interface, an Atari-specific iteration of the then-popular SCSI standard that transferred data at up to 10Mbps, or as the manual put it, "enough to fill the entire Random Access Memory (RAM) of the ST Computer in a fraction of a second." Hey, that was big stuff!

As with the Atari 8-bit line, the 520ST required an external power supply, though this would be remedied in later iterations of the platform. The left side of the computer had a cartridge slot. As with 8-bit computers and game consoles that came before the ST, cartridges contained ROM, booted instantly, and in the ST's case, supported up to 128KB. Most ST users never needed the cartridge port, unlike with the 8-bit lineup. But there were certain specific instances where it was required, such as plugging in security dongles for certain software packages and connecting external hardware for Macintosh emulation, among other niche applications.

Aside from the ST's appearance, the biggest immediate change from the 8-bit line was the sound and the feel of just using it. The ST produced different noises, such as the deep whirr of the SF354 external floppy drive and the click sound of the ST keyboard through the monitor speaker. Few praised the mushy feel of the keys, but to me, even that was an exciting change. Moving the mouse and clicking the two buttons was a huge change compared with entering command-line syntax. Even something as simple as double-clicking on a floppy drive icon and opening a window to see its contents was a novel experience.

The ST was one of the first personal computers to make use of new 3.5-inch floppy disks. These stored as much data on a single side (360KB) as a double-sided, double-density 5.25-inch disk. A 3.5-inch floppy disk was smaller but sturdier than the older kind—much more resistant to bending—and came with a metal, spring-loaded cover for the magnetic portion. Once you removed the disk from the drive, the cover would slide back over to protect it. It was an improvement over 5.25-inch disks on all fronts and would be the right kind of flexible storage to carry the ST platform forward.

TOS

By now everyone is familiar with typical graphical UI conventions in Windows or macOS. I'm sure I don't have to explain what a window or a trash can is. But it's worth a quick look at how the ST's interface was set up because it was one of the first to arrive. To many computer users in 1985, the GEM desktop was a breath of fresh air—or possibly a step backward, if you remained smitten and happy with the aforementioned command-line interfaces. (Some of the back-and-forth still persists today.) Nonetheless, it was the GUI revolution that helped propel computers into the mainstream over the next few decades.

Earlier personal computers were based on text. For example, with Atari's older 8-bit computers, you usually booted into either BASIC, which was built into the later machines; DOS, which could be set to autoload from a disk (via DUP.SYS) and presented a menu of file operations; or a cartridge or disk that took you to a program you wanted to run once it loaded. There were also some lesser-used modes such as

Atari Computer Memo Pad on the 400/800 and the XL and XE Self-Test mode. PCs running MS-DOS booted to a command line, or if there was an AUTOEXEC.BAT file on the boot drive, it would execute a series of DOS commands in that batch file first. With the ST, the process was completely different. The OS booted into the desktop, which was mostly blank save for three icons on the left and a menu bar across the top. Two icons were for the floppy drives (A and B) and the third was the Trash. You moved the mouse, which controlled the on-screen arrow-shaped cursor, to select those or to choose an item on one of the drop-down menus. For the ST, it was Desk, File, View, and Options, each of which offered commonly used commands, such as for sorting the list of files that were showing in a window by name or type, or for setting the current screen resolution.

Many of the conventions in GEM would still look familiar today. The interface operated around the concept of windows and icons, which represented objects you'd typically find in an office environment, such as pieces of paper (files) and folders (directories). File cabinet icons represented disk drives, while a trash can offered a place for deleting unneeded files. Other elements included dialog boxes, buttons, and drop-down menus. Windows had horizontal and vertical scroll bars, and they disappeared (or became solid) if the window was large enough to contain all of the items in that storage location. You could click, hold, and drag items around, or draw a box around multiple items to affect all of them at once. Copying items from one window to another—say, to back up a letter you wrote or some programming code—was easily accomplished by clicking and dragging. You could close windows, resize them, or expand them to the full size of the desktop using icons in the corners.

Several file types on the ST indicated executable programs, including PRG, APP, and TOS (the last of which didn't need to run in GEM). Sometimes software came on a disk inside a folder named AUTO. That meant the disk would automatically boot, bypass GEM, and load its contents when you first power up the machine.

Atari had originally designed TOS to be built into the ST's ROM chips, but they didn't finish the OS in time for the first machines to ship this way. As a result, the first batch of STs out of the factory required you load TOS from disk to boot into the computer. I had one of these models myself; my trusty (and now long-departed) 520ST booted via floppy disk. It displayed a cycling series of rainbow colors during the boot sequence, and let you familiarize yourself with the mouse by moving the "bee" cursor around the desktop.

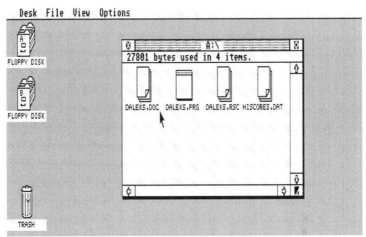

Figure 2.1: The 520ST's TOS desktop brought what was then a cutting-edge, mouse-driven graphical interface to a computer that cost less than $1,000 for the first time.

ST users quickly became familiar with error codes. At first, they were depicted by a varying number of mushroom cloud explosion icons, which I remember thinking were pretty intense. These were soon replaced with the now-familiar bomb-with-a-fuse icon, beginning with TOS 1.00 in ROM (instead of RAM). Often, the reason for the error laid somewhere with the software you were running, but occasionally it was hardware related. With early 520STs there was what came to be known as the dreaded "drop" trick. This is what you did when the machine began to freeze up unexpectedly; at some point, it might never boot at all anymore. It happened to me on a semi-regular basis. To resolve the problem, you had to lift the back of the chassis off of the desk by a couple of inches, and then let it drop back down. The resulting slam would help reseat the chips on the motherboard. Sure enough, the machine would boot up again. The thought of doing this to an Alienware PC or an iPhone today would give me a heart attack.

You could also customize GEM by adding desk accessories. These small programs, commonly denoted with the ACC filename extension, let you add capabilities to TOS that didn't come with the system, such as calculators, notepads, and measurement converters. On early 520ST systems that loaded TOS from disk into RAM, if you also installed several desk accessories on top, you could encounter memory issues when you tried to run actual programs. The easy way around this was to rename a desk accessory file by changing the ACC extension to something else so it didn't load on startup.

There were some key differences between GEM and the Mac worth pointing out. Macs used 32-character filenames, and they could contain upper- and lowercase characters and even spaces, while ST files were restricted to the IBM DOS 8.3 standard in all caps. Scrollbar behavior within windows was a little more limited and felt stiff. Subfolders opened in the same window, rather than separately; you could make a new window to have two open at once, but it was an extra step. Clicking the Close box didn't close the window if you had navigated to subfolders. Instead, it took you one level up. Finally, TOS did not support multitasking, at least until the very end of the ST's time on the market; the Mac had support for cooperative multitasking, which let you run several programs at the same time.

Little of this mattered to ST owners. The ST delivered most crucial aspects of the Mac—especially with the SM124 monochrome monitor, which offered 640-by-400 resolution and compared favorably with the 512-by-384 desktop the Macintosh delivered on its 9-inch black-and-white screen. There were hundreds of little details about how a graphical user interface operates we now take for granted, but that were all new then.

Although the GEM desktop was fun to mess around with, you really couldn't do anything productive with just the ST and its built-in operating system. You also needed extra software, the same as with earlier 8-bit computers. ST owners would soon have plenty to sink their teeth into, but at the beginning of the platform's time on the market, they had just the two choices that came bundled with the computer.

Atari Logo (Atari, 1985)

If you were going to program the ST to create professional-level applications, you would have probably used a compiled language such as C. Atari included a C compiler (Alcyon C, from Digital Research)[1] with its software development kits for the ST platform, and soon you would be able to buy C compilers at retail.[2] GEM itself was coded in C. Programming in C meant easy-to-read code, and thanks to the compilation step, your program ran much more quickly as machine language only the computer understood.

If you just bought the ST and wanted to learn programming for fun, though, there was no sense diving in that deep. Logo was perfect for this. The education-focused Logo was an interpreted language. That meant you entered a list of commands and, when you were done, you "ran" the program. The program then executed each instruction, interpreting it into machine language the computer could understand on the fly. This left out the compilation step, which made debugging much faster, but also meant slower performance as the code was interpreted in real time.

If you were like me, you probably thought Logo had a lot to do with turtles and didn't know much else about it. But it did have some power. The language supported lists and variables, and was simple enough to learn that you could get started with just three commands.[3] The turtle was a virtual stand-in for a robotic device used back in the early days of mainframe programming. In Logo, you could use turtles to draw, make charts, or solve geometry problems, among other things. And thanks to Logo's simple error messages, it was easy to figure out where your code went wrong. I had played with Logo on the Atari 800, but it was nice to give it another go with a GUI and multiple windows. A GUI, however rudimentary, made for a nicer programming environment. You could code in one window, see the results of your program's execution in a second window, and debug the code in a third.

Today, the Atari ST version of Logo is largely forgotten. There are better ways to program the ST, of course, and if you're looking for an education-focused language to get started with on today's computers, there are now much better options, such as Scratch, Kodu, and maybe Python for 8-year-olds and up. Back then, most ST owners weren't all that excited to program in Logo, and left this disk in the box or just fiddled with it a bit before moving on to ST BASIC, C, or assembly language programming.

ST BASIC (Atari, 1985)

BASIC was still where most of the 'beginning programming" action was, so it was natural many ST users (myself included) started here. No personal computer from the 1980s felt complete without a copy of interpreted BASIC for typing in or creating your own programs, so this was an obvious shoo-in. ST BASIC, which arrived on the ST in

October 1985, was essentially a new version of Digital Research's DR-BASIC, albeit optimized for the ST's GEM-based OS.

As with other BASICs, ST BASIC supported all of the usual command groups, including variables, strings, IF/THEN statements, GOTO and GOSUB branches, and the ability to PEEK and POKE memory locations. ST BASIC went further in that it let you access the GEM desktop and virtual device interface (VDI), and it offered some compatibility with the GWBASIC found on PC-compatibles.[4] ST BASIC featured a multiwindow interface for entering code, listing it, monitoring output, and debugging, which was a nice upgrade from the full-screen UI on Atari 8-bit BASIC, on paper at least. But in practice, it was clumsy. You had to use the mouse to switch between windows, and worse, the program decided for itself which of the four windows to make visible on screen based on what it thought you were doing. You could get around this in various ways, but it wasn't intuitive.

Although ST BASIC helped owners like me get started, it proved slow and riddled with bugs the more you dove into it. It had serious trouble performing floating point calculations and didn't let you do simple things such as choose the color palette for your program or play all three voices on the sound chip without complex workarounds.[5]

Remember this was back when many people buying a computer expected to either do some programming on their own, or at the least, type in some listings printed in computer magazines. That would fall out of favor, but it was still very much a part of personal computing in 1985. More advanced users quickly moved on from the bundled ST BASIC.

Books and Magazines

The excitement around the ST among computer enthusiasts was palpable from the beginning. Atari put out a modicum of television and print ads showcasing the ST, but newspaper and magazine articles were still the primary way to find out about the new computer—and, once it was released, the way you'd learn which new peripherals and software were worth buying and how to get the most out of the machine.

The top two Atari computer magazines by 1985, *Antic: The Atari Resource* and *ANALOG Computing*, both began to cover the ST from the moment they were announced to the public at the Winter 1985 Consumer Electronics Show. By the end of 1985, both magazines would run separate ST sections with articles and program listings specifically targeted at Atari's new 16-bit machine. Other, more generally focused computer magazines, such as *InfoWorld* and *Compute!*, as well as major newspapers such as the *New York Times* and the *Washington Post*, covered the ST announcement and launch with more of a broader brush—and set against the competitive landscape of the time, with Commodore and Tandy on the low end and Apple and IBM on the high end and business side.

For those who wanted more in-depth info than they could get from any of these sources, Abacus was first out of the gate with a library of ST explainer and programming books. This lineup, heavily advertised in the aforementioned magazines, gave ST owners an instant close look at the insides of the machine's hardware and software that went far beyond anything Atari provided in its own documentation. Revised editions corrected some mistakes, but these books were invaluable tools along with the monthly magazines mentioned above.

Books from other publishers soon followed, including one by Thomas P. Skinner called *Assembly Language Programming for the 68000 Family*, and First Publishing's *The Anatomy of the Atari ST* and *The First Atari ST Book* (but was it really?). *STart's* Special Issue Number One (published late 1987) had a story in it called "The well-stocked ST library—what should be on your shelves" that covered 18 books, some ST-specific and some for more general programming, plus a nod to *Gödel, Escher, Bach: An Eternal Golden Braid*, which every nerd had on their bookshelves in the 1980s regardless of whether they read it. The story also had a sidebar covering the 12 Abacus books that had been published to date for the ST. More would soon follow.

ST Writer (Atari, 1985)

ST Writer began life essentially as a straight 16-bit port of the 8-bit AtariWriter cartridge, right down to its visible carriage returns and complete lack of mouse and window support. ST Writer was meant to be a stopgap solution until Digital Research finished GEM Write, a homegrown word processor that…never materialized. Digital Research and Atari blamed each other, with DR saying part of the problem was Atari's last-minute switch to providing TOS on disk instead of in ROM chips as originally promised, which reduced the available memory on the machine.[6]

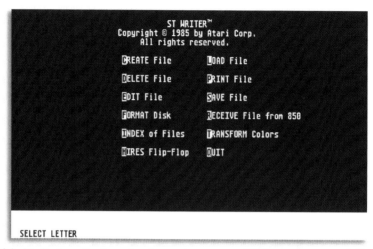

ST WRITER™
Copyright © 1985 by Atari Corp.
All rights reserved.

CREATE File   LOAD File

DELETE File   PRINT File

EDIT File   SAVE File

FORMAT Disk   RECEIVE File from 850

INDEX of Files   TRANSFORM Colors

HIRES Flip-Flop   QUIT

SELECT LETTER

Figure 2.2: Atari's free afterthought of a word processor, ST Writer was essentially an 80-column version of AtariWriter and made zero use of the ST's GEM desktop (at least at first).

Two people were key in bringing ST Writer to life. Programmer Dan Oliver ported the AtariWriter editing code to the ST in assembly, while John Feagans adapted the formatting portion in C. "I decided to write this after reading a review of the ST that said 'it doesn't even have a word processor,'" Dan Oliver said in a 2015 comment on Atarimania. "John Feagans wrote all the code for sending to the printer." The whole project was wrapped up in two weeks, and ST Writer ended up being all the word processor many (if not most) ST owners needed. And because it was free, it was even more compelling than it was on the Atari 8-bit computer line.

ST Writer greeted AtariWriter users with a familiar menu screen. It was here you created, deleted, and edited files, as well as re-saved them or even formatted a disk if you needed to. An option to "receive file from 850" let you transmit an AtariWriter file from your Atari 800 (via the 850 interface). You could also Transform the colors between white text on a black background or black text on a white background. In edit mode, the program's interface was mostly blank space for you to write in, with a strip along the bottom that contained a ruler, how much free memory remained, and the line and column of the cursor's current position. Pressing Esc brought you back to the main menu screen.

ST Writer included most of what you needed to create documents and write just about anything, with the exception of font choices. You could create headers and footers, justify text, create double columns, and find and replace text, just as with AtariWriter on the Atari 800. I liked ST Writer immediately when I downloaded it for my 520ST because of the 80-column support and because of the white-text-on-black-screen option. Today's Macs, PCs, iPhones, and Android phones are all getting various iterations of what's now called Dark Mode, because it's easier on the eyes and also looks cool. The ST had that in 1985.

An interesting story is that ST Writer may have died a quick death were it not for the efforts of one enthusiast. Atari ported its AtariWriter code to the ST and promptly forgot about it. The company wanted to move onto other paid products that could bring in revenue. According to a story in the Winter 1986 issue of *STart*, Dr. Bruce Noonan "wrangled" the source code from Atari and then spent the next year fixing bugs and adding features.[7] And there were many; according to the story, double-column printing didn't work right with double-spaced text, and headers and footers were janky, among other issues.

Thanks to Dr. Noonan's continued efforts, ST Writer was quickly improved. Many ST owners used ST Writer the entire time they owned the machine. *STart* magazine also included it on the floppy disk packaged with many of its issues. For a more comprehensive look at ST Writer, I recommend InverseATASCII's S2E41 episode of his 1632 ATARI podcaST, which focuses exclusively on the program.

1st **Word** (GST Holdings, 1985)

Even though I was an avid ST Writer fan on the ST, I did see the benefits of GUIs for word processing early on (it was hard to miss, honestly). Back in the late 1980s, our high school lab was stocked with then-new Macintosh SE machines. Even though I used ST Writer all the time at home, my favorite word processor to use on these lab computers was MacWrite. I loved the simple GUI and the ability to choose what fonts and styles I wanted, and to then see them on the page as they would print out on paper. I honestly don't remember if there were other word processors installed on the 20MB hard drives.

Although ST Writer didn't have a GUI, ST owners did get their free graphical word processor—it just took a few extra months. Atari acquired 1st Word from GST Holdings in December 1985 and soon began bundling the program with every complete 520ST system.[8] This word processor gave ST owners what was likely their first taste of writing in a graphical user interface, complete with drop-down menus, multiple windows, and what-you-see-is-what-you-get (WYSIWYG) editing of your document.

The last point, combined with the ST's 80-column display, meant you could preview how your document would look on a standard piece of paper without having to use your imagination, and without having to waste paper printing test copies and then making improvements. 1st Word displayed bold, italic, and underlined text on screen, without ugly formatting codes, and could accurately show whether the text was centered or justified. You could also move, resize, scroll, or zoom in and out of windows, and have up to four documents open at once. A built-in help function meant you didn't need to consult the printed manual all the time.

The program still lacked some key features we've since grown accustomed to—namely, the ability to see changes to your existing text without having to force a refresh of the visible formatting. (This meant 1st Word was really WYSIWYGAPAB, for what-you-see-is-what-you-get-after-pushing-a-button.) There were also no visible rulers or margins, although what was shown was enough that you still didn't have to "preview" your document before printing in most cases, as a June 1986 review in *Antic* pointed out. Most importantly, 1st Word still didn't support multiple fonts, unlike Macintosh word processors, and there were some visible bugs in the launch version, such as underlined text disappearing as you started typing on the next line. The *Antic* review even mentioned a search-and-replace bug that let you type past the end of the line in the dialog box right onto your actual text (although the program didn't crash). It also didn't support variable spacing or variable pitch text, both of which ST Writer supported.[9]

The ST should have come with some kind of GUI-based word processor right at launch. And 1st Word, already months late, was missing some crucial features. Nonetheless, it did the job nicely, and it also came with an ASCII text mode that proved especially useful for programmers.

NEOchrome (Atari, 1985)

Earlier computers had their share of paint programs, which let you "paint" on the screen using the joystick, or with a pad such as the Atari Touch Tablet or the KoalaPad. But the mouse-driven NEOchrome marked the beginning of a new era. Here was a program that let you easily choose icon-based paint tools and colors by clicking on them, and then create art in an intuitive fashion. Even the ST's "low-resolution" 320-by-200 mode was equivalent to the highest offered on the Atari 800 (320 by 192), and on the ST you could put any 16 colors on the screen from a palette of 512.

Programmed by Dave Staugas (who also worked on the ST's operating system) and Jim Eisenstein, NEOchrome also included a special color-cycling mode that delivered a sort of pseudo-animation look. The famous Atari ST "waterfall" picture that appeared in magazines everywhere was thanks to NEOchrome and this effect. Although Mac-Paint on the Mac was first, NEOchrome was many people's first foray into drawing on a computer with a mouse. It was even nicknamed "JackPaint" in a reference the Mac. Various beta versions of the program (v0.5) began dropping in October 1985, and Atari released a 1.0 version in September 1986 that remained freely available. It was also available for download on CompuServe.

NEOchrome included a lot of what we now expect to find in any paint program, such as a pencil, an eraser, a paint brush, a spray can, and a paint bucket, along with tools for creating shapes and inputting text. By the time the program hit v1.0, it included 40 different brush and spray patterns, five text styles, six text sizes, and two character sets. The v1.0 version also featured the Jack Knife, a freeform tool that let you cut out something in order to delete it or move it somewhere else. You could choose colors using an on-screen map of all 512 in the ST's palette (with 208 showing at any one time, you could scroll to see the rest). NEOchrome also included a wipe-screen effect to transition from one picture to another in a slideshow.

In an interview in the spring 1987 issue of *Atari Explorer*, Staugas said they wrote NEOchrome because they needed a tool to create the ST's boot screen, and also one to enhance some images created on the Atari 800 to take advantage of the ST's graphics prowess. "Neo started off as a primitive pencil to change individual pixels on the screen, with a zoom window to show the image close up—a 'fatbits' window. At the time, I called the program 'Fat' in honor of the fatbits." Eisenstein added, "[When] we found out that the file table on an ST disk was also called a FAT (File Allocation Table), we needed a new name." (Mac-Paint had a FatBits window a year earlier, but we'll let it slide.)

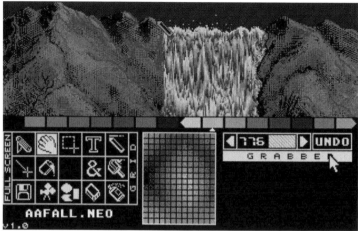

Figure 2.3: The ST's first (and free) paint program, NEOchrome quickly became iconic thanks to its appearance in pervasive early ST advertising.

In explaining the interface design, Staugas said, "It was basically the trick with the horizontal interrupts and the magnify window that is always on. Because the program is based around the magnify window, you need to have a certain amount of space in which to put it." Eisenstein said they used NEOchrome to debug the graphic parts of the operating system, and that it helped set the stage for the blitter chip (more on this later), because they could test right away what wasn't working correctly.

NEOchrome didn't support mono monitors or even medium resolution in color—it was strictly 320-by-200-by-16. The program was fast and easy to use on any ST, and thanks to its slideshow viewer, you could see all of your creations in order—something we take for granted today, but was completely new then.

DB Master One (Stoneware, 1985)

DB Master One, provided free to ST owners, was an excellent entry-level, non-relational database for typical organizing tasks. As Abacus's *Presenting the Atari ST* explained, a database could be thought of as a file cabinet where you place records. The difference between a file cabinet and a database program is you could access the program's data quickly, and you could choose new sorting methods and execute them in a flash.[10] "I assumed that since Atari was giving it away with each complete 520ST system purchased before Christmas, it couldn't be worth selling," Christopher Chabris wrote in a June 1986 review in *Antic*. "I was wrong. DB Master One is an excellent GEM-based program that should be able to handle most users' file-management needs."

DB Master One consisted of two separate programs: MakeOne and UseOne. MakeOne displayed an empty window; here, you could place fields and labels using the mouse. You could also use MakeOne to edit existing forms. UseOne is where you used the database you created; it let you add, delete, and edit records. A nifty Splat menu came with predefined layouts for things such as checkbooks and mailing lists. You could add record after record, and then print the results or save them to disk. Although DB Master One was free, Stoneware charged $25 for 30 minutes of support and included an order form for it in the package.

The program supported files up to 320KB in size, 100 fields per form, fields up to 3,000 characters in size, and up to 3,000 bytes per record. Chabris noted the program kept the entire database in memory, which was something the 512KB ST enabled you to do. You would have had a much tougher time of this with the 64KB and 128KB home computers common in 1985. All told, DB Master One was a useful freebie for Atari to provide with new ST computers. In 2018, B&C ComputerVisions was still selling shrink-wrapped boxed copies of DB Master One on eBay, thanks to its seemingly endless long tail of old Atari stock. B&C owner Bruce Caruso wrote on the eBay entry, "Note: I doubt there is support at this time." I have a feeling he's right.

Sometimes this program was bundled with a free game on the same disk called Megaroids. Let's take a look at that next.

Megaroids (Megamax, 1985)

As a showcase for Megamax's upcoming new C compiler, the company released Megaroids, a polished Asteroids clone that used the keyboard for controls. You could rotate your ship, thrust, fire, and enter hyperspace, as well as pause the game with the Escape key. The medium-resolution, four-color interlaced (640-by-400) graphics looked sharp, with shaded green asteroids and a white fighter ship, and the game looked even better in monochrome high-resolution mode (noninterlaced at 640-by-400).[11] Animation was super-smooth throughout; the enemy alien ships even had a rotating band of thrusters that the arcade game lacked, and the asteroids themselves contained significant shading to make up for the lack of vector graphics. The physics and sound effects were spot-on as well. The game was another welcome freebie with every new ST computer beginning with the 1985 holiday season. If you were like many early customers, Megaroids may well have been the first video game you played on the ST.

Going Online

One of the biggest perks of owning a home computer in the 1980s was connecting to the outside world. These connections came in the form of both paid services such as CompuServe and GEnie, and in the spirit of community hobbyists everywhere, free bulletin board systems (BBSes) that let like-minded Atari ST fans leave messages for each other, download new software, and otherwise tap into the latest news and gossip for their favorite platform.

To get online, of course, you needed a modem. These devices predated the ST, and Atari sold some of its own models, so there was no initial need to buy something special such as the 850 interface just for the company's new 16-bit computer. You simply had it to plug one into the ST's RS-232C modem port and install some terminal software such as the VT52 emulator, which Atari made available for free shortly after the ST's release. Some users marveled at how a complete ST system could serve as a VT52 terminal for less than the cost of a dedicated piece of hardware.

This is going to sound lame, but one of the biggest changes for me in moving to the ST was I could finally read online BBSes in 80 columns. It wasn't just about AtariWriter. I never bought an 80-column board for my 8-bit machines, so I had always called BBSes and even ran my own in 40-column ATASCII mode. The ST didn't support ATASCII mode, but it did support the wider print-like 80-column format. Nonetheless, it was fun to go online, talk to other users in message bases, find out which desk accessories and disk utilities were worth using, and download freely available software.

You could also compress files the way you can today, and in fact it was much more necessary then because of how expensive storage was. But you needed to find and install a program first. ST users favored the ARC file format. You couldn't get far, especially online, without some way to "un-ARC" downloaded programs.

I remember being so proud of my 13-year-old self for starting a big conversation in one ST message base about the horrible Chernobyl nuclear accident in 1986. I'll never remember *which* BBS the message base was hosted on, aside from that it was in Brooklyn or Manhattan and therefore a local call for me as with all the others. Aside from being a dopamine buzz to seeing your thread appear many times in a public message base—foreshadowing the thrill we all get when someone "likes" our status update on Facebook or Twitter—I remember this precisely because there weren't enough characters in the subject line to hold the entire name, so the thread subject on all the replies all ended in "Chernobyl nuclear accid" instead of accident. There was nothing I could do about this once the thread was started. (I haven't the faintest memory of what was said in the discussion.)

Soon we began to see more professional-level programs arrive on the platform. Let's take a look at two of these.

Degas (Batteries Included, 1985)

The Toronto-based Batteries Included first developed a reputation for quality productivity software on 8-bit computers—most notably Paperclip, the popular word processor available on both Commodore and Atari machines. Its first application for the ST was quite different, though. The name Degas was clearly a call out to the famous Impressionist, but the company said it also stood for Design and Entertainment Graphics Arts System. Degas was a bitmapped paint program that was split into a full-screen drawing window, giving you total focus on your work, and a full-screen menu that you brought up with a click of the right mouse button.

Degas featured 15 brush shapes and 38 fill patterns, plus space for user-definable ones, and there was an Undo facility. The program was a clear step up in features from NEOchrome; some of the more notable additions included an airbrush that let you control the paint flow (as opposed to the spray can in NEOchrome, which didn't), automatic shadow and border tools, and impressive font flexibility. Unlike NEOchrome, Degas also worked with medium-resolution color and high-resolution mono images.

Degas was the brainchild of programmer Tom Hudson, fresh off his stint at *ANALOG Computing* magazine, where he was responsible for hits such as the Tempest clone Livewire on the Atari 8-bit. Hudson and co-creator Gary Yost nearly chose Antic Software to publish his new product, but in the end went with Batteries Included instead.[12] Batteries Included heavily advertised Degas in both *Antic* and *ANALOG Computing*. One iconic ad showed a colorful yellow-and-blue bee on a red background and a mock-up of those 3D guys in the video for Dire Straits' "Money for Nothing," painted by Tom Hudson and John Bell. In its February 1986 issue, *Antic* magazine launched a $2,000 art competition in tandem with its published review of Degas, including two $500 grand prizes and a selection of software from both *Antic*'s house catalog and Batteries Included. Degas on the ST did much to counter the Amiga's heavily artist-focused introduction and advertising of the time. The Amiga's launch event famously included Andy Warhol filling a picture of Debbie Harry with color using the Amiga 1000, a mouse, and the program GraphiCraft, all while the real Debbie Harry looked on.[13] Even without the star power, a Degas-equipped ST held its own against the Amiga and quickly became the go-to choice for a commercial paint program for Atari users.

Megamax C (Megamax, 1985)

Advanced programmers who had moved beyond BASIC and Logo and wanted to develop commercial software soon had numerous options. Perhaps the most popular was Megamax C ($199.95), which was sold as a complete development system that could turn out finished executables running under GEM. Originally a Mac product, Megamax C included in-line assembly for 68000 code, one-pass compiling, six register variables that reduced code size with pointers and integers, support for floating point and batch processing, and a code optimizer in post to tighten up your code. The compiler also included a resource construction program for creating menus, dialog boxes, and icons, as well as a UNIX-style system library, a library linker, a GEM routines library, a disassembler, and full documentation.

A September 1986 review in *Antic* noted it was the only C compiler so far to fully support creating GEM programs, and its environment shell "makes program development a joy." Reviewer Mike Fleischman timed an example program and found the competing Alcyon C in the Atari SDK compiled and linked his code in 6 minutes, 7 seconds, and the resulting 12KB code took 2.47 seconds to run. Megamax C compiled the same code in just 1 minute, 34 seconds, and generated 6KB for the same code, which took 2.28 seconds to run. Part of the speed is that Alcyon C was a three-pass compiler. Megamax C did it all in one pass, Fleischman wrote. The only limitations in the initial version were a 32KB ceiling on both code blocks and array size.

As we discussed earlier, Megamax released a free copy of Megaroids, a polished Asteroids clone that was developed in Megamax C—probably as shrewd a marketing move as there ever was, especially because the source code for the game was included with retail copies of the compiler. Megamax touted in ads its compiler was already used by Batteries Included, FTL Games, and Supra Corporation. Other popular C packages for the ST included Mark Williams C, Lattice, and GST, and Megamax C itself morphed into Laser C a few years later.

ST Gaming

As with its 8-bit brethren from Sunnyvale, the Atari ST quickly became a formidable gaming machine. The Atari ST's powerful processor, color graphics, and aggressive price point compared with the Amiga, the IIGS, and the Macintosh made it a go-to 16-bit computer purchase in the mid 1980s. Early on, ST games showed an unprecedented level of detail and complexity, and enabled mouse-driven adventure games and sharper sprite resolution that simply weren't possible on 8-bit machines.

Some top-name video game developers programmed on the ST, including Peter Molyneux, Doug Bell, Jeff Minter, Eric Chahi, Jez San, and David Braben. The platform gave rise to renowned third-party studios such as Psygnosis, Microdeal, Rainbird, FTL Games, Cinemaware, and MichTron, and boosted the fortunes of Mindscape, Epyx, MicroProse, SSI, Accolade, Lucasfilm Games (later LucasArts), and Sierra On-Line (later just Sierra). Delve a bit deeper, though, and in some cases it was two steps forward, one step back. As we covered earlier, the ST didn't have separate coprocessors for graphics and sound, even though its main processor was much more powerful than what the original Atari 400 and 800 computers contained. At first, there was some lost smoothness in animation before programmers learned ways to compensate for the missing hardware. In many ways, gaming on the ST was still a significant step above what the 8-bit Atari line was capable of.

As we go, I'll talk about Atari ST–exclusive games when applicable. But mostly, I'll discuss important titles that may have seen ports on other platforms, or even have originated on other platforms first, but that remain significant for the Atari ST from a historical perspective and offer a unique gaming experience on it. We'll get to games from all of these companies and more.

With that, let's start in earnest with a proper ST conversion of an arcade classic.

Joust (Atari, 1985)

Atari's 16-bit port of Joust, the popular Williams coin-op, is pitch-perfect. The ST may not have had enough hardware to declare it undeniably superior to the 800 and 5200 version, but this game completely masked the fact, as it showed up the 8-bit platform conversions. I've covered Joust already in both of my previous books on the 8-bit computers and the 2600, so I'll skip the details of how this game works. Suffice to say, everything missing in earlier iterations of Joust were present here: The colorful, animated attract screen at the proper size, instead of the smaller versions on the Atari 8-bit and the 2600, and now complete with dual high score tables; the full-color birds for both the player and the three enemy types; the detailed, animated flame burning the edges of the bottom platform on level 3; the troll's creepy, mottled hand in full splendor; the hatching eggs that properly reveal just the warrior, upon which a new buzzard appears and arrives to collect its rider, instead of the entire fully formed pair sprouting at once from the egg… It was all there, right down to the same screen font Williams used in the arcade.

Back in the day, I'd show off the power of the ST to a friend by firing up this game. Everyone knew Joust. And anyone who played it in the arcade, or who had played an inferior home port, could see the difference immediately. This probably made me look like a jackass more than I realized—"look how much better my computer is!"— when I never said or thought anything of the sort. I was just excited at how it was possible to get a true facsimile of an arcade game at home, after years of disappointment across so many other platforms. If I *had* to levy a complaint, despite all of the proper elements appearing, it's that the ST port played a bit slowly. Everything was fine at the start of a level, but then the action began to slow down and flicker as more birds appeared. Nonetheless, the ST conversion of Joust was easily the best ever to appear outside of the arcade coin-op.

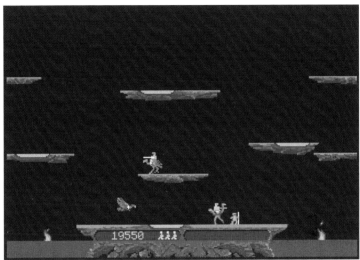

Figure 2.4: The 1982 arcade original arrived on the ST as a pitch-perfect conversion that was almost impossible to distinguish from the coin-op Joust.

The Rugby Circle, which consisted of 23-year-old Robert Lech and 19-year-old Troy Dahlman, developed Joust for the ST. They started by buying a $4,500 pre-production ST—one of the first 20 Atari made available for purchase. Later, the duo bought a second machine from Atari after the company dropped the price to $1,500.[14] Joust proved to be a difficult game to convert. After running into trouble trying to get source code and original art assets, the two developers ended up snapping pictures of the arcade coin-op in one of the few arcades that still had the machine, taught themselves C, and in the process, created a commercial software sprite program purely as a utility to aid them in programming Joust.

C.O.L.R. Object Editor (Antic Catalog, 1985)

The Rugby Circle programmers developed C.O.L.R. Object Editor to create software sprites for Joust. But *Antic* magazine editors saw the program's potential right away. "Nice birds, we said," wrote Gigi Bisson for the November 1985 issue, during a private demo of Joust. "But we began drooling over the graphics editor. We knew ST users would need a graphics utility tool right away and here it was. *Antic* immediately contacted Bob and Troy, and C.O.L.R. became the first ST product in the Antic Arcade Catalog."[15]

"We never dreamed the graphics editor could be a commercial product at all," Troy said in the article. But it didn't matter. "The game wasn't even finished," Bisson wrote in *Antic*, "and they already had a product—the first commercially available programmers' tool for the ST." The ST lacked the 8-bit Atari's fabled Player/Missile graphics. Instead, it employed something called a bit block transfer (BitBlt), which would have been slow if it weren't for the ST's much faster 68000 processor. "ST developers have reported up to 80 sprites zipping around the screen simultaneously," according to the article.

C.O.L.R. Object Editor wasn't paint software as we know it today. It was a genuine sprite editor, a cursor-based drawing program within GEM that let you create bitmapped pictures using the mouse. When finished, the program could then save each one as a byte-array data file on disk. The program gave you the ST's full (low-resolution) 320-by-200-pixel workspace, and featured a small zoomed-out version in the top-left corner of the screen so you knew where in an image you were currently working. You could open picture files from other ST graphics programs inside C.O.L.R. Object Editor.

Despite the program's historic placement in *Antic* and the success of Atari's Joust conversion, I haven't been able to turn up other instances of the Object Editor being used to create software. It's still a prime example of the rush to build out the ST's new software catalog, and how programmer-utility-heavy said catalog was at the start. It's always a mad rush to beat the chicken-and-egg problem of developing new software for a platform no one has yet, but that could well take off quickly, so you don't want to miss your chance to get in early even if there's no money in it at first.

Ultima II: The Revenge of the Enchantress (Sierra, 1985)

Sierra was one of the first companies to release software for the Atari ST. It began with the only Ultima RPG it had the rights to. Ultima II was the first game from the already-popular series to reach the ST, and was one of the first games overall to arrive on Atari's then-new 16-bit home computers shortly after their release in June 1985. Ultima II isn't as well remembered as some of the later installments in this venerable series, but it was a solid game nonetheless.

The evil enchantress Minax has taken over the world—originally Earth, but later redefined as Sosaria for retroactive consistency—as revenge for her lover Mondain's defeat in Ultima I. In this game you controlled one character, rather than a party of characters of different classes as in some of the later installments. Ultima II was a larger game than the first. It also took place in different time periods you accessed via "time doors" while on the overall quest to defeat Minax. The game was the first in the series to feature animated tiles for water and other features of the landscape and in-game characters.

Sierra's ST conversion, adapted by Eric Heitman, added drop-down menus you could use to equip your character, and you could control movement with the mouse. I never found this helpful, having cut my teeth on the 8-bit Atari versions with full keyboard control, so I just replayed the game using the ST's keyboard. If I hadn't solved the game on the 8-bit, maybe I would have done so on the ST, although others have complained about how clumsy the UI was. The game also ran from within TOS, not on a self-bootable disk. The ST box included a full cloth map and an amusing, well-written manual.

Two other major differences stood out on the ST. The first was the color scheme; unlike every other Ultima port I've ever played, Ultima II on the Atari ST had its colors reversed so the background was white all of the time instead of black. The background flashed black momentarily whenever you attacked or cast spells in the appropriate tiles. Second, thanks to the game's four-window interface on the ST, the main view was smaller than normal. But you always saw what was in your inventory and the name of the town or time you were currently in. This made it easier to get around and also showed you immediately if a thief had swiped an item from your inventory, as the Ultima Codex site pointed out.[16]

The GEM enhancements here in Ultima II laid out a path to point-and-click adventure games that only became possible on the ST, Mac, Amiga, and later computers with mouse-based graphical interfaces. Porting the game was also a significant feat, as programmer Richard Garriott famously coded Ultima II in assembly language on the 6502-based Apple II, the first game he did that for instead of using compiled BASIC. According to the second edition of *The Official Book of Ultima,* Garriott battled with Sierra about royalties for the PC port of this game, leading him to break camp and start up his own company, Origin Systems.[17]

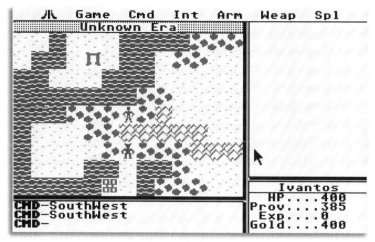

Figure 2.5: You may have defeated Mondain in Ultima I, but now it was time to defeat his lover in Ultima II—and also work out how to graft a mouse-based interface onto a classic keyboard-based CRPG. Probably not like this.

Infocom

One of the earliest developers to release games for the ST was Infocom, the fabled purveyor of interactive fiction—text adventures with sophisticated parsers, voluminous area descriptions, and often fiendishly difficult puzzles. Infocom released a slew of titles for the ST in short order, as the company's Z-machine interpreter made it easy to recompile each game for the new platform. This let ST owners take advantage of a well-developed text adventure library right of the gate in the second half of 1985, and with the added benefit of an 80-column screen to play them with. The ST received ports of a variety of Infocom titles including the Zork series, the Enchanter trilogy, The Hitchhiker's Guide to the Galaxy, and more. A good portion of the first batch of software titles to hit retail for the ST were from Infocom, helping to bulk up retail store shelves and the accompanying price listings in magazines.

The ST's increased memory also allowed for more in-depth gaming, which Infocom moved to take advantage of quickly. That lead to 1985's A Mind Forever Voyaging, the first ST title the company released that wouldn't ever be available for 8-bit Atari computers. In this politically minded game by veteran Infocom developer Steve Meretzky, you played as PRISM, the world's first sentient computer. Your goal was to run simulations of the future to see the possible results of a sweeping new government plan. The game served both as an immersive, futuristic science-fiction game and a critique of some of the Reagan administration's policies.

There was nothing ST-specific about A Mind Forever Voyaging; the game also came out for the Amiga, MS-DOS, the Mac, and even 128KB-equipped Commodore 128s and Apple IIs. But it's notable for its use of version 4 of the Z-Machine interpreter and that 128KB memory requirement, both of which lead to the then-new designation "Interactive Fiction Plus" that Infocom also bestowed on Trinity. An early ad quoted *Newsweek* as saying, "A Mind Forever Voyaging uses the expanded memory to breathtaking effect, creating a richly imagined anti-Utopian future-world. AMFV isn't *1984*, but in some ways it's even scarier." A Mind Forever Voyaging was a sales disappointment in its time, but today it is increasingly recognized as a historic achievement in interactive fiction thanks to its depth and its parser's 1,800-word vocabulary.

SunDog: Frozen Legacy (FTL, 1985)

FTL Games, one of the first third-party ST developers, made a huge splash with this enhanced conversion of the company's already-popular Apple II game. The result was jaw-dropping on the ST, with massively improved graphics. SunDog: Frozen Legacy was an entire self-contained sci-fi world on a single 3.5-inch disk. This space exploration and trading game, developed by FTL's Doug Bell, let you visit more than 50 cities on 18 planets grouped into 12 star systems.

After creating a character, you began with an inherited star freighter and a signed contract to build up a new colony called Banville on the planet Jondd. You had to locate and deliver all the construction materials, and then find the cryogens stored in warehouses and bring them back to the colony. Along the way, you'd have ample opportunity to trade cargo, fend off pirates, repair and refuel your ship, and dodge muggers on foot in cities.

You controlled the game with the mouse. There was a cursor pointer for most actions that then you performed by clicking the left button. For example, you could walk around your ship or in a city by positioning the cursor where you wanted to go and then holding the mouse button. The right button brought you back to the previous option, or if there wasn't one, it displayed your status and inventory. It also let you enter pods, ships, and doorways.

Your ship, the SunDog, had six engineering bays: warp drives, sub-C engines, guns, shields, tactical, and pilotage. You needed to keep an eye on these throughout the game. You could navigate to star systems and planets using 3D maps, or enter combat with a window, radar, control panel, warp charge, and ship status display. During combat sequences, stunning graphics showed off the ST's capabilities in real time as you battled space pirates from your ship's deck. The ship held stores and lockers for packing away your cargo.

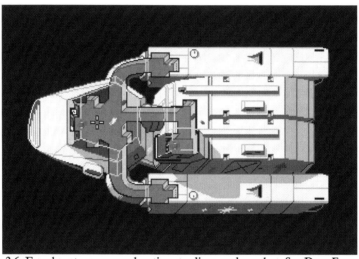

Figure 2.6: Equal parts space exploration, trading, and combat, SunDog: Frozen Legacy was a triumph. To this day, people are trying to resurrect or remaster the game for new platforms.

You could also depart your main ship and travel down to the surface of planets, where you'd engage in battles on foot, deposit or withdraw cash in banks, trade for items at exchanges, or enter bars, where even the slot machines worked, to get information from others. I remember spending many hours buying and selling pistols privately in bar booths for a profit. "The strongest feature of SunDog is its incredible attention to detail," reviewer David Plotkin wrote in the July 1986 issue of *Antic*. "Everywhere you turn, there's something to see and explore."

SunDog went on to become the Atari ST's best-selling game until Dungeon Master took the crown in 1987. In a 1999 interview with *PC Zone,* legendary game designer Richard Garriott called SunDog his favorite game of all time, and said it was "basically Ultima meets Wing Commander."[18] Some SunDog fans have wondered whether the popular indie space game Faster Than Light (FTL), which was released in 2012, has anything to do with this 1980s classic. Vintage computing historian Benj Edwards asked the developers of FTL point blank in an interview several years ago if there was any connection. They swore it was a coincidence.[19]

Numerous efforts have been made and abandoned to reboot Sun-Dog throughout the years. Although I'm still hoping that happens, in the meantime the original is still immensely playable. One caveat: It hasn't happened to me recently, but I remember this game occasionally freezing up and trashing my saved character, which was incredibly frustrating and a not-uncommon fact of life when gaming on a computer in the 1980s. If you play today, make a copy of your save disk often, or play in an emulator where you can save the game state as a backup.

Time Bandit (MichTron, 1985)

An arcade and adventure game in one, Time Bandit put you inside 16 different worlds that comprised more than 3,000 screens, with the goal of grabbing as much treasure as possible while fending off monsters. You had to find 16 missing artifacts—one from each world—in order to conquer the Gates of Time. Part Gauntlet, part Gateway to Apshai, the game featured worlds set in different time periods, including the Old West and space travel, with enticing names such as Ghost Town, Castle Greymoon, Sentinel, and Bomb Factory. Three of the included worlds were genuine miniature text and graphic adventures, where you can interact with non-player characters and talk to them via text. A distinctive world called Shadowland sent up the arcade game Pac-Man; as part of solving the world, you had to eat the dots.

You travelled to each world by way of time gates that appeared when you first started the game; you had to shoot enemies as you ran to each gate. Move through one, and you'd transport to the first level of that world. Each world contained 16 levels, labeled 1A through 4D. To complete each level, you needed to find the keys and use them to open locks, one at a time; once you finished, you had to locate the Way Out, upon which you then chose another land to enter. The next time you returned to that world, you would advance a level. Along the way, you had to collect treasures, which multiplied in points (called cubits) the more you found. You could also shoot an array of evil guardians to get points and increase your bravery level. The enemies came in through various portals, similar to what happened in Gauntlet.

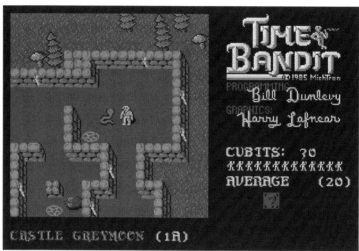

Figure2.7: The ST received an early gaming boost with Time Bandit, a fast, addictive arcade romp through time and space that delivered hours of intense action.

Some of the levels featured one-way doors that meant you couldn't return the way you came. Others featured a series of green arrows that carried you at high speed from one place to another. Red transporter disks let you travel long distances quickly, and there were the usual array of pits and ladders you'd find in a normal platformer. You received 14 lives to start (not 10, as the manual says), and another life every 1,000 cubits; lives came and went quickly as part of the fast-paced action. According to the November 1986 review in *ST-Log*, it's "unlikely you could ever finish every micro-world through all 16 levels. The authors don't believe it can be done, either."

A built-in two-player mode gave each player a square view of the landscape. One player was yellow and the other was blue; you could cooperate to clear levels or just attack each other. The view of the playfield in two-player mode was smaller than it would have been for a single player, but there was zero slowdown. You could play the game with the keyboard, but it was much better with a joystick, and in two-player mode at least one person had to use one. When one player died, that player became a Shadow, which could then "haunt" the other player and steal treasure—or just help out by shooting guardians.

Bill Dunlevy and Harry Lafnear originally developed Time Bandit for the TRS-80 (pre-Gauntlet, and the same time as that game's APX precursor Dandy for the Atari 8-bit). Time Bandit is addictive to play even today, thanks to its colorful pseudo-three-dimensional graphics, in-depth levels, and sheer speed. Despite the lack of hardware scrolling and hardware sprites, Time Bandit proved early on the ST could deliver steady animation thanks to the 68000's inherent power and speed. If you squinted on some of the more crowded levels, you could still see a slight choppiness that you wouldn't see on an Atari 800 game. But Time Bandit's vibrant color and massive game world clearly set this title in the 16-bit era. The game consisted of 350KB of machine language code; it filled up an entire single-sided 3.5-inch floppy disk, and you could save your game in progress on the same disk. The only thing missing was in-game music. Sound effects were also few and far between.

MichTron billed Time Bandit as "the biggest, fastest, most detailed game ever designed for a home computer." The company wasn't wrong. In the September 1986 issue of *Byte,* reviewer Jerry Pournelle called Time Bandit "the best arcade-type computer game I have ever seen." *Antic*'s review said Time Bandit "has the credentials to someday qualify as a true classic for the ST." I received this game with my 520ST and played it constantly. It was a fun antidote to the turn-based RPGs I was buried in, and scratched an arcade itch that otherwise took the ST some time to build up a library for.

When the ST arrived at retail, the expected launch library of compatible software was essentially nonexistent.[20] But things started to pick up through the rest of 1985. In December, Atari began to bundle free programs with every complete ST system sold for the holidays: ST BASIC, Logo, 1ˢᵗ Word, NEOchrome, DB Master One, and Megaroids. This gave you two programming languages, a word processor, a paint program, a database program, and a free game, all right in the box with the computer. (I'm almost positive this is the packaged I received, because I had all of the original "bundle" disks with the sparse white labels.)

Although disk-based software was still the norm in 1985, the future was looking rounder, shinier, and more colorful. A good portion of the early coverage around the ST, and other 16-bit computers for that matter, centered around the possibilities of this just-invented CD-ROM format and its ability to store up to *600MB* of data on a single disc, or the rough equivalent of a couple thousand floppy disks. *Antic* magazine featured CD-ROMs for the ST as its October 1985 cover story, and in its December 1985 "ST Shopper's Guide," it said the first software available would be the Grolier Encyclopedia, and that "by itself, CD-ROM technology is enough of a reason to buy the ST." [21]Analysts, tech media, and enthusiasts engaged in a kind of collective delusion, with varying stages of doubt followed by signs that no, really, Atari's CD-ROM drive is coming Real Soon Now.

The "upcoming" CD-ROM drive hovered in the background for most of the ST's tenure. At one point, it even received a price and release date. Three years after the ST launched, the choirs were still singing about it. Here's *STart,* from the Summer 1988 issue: "The Atari CD-ROM player … is well on its way … At about half the price of competing CD-ROM decks (approximately $599), it will be difficult for other companies to compete. The machine is slated for release late in the second quarter of 1988." No CD-ROM drive appeared. In 1990, *STart* ran a story called "Is Atari's CDAR-504 Finally Ready to Ship?" Although by this point it finally had a model name that would stick (earlier references to a CDAR-500 had disappeared), this article consisted of four more pages of wish fulfillment. It included a list of imaginary CD-ROM software titles that were in development, along with hopeful claims such as "the CD-ROM is finally ready to ship and, in fact, should be at your local dealer as this story reaches you." A developer was quoted as saying, "I believe it's really going to happen this time."

It didn't happen. The closest it ever came to release was a prototype model. It's tempting to blame Tramiel's notorious penny-pinching or management snafus for this, but it was just too early for optical discs. Although Microsoft first sold CD-ROM software for PCs in 1987, most people associate CD-ROM drives with the 1990s, as that was when they first became popular and prices had come down enough for them to be feasible additions to the average PC or Mac. It's not a surprise the cost-conscious Tramiel never pulled the trigger.

To be fair, the CDAR-504 did "exist" in the end; a few dozen drives made it to developers, and sometimes one of these occasionally appears in the wild today. But the CDAR-504 was never sold at retail. A revised CDAR-505 was also announced, but that one never materialized.

Nonexistent CD-ROM drive aside, by most accounts, the ST's launch was solid. The general inkling was Atari Corporation sold a good number of units out of the gate—50,000 by September, as reported by *InfoWorld*,[22] with 10,000 in the US by October alone.[23] But there still wasn't enough software available for the machine. And although a number of popular publications had begun covering the ST in part, there weren't any dedicated ST magazines just yet. This would all soon change for the better.

3 | Mainstream

The ST's software library grew massively in 1986, a feat made possible because Atari Corporation ensured the ST was an open platform right from the beginning. This was in stark contrast to what the former Atari Inc. did with the 400 and 800, where it not only withheld internal specs and programming information from third-party developers, but also threatened to sue them if they made software—mistakes that cost the 8-bit platform a precious couple of years before Atari relented and its software library truly took off. By the middle of 1986, 1,500 developers were creating ST software worldwide, according to Atari Corporation president Sam Tramiel.[1] Big chunks of that number worked in Europe rather than the US, but a healthy software selection had become available in US retailers as well. In the beginning, vendors were understandably hesitant to jump into the ST market, given Jack Tramiel's ruthless reputation from Commodore. But there was genuine progress.

Thanks to the sudden influx of programming tools, third-party developers could now get started on their own and not necessarily need Atari's SDK. Soon it became common to see large, multipage magazine features covering diverse programming topics such as artificial intelligence, engineering, and fractals, all with type-in code specifically for the ST. Plus, then-current 520STs enabled upgrades to 1MB memory by soldering in new chips, and kits began to appear on the market letting you do this more easily.

One popular commercial that ran in the UK showed people pulling off various masks to demonstrate how much the ST could do. A booming, echoing voice said:

Any machine can play games with you. But as a real computer, I can also help with education. Give people the power to be successful. Enable them to create music and produce extraordinary images from my artist's palette. It is I, the Atari ST: A real thing, not a plaything.

While the 520ST was already doing well, Atari dropped a new product on the market—and at a surprising price point.

Figure 3.1: In 1986, we got the perfect mainstream 16-bit Atari computer: the 1040ST. This model doubled the memory, marking the first time a 1MB personal computer cost under $1,000. Credit: Bill Bertram

Atari 1040ST (1986)

Atari announced the 1040ST at the Winter 1986 Consumer Electronics Show, once year after the company first introduced the ST platform. The 1040ST came with several significant and desirable upgrades compared with the 520ST: 1MB RAM instead of 512KB, an internal power supply, and an internal double-sided 3.5-inch floppy drive. The last two changes made for a considerably more compact desk setup, even despite the system's deeper enclosure. The MIDI ports were also moved to the left side, which made them more easily accessible. The 1040ST cost $999.99 at launch. This made it the first personal computer to offer a megabyte of memory for under $1,000, leading *Byte* magazine to put the 1040ST on the cover of the March 1986 issue. The new models included TOS on ROM and a floppy disk with ST BASIC, Atari Logo, NEOchrome v0.5, and the VT52 Terminal Emulator.

Print advertisements played up the 1040ST's strengths, and (at least in my opinion) were more effective than Atari's usual muddled messaging. One showed the front of a red Ferrari with the ST on its hood, saying: "The ST Computer Line From Atari. It's like getting the power and speed of a Ferrari for the price of a Ford." It also showed the famous NEOchrome waterfall image, and included a spec comparison chart that presented the 1040ST as more capable and less expensive than the Amiga, PC-AT (286), Macintosh, and even the 8-bit Apple IIc. (To Atari's credit, the chart showed the Amiga did have the widest color palette at 4,096 colors, though it left out how the Amiga can also show 64 at once instead of 16.) Another magazine campaign played out as three separate quarter-page ads, talking up the system's ability to deliver 1MB of memory, 8MHz speed, and standard modem and printer interfaces for under $1,000, complete with a monitor and disk drive.

A couple of things on the 1040ST came in for criticism, most notably the new location of the two joystick and mouse ports. To make room for the floppy drive on the right side, Atari moved those ports to the bottom of the computer in a recessed opening toward the front. That meant whenever you wanted to unplug the mouse and plug in a second joystick, or vice versa, you had to lift the entire machine. It would put stress on the rear connectors and wiring unless you also shut down the entire computer and disconnected everything first. This wasn't a huge day-to-day impediment unless you played a lot of two-player games, where loading them meant you had to disconnect the mouse, which you would then need to reconnect to boot the next game if that disk didn't autoboot.

Atari also announced new "m"-designated models that included an RF modulator, letting owners hook these machines up to a standard color television. A new "f" designation meant the floppy drive was built into the machine—standard since day one on the new 1040ST, but later applied to new 520ST revisions as well. The new machines began shipping in March in both the US and UK. Various combinations of STf, STm, and STfm were shipped to different countries in a somewhat scattershot rollout.

All told, I still consider the 1040ST the archetypical ST computer. Short of an enclosure that combined the monitor and CPU, such as with the diminutive Macintosh Plus, the 1040ST system looked a lot more integrated with just the computer, mouse, monitor, and keyboard on your desk. Later models in the line would soon beat the 1040ST in both power and flexibility, with niceties such as internal hard drives and faster graphics. But the 1040ST to me represented the earliest "best" ST and the one that was the most desirable for its time, even though the competition had an extra year to catch up by this point.

New Storage Options

The SF314 was a double-sided 3.5-inch floppy disk drive for the Atari ST line similar to the one built into the 1040ST. The SF314 was the same physical size as the SF354, but offered 720KB of storage on a single disk instead of 360KB. Atari had announced the SF314 as early as April in 1985, but it didn't start shipping in quantity until sometime in early 1986 along with the 1040ST. An SF314 made perfect sense both as an upgraded second drive for SF354-equipped 520STs as well as a second "Floppy Disk B" for 1040STs that already had double-sided capability. Soon Atari stopped promoting the single-sided SF354 in the US and only sold it in the UK alongside the remainder of its lower-cost 260ST production run.[2]

PC owners had already begun to discover the joys of hard drive storage. A hard drive could store a hundred floppy disks worth of data or more, all accessible with a single keypress or click of the mouse. Except for backups, transfers, and the occasional copy-protection scheme that required the original disk, you could install your software once and then fire it up at will whenever you wanted to. Hard drives were also much faster to read and write data than their floppy disk counterparts. The SH204, Atari's first hard drive for the ST, featured a 20MB capacity. It was about the size of a shoebox, maybe slightly lower in height. It connected to the ST through the DMA port on back, and a driver loaded from the drive when you booted the machine.

The SH204 launched at $699.99, but quickly faced heated competition from third-party manufacturers such as Supra Corporation, which worked to undercut whatever Atari offered. Often, it succeeded. Among the most popular third-party hard drives for ST owners, SupraDrives were easily recognizable by their shoebox-size design and prominent logo (written in black script) on the front panel. Supra Corporation sold the drive in 10MB, 20MB, 30MB, and 60MB varieties at first, beginning at $549 for the 10MB drive early on. Soon the company began offering 120MB and 250MB drives as early as 1988 as well. The enclosure was noticeably smaller than Atari's SH204 while boasting the same 20MB capacity.[3] The rear panel contained the power switch, while the front panel had a power LED. Out of the box, it was partitioned as two 10MB drives (called C and D), though you could reconfigure that with up to four drives.

The SupraDrive also worked with 8-bit Atari computers. "10 million bytes at your fingertips," went the October 1986 *Antic* story first covering the drive. It went on to say the magazine office's own Supra-Drive contained every 8-bit program the company ever published with more than 7MB to spare. For the ST, *Antic* marketing director Gary Yost ran the magazine's software publishing arm and had apparently filled 16MB of his 20MB ST hard drive "with every program from the catalog, all the early versions of each program, all his correspondence with the software authors, and all the Tim Oren Antic Online professional ST programming articles. Gary clicks his mouse through on-screen arrays of folders, files, and menus with virtuoso speed." The story said readers seemed to use hard drives the most for operating BBSes on the 8-bit side, and professional software developers and business owners took to it as well.

Out of all of this grew the invariable precautions about data loss. A *STart* article noted with the SupraDrive, you should be using TOS in ROM, because earlier disk-based TOS could "adversely affect" the use of the drive, and you should "never copy a file to itself because of a bug in the TOS operating system that may wipe out the entire hard disk if you do so." Worse, the article said to pay attention to the manual's reminder to backup files periodically, and critical files at least daily. "Speaking as one who just recently lost the entire contents of a hard disk and did not have it backed up, I am living testimony that a hard disk mishap can make a grown man cry." This still happens to grown-ups today, but many of us can vouch for how easily hard drives used to fail. A good friend of mine told me he would rebuild and reinstall the drive in his Macintosh SE a lot, because "hard disk crashes every few months" were just a fact of life and you dealt with them whenever they happened. For all of the Windows blue screens and Mac kernel panics I've seen, I'm glad computers no longer routinely trash their boot drives.

Productivity Software

After a slow start, the ST quickly began to build up a library of application software that made it much more of the proper low-cost Macintosh alternative Tramiel and the ST engineers had envisioned (even if they didn't call it such).

1ˢᵗ Word Plus (Pacific Software, 1986)

Despite the availability of the free ST Writer and 1ˢᵗ Word, many third-party word processors for the ST quickly hit the market, such as Habawriter and Papyrus. Arguably the most popular of the first-year bunch was 1ˢᵗ Word Plus, a natural upgrade for anyone who worked with (or tried to work with) the bundled 1ˢᵗ Word that came with their new 520ST computer. Unlike the original, 1ˢᵗ Word Plus was exclusively a retail product. It bundled in GEM Paint for creating pictures and GEM 1ˢᵗ Mail for form letters, and could show both words and pictures in-line simultaneously.

The program featured word processing and ASCII modes, the latter still good for coding or writing straight text as before. It also cleaned up some of the bugs and limitations of 1ˢᵗ Word, and included file statistics for the number of words your document contained, its length in pages, and so on. It also supported multiple kinds of page breaks, as well as footnotes and superscript numbers that stayed together on the correct pages even if you edited and expanded text later on. Unfortunately you still had to "reformat" the text on the page after making changes before you could see them represented visually.

The program included a spellchecker and a 40,000-word dictionary, though a Winter 1987 review in *STart* strongly urged 520ST users to save their files before attempting to load the dictionary into memory: "The first time I tried it the program bombed; I could only get spelling to work by removing one of my existing desk accessories." Removing desk accessories was a fact of life whenever you needed to squeeze the last bit of memory out of the 520ST.

Digital Research also sold GEM 1ˢᵗ Word Plus as a PC product, and said that version let you work with other software from the company like GEM Graph for creating pie charts and bar graphs. That made it a kind of proto–Microsoft Office combination that offered an alternative to using separate word processor and spreadsheet apps, as well as suites such as Ashton-Tate Framework on the PC side.

Figure 3.2: Timeworks sold numerous productivity applications for the ST, including Word Writer ST, Data Manager ST, and SwiftCalc ST.

Word Writer ST (Timeworks, 1986)

Timeworks distinguished itself with powerful productivity software that took advantage of the GEM-based interface on the ST. Its first application was arguably the most important, or at least it had the widest potential user base. This well-packaged word processor ($79.95) featured a 90,000-word dictionary and spellchecker. It sported a GUI that was similar to the one found in 1st Word and 1st Word Plus. A visible ruler displayed tab stops and margins, and you could scroll around your text with the cursor keys or with the scroll bars. One big change was at the bottom of the screen, which showed one or more rows of labeled "Quick Keys" (function keys) that saved you from using the drop-down menus all the time.

Unlike 1st Word Plus, you couldn't insert or manipulate images; it was strictly a text-based word processor. You also couldn't add to the dictionary with custom words the way you could in 1st Word Plus, though the program would at least remember words it didn't know for the duration of your editing session so it didn't keep flagging them repeatedly. It supported word wrap, and unlike with the two 1st Word products, you could see your changes without having to manually reformat the screen first.

A reviewer in the Summer 1987 issue of *STart* gave a good summary of how GEM-based word processors sat in the lineup versus the free ST Writer and 1st Word. "Personally, I use only two word processors: ST Writer and Word Writer ST," consulting editor Matt Loveless wrote. "I use ST Writer for long documents that don't require sophisticated formatting; it's fast and makes major editing a simple job. I use Word Writer ST for short letters and notes (less than five pages) because it is so easy to get the document to look exactly like I want it to; to do that in ST Writer would require two or three trial printouts and a lot of parameter tweaking."

A few other nits mentioned in the review: You could easily out-type the display and have to wait for it to catch up. And the built-in outliner was basically useless; nothing you did on it seemed to line up correctly.

Thunder! The Writer's Assistant (Batteries Included, 1986)

Thunder! ($39.95) was the kind of program that would soon be subsumed into word processors and office suites: a real-time spelling checker with a 50,000-word dictionary. But for a time, it served a real purpose and was a valuable accessory. It corrected your spelling as you typed, something Microsoft Word couldn't do until 1993, when the feature was introduced as AutoCorrect. Today, we only think of auto-correct when our phones change our text messages to "ducking." Oh come on, that's totally happened to you.

Back in 1986, Batteries Included billed Thunder! as more than just a spellchecker: "Thunder! is also a document analyzer and a quick typist abbreviation expander!" Apparently it was also an exclamation-point inserter, but besides that, it would read a document you gave it after the fact and analyze its "readability score." The latter figured out how readable your copy was by measuring its grade level you wrote at and how many words, sentences, paragraphs, and even syllables were in your text. And Thunder! changed abbreviations to the correct spelling automatically as a kind of ever-present macro function for things you typed often.

One half of the program was a simple desk accessory you could pull up at any time. As a result, Batteries Included claimed the program worked with all kinds of word processors, databases, financial, and personal productivity software. The desk accessory worked in real time, and you could also turn it off so it didn't consume memory if you didn't need it. The other half stood alone and let you feed it documents after the fact. As with a few other things we've covered so far, I'm including this primarily for historical reference; it's not anything you'd want to use today. That is, unless you're of the flintiest kind and still type in documents not just on the ST, but in a program that doesn't already have a spellchecker.

Spreadsheets

Spreadsheets are no one's definition of exciting software, but with the advent of VisiCalc on the Apple II in 1979 and Lotus 1-2-3 on the PC in 1983, they quickly became the staple of businesses large and small—and a reason to put a computer on every worker's desk. Microsoft Excel, a spreadsheet with a graphical user interface, was released in 1987 and eventually supplanted Lotus 1-2-3 as the industry standard. The ST never received a port of Excel, but it did get its own GEM-based spreadsheets, some of which beat Excel to market. ISD Marketing's VIP Professional was heavily advertised early and may have well been the first—and is that a qualified "first." It arrived at retailers in December 1985 at an introductory price of $99 before going up to $179—albeit with a catch, as reviewer Gil Merciez wrote in the May 1986 issue of *Antic*.

"The impressive, shrink-wrapped package featured screenshots of drop-down menus and windows on a desktop spreadsheet," Merciez wrote. "Only after opening the package and scanning the 'Read Me First' pamphlet did I discover that the VIP I had just purchased was a 'text version' minus the GEM interface." And that was after months of delays to begin with, because the company first announced the software right around the time of the ST's release. "The GEM version, explained the pamphlet, was too large to fit into the memory of the ST with TOS still disk-based," Merciez continued. "As soon as TOS ROMs were available, I would be able to get the GEM version I assumed I had already bought—for an additional $19.95." Merciez went on to write the text version was so full of bugs as to be totally unusable, and customer service representatives refused to talk to customers without filled-out registration cards mailed in. After litigation between the developer and a company that was distributing the product, things began to settle down and VIP Professional went on to have a long life on the ST platform.

The program was more than just a 1-2-3 clone, as it also included presentation and database modules, making it a kind of miniature office suite all its own. It worked with Lotus templates, and offered up to 8,192 rows by 256 columns arranged in a grid. In addition to scores of formulas and labels, you could easily resize the rows and columns and add macros. The database portion of the program allowed for budgeting, financial planning, and tax preparation, while the graphics portion generated bar graphs, pie charts, line graphs, and x-y graphs.[4]

Later on, the ST saw more capable products such as LDW Calc, 3D-Calc, and Timeworks' SwiftCalc, all of which contributed to making the ST a viable and even advanced machine for business use at a time when the distinctly non-graphical MS-DOS was dominating the US market.

GFA BASIC (MichTron, 1986)

It became clear ST BASIC wasn't going to cut it for serious programmers. The ST was a fast 16-bit computer, and the last thing you wanted was to not be able to take advantage of that speed in your own programs, even if you were programming in BASIC. Fortunately, third-party developers came to the rescue relatively quickly. MichTron soon released GFA BASIC, a program developed by Frank Ostrowski. The company billed it as a compact, high-speed structured language interpreter that took just 57KB of memory and ran your programs as fast as compiled Pascal.

GFA BASIC included support for various GEM features by keyboard, and didn't need line numbers.[5] There was also a compiler available. The main window was clean save for a two-row inverse menu bar at the top with commonly used editing tools. You could code in all three of the ST's graphics modes. Later iterations of GFA BASIC added hundreds of additional commands and what MichTron said was a 40 to 60 percent speed boost, all while remaining retroactively compatible with programs written in previous versions of the interpreter.

The market for BASIC interpreters soon grew much more crowded. At one point, at least five different BASICs were available to ST owners, with others announced if never quite reaching the market.[6] But GFA BASIC was considered by many to be the standard, at least before you moved up to 68000 assembly or C. After the Atari ST, GFA BASIC was ported to the Amiga, MS-DOS, and Windows, and stuck around until around 2001. Most famously, Eric Chahi used GFA BASIC in part to develop the stunning game Another World, which we'll get to later in this book.

Graphics Software

The ST's powerful graphics abilities may have been second to the Amiga's, but they were still far ahead of what clunky MS-DOS computers and ultra-expensive, black-and-white Macintoshes offered—to say nothing of what you could get on any 8-bit platform.

Degas Elite (Batteries Included, 1986)

Batteries Included quickly followed up the resounding success of Degas with the higher-end Degas Elite ($79.95). Its interface resembled that of Degas at first glance—a good thing. You still drew with the mouse on a work screen and then pressed the right button to engage a full-screen menu of tools and options. One key change was the program was now fully GEM-based, so on the menu screen there was now a menu strip across the top, a color bar beneath that, several dozen command boxes, and a fill pattern view. This also meant you could access desk accessories to work in tandem with Degas Elite.

Another key difference was Elite supported up to eight separate work screens on a 1MB machine, or four if you had a 520ST. You could cut a picture out of one and use it as a brush on another, or paste that picture into several other screens. The program also had a new Blocks mode, which let you manipulate portions of your image as a block for stretching or skewing.

Batteries Included touched up some other weird UI details of the original Degas; in Elite, for example, you could more easily choose a fill pattern without having to cycle through all of them again to get to the one you wanted. A new Animate facility added four color cycle sequences you could set to perform simultaneously. The Fatbits window now zoomed in at up to 12x in magnification, and Degas Elite also had a slideshow viewer similar to the one in NEOchrome. Batteries Included soon stopped selling the original Degas, and Degas Elite went on to remain one of the premiere graphics programs for the ST platform throughout its tenure.

Aegis Animator (Aegis Development, 1986)

The Amiga quickly distinguished itself with its visual art abilities, thanks to programs such as Aegis Animator, but the ST wouldn't be left out. Aegis Animator made its way to the ST a year later and brought with it a couple of new features and some extra performance along the way. The program's print ads promised to turn your computer "into a full-function animation workstation capable of creating any time of moving computer/video storyboard."

Aegis Animator, developed by Jim Kent for the Amiga and then the ST, included tools for metamorphic, cell, and color cycling animation. You could animate objects by changing their relative position, shape, and size, and control the program's palette and animation speed. The program used a technique called tweening, where you sketched out the key positions for animation to tell the story, and then the program interpolated the in-between images in order to produce a polished animation sequence. The in-between images could be as a frequent as $1/60^{th}$ of a second to match the monitor's refresh rate. The more objects you added into the project, the less smooth it could become as you ran into processing or memory limits. There was even support for a command language. One trick the review mentioned is if you were recording the output, you could halve the global speed and double the tape playback rate to buy Animator more processing time on the ST.

A June 1987 review in *Antic* mentioned Aegis Animator was used in a Parliament music video ("Do you want shake with your fries?"), and that Oingo Boingo played a taped Animator sequence on a giant screen on stage at its concerts. Animator didn't create Pixar-quality movies—nothing would on a computer that supported just 512 colors, with 16 at any one time, and a maximum resolution of 320 by 200. Instead, Aegis positioned the program as a tool for building advertisements, business demonstrations, or simply pure artistry you could then output to a VCR for titling and special effects. The optional Art Pak ST added hundreds of animals, buildings, trucks, cars, and scenery objects, all within the same color palette so they were prematched to work together.

FujiBoink (Xanth Park, 1986)

The Amiga's famous bouncing ball demo captured the public's imagination upon the platform's introduction, so the ST clearly needed its own. At first, Atari responded with fairly mediocre demos for the 8-bit and ST, but then another group decided it wanted to far surpass this. The result was FujiBoink, released first for the Atari 8-bit platform and then for the ST.[7] The program displayed a red-and-white checkerboard pattern on startup. Then the Atari Fuji symbol appeared, complete with cascading rainbow colors on the front. After a few moments, it fell and began bouncing around the screen while rotating, revealing its shiny blue sides and rear panel along with a translucent shadow on the background. The entire demo was rendered at an impressive 60 frames per second.

As programmer Xanth Park explained in *STart* magazine, the effect was an illusion. It wasn't rendered the way we expect today; instead, it was basically a cartoon, with 32 predrawn frames showing the Fuji symbol in various stages of rotation and color. The demo made use of various "bit planes" to overlay the Fuji frames onto the checkered background in a way that made the shadow more realistic. Overall, it was a kludge, albeit an impressive one that masked the lack of actual polygon rendering and the loss of the 8-bit Atari's hardware color cycling capability. Back then it was a fun diversion to power up FujiBoink and impress people with it, because it was a quick-and-dirty way to show off the ST's graphics prowess. I guess bragging rights were more important to me than I realized. But when you were talking about a computer this cool, it was hard to contain your excitement.

PrintMaster (Unison World, 1986)

Many 8-bit computer faithful were familiar with Brøderbund's The Print Shop for all their dot matrix card-making and sign-printing needs. Unison World's PrintMaster quickly took up the mantle for the ST, letting owners print letterhead, signs, greeting cards, calendars, and multipage banners, just as with the older program. PrintMaster included 11 borders, eight fonts, more than 100 icons, and 11 patterns. You still couldn't create some of those on your own, but at least you could edit your own small (88-by-52-pixel) images for use in your productions.

A July 1986 review in *Antic* complained about PrintMaster's frequent disk access, probably because the program was developed before TOS ROM chips were available and Unison World wanted to make sure machines with less RAM available would still run it. In addition, the original PrintMaster didn't support menu bars, windows, and other GEM-based features, a problem it shared with ST Writer. On the plus side, and unlike with The Print Shop, PrintMaster let you add a second graphic to any design. You could also use different fonts on different lines and change the styles and sizes from line to line.

PrintMaster was a fine substitute for The Print Shop on the ST, and it worked with many different dot matrix printers. Today we've largely moved on from printing out things like this on a day-to-day basis—if there's interest in anything with physical output, it's 3D printers. But PrintMaster harkens back to a time when printing out a Happy Birthday banner or handing a custom greeting card to a friend was a nifty trick and much appreciated, especially if you didn't have Facebook to remind you it was their birthday in the first place.

Music Software

The Atari ST was soon going to change the world of music recording, thanks to its built-in MIDI ports and reasonable pricing. Within a year of the ST's release, we began to see programs hit the market that took advantage of the ports. Some of these were type-in programs, such as Simple Sequencer in the first issue of *STart*, but the ST quickly secured the attention of professionals in the music industry—and professional software developers that wanted to cater to them.

Pro-24 (Steinberg Research, 1986)

One of the first companies to take advantage of this was Steinberg, which opened for business in 1984, just a year before the ST was released. The Hamburg, Germany–based music software company is most famous today for Cubase, its popular digital audio workstation software for PCs and Macs. Steinberg started with simpler MIDI sequencers, first with Pro-16 on the Commodore 64 (which saw limited take-up, because you needed to buy extra MIDI hardware to use it) and then Pro-24 on the Atari ST, which put the company on the map.

"Thinking of going 24-track?" asked *Sound on Sound* magazine in the July 1986 issue. "If you are, and your musical output is primarily synthetic in origin, then Steinberg Research's Pro-24 MIDI sequencer for the Atari 520 and 1040 micros could prove an inexpensive alternative to upgrading your existing tape recorder."[8] Pro-24, as its name implies, offered 24 tracks of recording, eight more than Pro-16. The interface was laid out similar to that of a tape recorder, with a transport for recording, playing, fast-forwarding, and rewinding. Across the top of the screen were 24 buttons that showed which track you were recording on, along with virtual "LEDs" that signaled how loud each track was.

Where Pro-24 really shone was in its new editing features, which included quantization for making your recordings "tighter" and more on the beat than you had played them on the keyboard, and a step sequencer grid for building drum tracks with the mouse. In version 2.0, Pro-24 would also gain full musical notation, so you could see the treble and bass clefs of your music on screen and edit it there as well, and MIDI System Exclusive (SysEx) support for automatically switching and editing sounds on a synthesizer. Pro-24 came with a hardware dongle, a plastic key that plugged into the ST's cartridge port and prevented people from copying the program. The ST soon began to see a ton of MIDI software, but Steinberg nailed the formula out of the gate with Pro-24.

The Music Studio (Activision, 1986)

You didn't have to be a professional musician to have a ton of fun with playing or even composing music on the ST. Activision's The Music Studio was heavily advertised in computer magazines and was one of the most enjoyable music programs I had ever played with. Although it wasn't going to replace serious MIDI recording software such as Pro-24, it had a completely different mission: It let you make music even without a synthesizer keyboard attached to the ST. With The Music Studio, you could compose new music or transcribe existing tunes with the mouse, note by note and track by track, onto an actual piano staff with treble and bass clefs. Each song could have up to 15 instruments, with three voices playing at any one time. Once you were done, you could save each tune to disk or print it out as sheet music.

The program also came out for 8-bit computers, but with those, you needed to use a joystick. The 16-bit ST port worked with a mouse and had considerably higher-resolution graphics. The program supported adding lyrics to songs, and you could transpose an entire song to a different key. There was also a nifty Music Paintbox option that let you paint notes on the screen using the mouse and different colors. A Design Instrument screen gave you a miniature on-screen synthesizer to play with, letting you change a sound's attack, decay, sustain, or release (ADSR envelope) or visually modify a timbre's volume and duration. The Music Studio supported MIDI, so you could record or play back music using an externally connected synthesizer keyboard.

No one confused The Music Studio with a proper music sequencer, but it was perfect for its intended home market. The Music Studio was light-years beyond something like Atari's 1979 Music Composer cartridge for the 400 and 800, or even some of the more advanced player-only files that came out several years later. And although you only had three voices to work with on the ST instead of four as on the 800, Music Studio's full graphical interface and mouse support made putting together tunes an absolute joy.

First ST Magazines

Both *Antic* and *ANALOG Computing* soon began to run out of room for the increasingly necessary ST coverage in the magazines, thanks to the still-flourishing 8-bit home computer market. In the first half of 1986, both publications spun off ST-specific magazines called *STart* and *ST-Log,* respectively. *STart* began life as "the ST quarterly," with Summer 1986 as its first issue, although it soon became bimonthly and then monthly. *ST-Log* published monthly beginning in April 1986 first as a separate supplement to *ANALOG Computing* before standing on its own. ST-focused magazines had even better success in the UK, with *Atari ST User* (1986–1994) and *ST/Amiga Format* (1988–1989) leading to *ST Format* (1989–1996), and *ST Action* (1988–1993) all quite popular.

At least in the US, you could tell from reading *STart* and *ST-Log* that new products were slow to arrive, as I've realized in retrospect when researching this book (although I don't remember thinking about it at the time, as I was too excited about my new computer). For example, the first two issues of *STart* barely contained any product reviews, even though by the time the Summer and Fall 1986 issues arrived we were already passing the one-year mark for the platform's availability at retail. As the next couple of years wore on, there was much more of a palpable sense the ST was here to stay and it was worth covering. But looking back on it now, when reading the first issues, again you get a distinct "so where was the party?" feeling.

Figure 3.3: The ST sections of *Antic* and *ANALOG Computing* soon outgrew the space they had in those magazines, so the two publishers launched *STart* (pictured) and *ST-Log*.

Even some of the software I've already gone over here in this book, which to me was super-exciting, barely received any coverage. For example, Time Bandit didn't get a review at all I could find, except on the public television show *The Computer Chronicles*. SunDog: Frozen Legacy received one in *Antic* in July 1986, nearly a year after its release, but not in the other magazines. I can't help but look back and wonder what could have been, had more ST products received press coverage earlier.

Atari unveiled some other products throughout 1986 that didn't quite make the big time. One of these, the PS-3000, was an unusual combination of a 14-inch color monitor for the ST paired with a 3.5-inch single-sided (360KB) floppy drive in its base. It was like a nerdy version of a TV/VCR combo. According to Canada's Personal Computer Museum, the unit played both NTSC and PAL games, which was unusual, and was reported to be produced in a quantity of 1,000 units.[9] I've seen a few turn up in both forums and on eBay, but it's rare.

Nonetheless, the ST had already begun to influence the music industry, with top-name artists like Gary Numan getting on board early.[10] Producer Jimmy Hotz was a huge fan from the beginning, and convinced B.B. King and Fleetwood Mac to buy their own systems for making new records and for touring. And composers like Jay Ferguson began to use the ST for scoring to picture.[11] "Sometimes they change a scene by just a few frames, and that involves just a simple tightening up by increasing the tempo in your sequencer," said Ferguson in a 1988 *STart* magazine interview. "Other times, they make wholesale cuts in a scene. If you've input properly into your sequencing program, you can just cut and splice and take out neatly whatever you want."[12] This kind of thing is routine today, but it was brand new and the ST was at the forefront.

In September 1986, nine months after Shivji first gave an interview to *Byte* magazine about it, *Atari* unveiled its new blitter (bit-block transfer processor) graphics chip. The blitter chip, which Atari styled BLiTTER, sped up moving chunks of data from one portion of memory to another, especially screen image data. The result was a snappier GEM interface and improved graphics performance in games. Atari planned to include the chip in all future ST models. It even promised a blitter upgrade for existing 520ST and 1040ST machines, which got everyone excited, but never followed through with a retail package. Later STfm machines had the socket for it, at least.

Even without an additional chip, as we'll soon see, game developers were busy finding new and exciting ways to harness the ST's power.

4 | Gaming

Around the release of the upgraded 1040ST, the platform's gaming lineup came into full focus. Although SunDog and Time Bandit remained top sellers, plenty of other developers jumped on board early. The best titles were all examples of what could only be done on a 16-bit computing platform, and only with hardware as powerful as what was found in the ST. Let's start with a game that combined jaw-dropping visuals with mouse control and fast-paced arcade-style action.

Starglider (Rainbird, 1986)

Developed by then-22-year-old Jeremy "Jez" San, Starglider blended wireframe vector-style graphics with a delicately shaded, three-dimensional control panel. It's impossible for me to discuss this title without hearing its extremely mid-80s-rock music loop in my head, but I'll try. In this game, you piloted an Airborne Ground Attack Vehicle. You had to shoot anything that moved in the wireframe 3D landscape—and especially the invading Stargliders that looked like mechanized pterodactyls and glided over the planet's surface. You battled the enemy mostly with your ship's lasers, although you periodically had to launch a missile to take out a certain unit. Sometimes you needed to replenish your ship's missiles, shields, and fuel.

San clearly drew inspiration from the Star Wars arcade coin-op to create this game. Thanks to the luscious use of color wireframes, crisp sound effects, and a fast frame rate, the game delivered a realistic impression of piloting a spaceship in combat using the mouse. As ambitious and impressive as the first-person Rescue on Fractalus was on the Atari 800, this was another clear example of just how big of an upgrade the ST could be when properly programmed.

Figure 4.1: A couple of years before Atari's own Star Wars arcade game made it to the ST, Starglider delivered the same kind of 3D action, wireframe graphics, and a truly fancy cockpit.

In addition to the game manual, Starglider came with a 64-page novella by science fiction author James Follett. It revealed parts of the plot and strategies for staying alive, and contained clues for identifying the gadgets and indicators in your cockpit that weren't expressed in the manual. A May 1987 review in *Compute!* called Starglider a kind of "aerial BattleZone" and said its "mix of bright colors, rapid movement, and strategic excitement [will] bring you back again and again." It was tough to beat this title as a do-it-all example of why the ST would shine as a gaming platform for years to come.

Postscript: In the early 1990s, Jez San helped design the Super FX chip found in the Super Nintendo's Star Fox cartridge. San has since gone on to found multiple software studios for the Xbox and for mobile apps.

Major Motion (MichTron, 1986)

Major Motion offered ST owners a colorful, slightly more sophisticated derivative of the popular Sega arcade game Spy Hunter, which helped make up for the lack of an official 16-bit Atari home conversion. Your goal in this game, loosely derived from James Bond, was to defeat The Draconian League, a terrorist group that took over the highways with its deadly fleet of vehicles, and make car travel safe for regular people again. Along the way, you had to fight off cars with impenetrable armor, spikes coming out of their wheels, and side-mounted machine guns. An enemy helicopter constantly terrorized you from the sky, and there was even an evil-twin of your car the League had at its disposal.

To combat the enemy, The Firm gave you a special vehicle with deadly attack capability, hidden inside an 18-wheeler that continued to develop more weapons for you. The mouse controlled the car, oddly enough. You pushed the mouse forward or backward to accelerate or brake, respectively. Moving it side to side let you swerve to the left or right. The left mouse button shot the first weapon you'd get in the game, a double machine gun. Shooting League cars netted 200 to 400 points, while running them off the road earned twice as much.

All League cars were blue or black, and civilian cars were other colors; if you shot too many of those by accident, a fighter jet would come and blast you with a missile. Whenever The Firm's truck had a new weapon ready for you, a truck icon would light up white on screen. When that happened, you had to maneuver your car it to acquire the new weapon. Possibilities included oil slicks, air missiles, a smoke screen (all using the keyboard), and a quick turbo boost you could activate with the right mouse button.

Major Motion was one of the games that highlighted the ST's lack of hardware scrolling, as it was choppy. The physics were also a little weird; after all, you could move the car sideways even when it was standing still, and the mouse in general was a bit bizarre for a game that cried out for a joystick. These glitches didn't affect gameplay too much, as the action was otherwise consistent and challenging. I found Major Motion to be addictive but difficult when I was a kid; the enemy vehicles seemed fast and a bit scary, and I remember the truck sometimes even inserted itself in the way.

There was demand for a Spy Hunter clone; in addition to the 8-bit home computer ports that appeared after the arcade game's release in 1983, an NES port came out around the same time as Major Motion. The October 1986 issue of *ST-Log* listed Major Motion as the eighth top selling game for the entire ST platform up until that point. To play Major Motion today, either in emulation or on a real ST, you'll want to set the CPU clock speed to 8MHz—something you'll need to do with some other early titles as well.

Star Raiders (Atari, 1986)

Star Raiders is widely considered the killer app that helped launch the Atari 400 and 800. It remains a landmark piece of code that fit in an 8KB cartridge and delivered an action-adventure space game any *Star Wars* or *Star Trek* fan could appreciate, complete with fast pseudo-3D space combat, a galaxy map, hyperwarp drive, and four distinct difficulty levels. Atari wisely decided to bring this game to the ST sooner rather than later; programmer Robert Zdybel did the conversion, while Jerome Domurat handled graphics and animation.

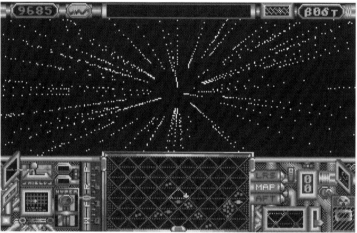

Figure 4.2: In some ways nothing would ever top Doug Neubauer's groundbreaking achievement on the Atari 400 and 800, but this nicely upgraded port of Star Raiders boasted much more detailed graphics, if a slower overall pace of play.

The result was impressive, but also a mixed bag. There were still four difficulty levels as before, and the goals were the same: Eliminate the enemy force before it destroyed you or all of your side's starbases. The ST's upgrades were immediately apparent. Your ship's dashboard was much more complex, and showed proper lights and controls. The galaxy map was now shown on the center radar screen; it was divided into triangular rather than square quadrants, which made it easier for the Zylons to surround a starbase. Enemy fighters and friendly starbases were more colorful and detailed, and there were more kinds of enemies and weapons than before.

Unfortunately, this version lacked the speed of the original, obtained through still-unbelievably efficient assembly code. Some people didn't like the slower pace of the ST game; Gauntlet developer Graham Tilley went so far as to say in a 1987 interview, after calling Star Raiders the definitive game for the 8-bit range, "Unfortunately the ST version is sadly lacking in the gameplay which makes the original so great."[1] Some Atari ads for the ST included Star Raiders as the example "gaming" screenshot, which may have seemed a bit out of touch, at least to current 8-bit Atari owners who already owned that game for years (though it looked so different new customers may not have made the connection).

Despite all the changes, Star Raiders was well worth playing. There was no way it could retain its killer app status on this new platform, nearly seven years after the first game appeared. But it was still immersive.

Adventures

One of the places where you'd see what the ST could do that 8-bit computers couldn't was in its more sophisticated adventure games. We'll start with an original property that was highly anticipated and truly compelling for its time, if ultimately flawed.

Brataccas (Psygnosis, 1986)

For many gamers, the name Psygnosis conjures up memories of the Sony PlayStation and its fabled Wipeout series—I was partial to Wipeout XL—as well as the developer behind the awesome Lemmings series and the long-running Formula One franchise. The Liverpool, England–based Psygnosis released more than 100 games through the year 2000 before becoming a wholly owned subsidiary of Sony Computer Entertainment Europe. There, it continued churning out well-received sequels for both the Formula One series and Wipeout before finally shutting down in 2012.

Less well known to most is that Psygnosis opened right around the time of the ST's launch and was behind some of the platform's best early games. The first game Psygnosis developed was also one of the first titles available for the ST, one that clearly showed off the ST's 16-

bit gaming prowess right out of the gate. Brataccas arrived amid considerable hype, as its ongoing development and launch were covered many times in the computer magazines of the day. This sci-fi adventure game featured good graphics, specifically a 2D-profile view with oversize characters and rooms. Your goal was to control a genetic engineer that figured out how to create a super-soldier, but didn't want to help the government do that; the government then declared him treasonous. He was forced to flee Earth to Brataccas, a distant mining colony on an asteroid, to clear his name from afar. As the protagonist, you had to explore Brataccas and talk to a series of corrupt outlaws in the colony in order to gather the evidence necessary to clear your name.

Unusually for an ST game, Brataccas ran in Medium resolution (640x200) instead of Low (320x200). This was the reason for its then-stunning screenshots and contributed to the hype machine surrounding the game. Unfortunately, the poor control system doomed the game to obscurity. Rather than having fixed controls, the game changes what each direction of the joystick or double push of the mouse button does depending what is happening on screen. The computer tries to interpret whether you want to walk, run, jump, fight, or pass through a doorway through a system called "implied action." As reviewer Michael Fleischmann put it in the June 1986 issue of *Antic*, "most of the time for me, it meant running into walls at full speed." Fleischmann wrote that one time it took him 20 tries to pick up an object off the floor.

If Brataccas was too cantankerous to be considered a genuine classic on the ST, it nonetheless served as a good mile marker and was one of many influential titles in the initial volley of software to arrive on the platform. Brataccas was indicative of the kind of in-depth gameplay the Atari ST made possible, and if you could somehow get used to the controls, it offered an engaging atmosphere and a good sci-fi story.

The Pawn (Rainbird, 1986)

Today we take photorealistic graphics for granted. But during the first several decades of home computer gaming, good graphics were hard to come by. Sometimes they were even designed as rewards for the player. As you progressed in a game, you'd get to see more and more beautiful images, or sometimes just one special one at the end. Rainbird's first graphic adventure took full advantage of this concept. At its heart, The Pawn was a text adventure similar to those that came out on 8-bit computers beforehand, but where this one shone was in its accompanying graphics quality. The game itself was also well done and surprisingly humorous, as it threw more than a bit of shade at its contemporary text-only competition.

Your goal in this game, at least at first, was to escape the mythical land of Kerovnia. The graphics weren't required to solve the game, which was a bit of a missed opportunity, but nonetheless were superb throughout. The Pawn's embedded parser won critical acclaim—not a small accomplishment considering how high Infocom had set the bar. Rainbird's advertisements claimed the game had a comprehensive 135-data-point understanding of the attributes of each in-game object. *Antic* called The Pawn "a little more stiffly written than some Infocom titles."

Perhaps the most obvious comparison in a historical sense is Myst. Myst's gorgeous 256-color graphics, sound design, and embedded QuickTime movies enabled greater immersion. The Pawn, released seven years prior to Myst, didn't compete, but it set the stage. You can also play The Pawn in a browser now thanks to a memorial site for developer Magnetic Scrolls located at msmemorial.if-legends.org—all the more awesome considering the game was coded in 68000 assembly language. The site's gone up and down a few times while I worked on this book, but it's worth a serious look.

King's Quest (Sierra, 1986)

No discussion of computer gaming in the 1980s would be complete without Sierra, the company that brought us the first and some of the best graphical adventures ever done. In this game designed by Roberta Williams, you were Graham, a young knight who must find three treasures scattered through the troubled Kingdom of Daventry in order to save it and become king.

The first Sierra adventures, such as King's Quest, which debuted in 1984 on the PCjr, were a kind of hybrid of text adventures (interactive fiction, like Infocom games) and graphic adventures (which show pictures, but still depend on text). Each game featured a mouse-controlled interface with fully animated graphics. Sierra referred to these titles as 3-D Animated Adventure Games, the 3-D denoting your ability to walk further into and out of the depth of each screen. In King's Quest, you controlled Graham with the mouse, intuitively pointing and clicking where you wanted him to go next. Whenever you wanted to examine objects, take something, or use it, you typed the command into the parser using the keyboard.

As with most adventure games of the era, you needed a pen and paper to map the game, though graph paper wasn't necessary in this case. Each screen had one or more exits; sometimes you needed to test them by moving Sir Graham to each edge and seeing if you could go somewhere else. All early Sierra adventures were scored using a points system that increased whenever you completed tasks in the game that were necessary to solve it. It was a good way to measure your progress, as you always knew the max score (in King's Quest it was 158), and that gave you a rough idea of how far along you were.

In 1987 Sierra repackaged the game using the now-familiar tan slip-cover boxes and renamed the title "King's Quest: Quest for the Crown," but it originally launched on the ST (and original IBM PCjr in 1984) without that moniker. Sierra fans may note King's Quest on the ST uses Adventure Game Interpreter 2 engine, an upgraded version of the original (a DOS rerelease that same year received the upgraded engine as well).

Either way, King's Quest was a natural fit for the mouse-driven Atari ST. This title set the stage not just for later Sierra games, but for LucasArts and other graphical adventures that dominated home computer gaming through the late 1990s. One ad for the game, like many of the era, said near the bottom, "Look for Sierra 3-D Animated Adventure Games at one of these fine dealers." It included a long list of local retail stores broken down by state. Those were the days.

Space Quest: The Sarien Encounter (Sierra, 1986)

Few heroes in video gamedom were as storied as the inept janitor Roger Wilco. And by few, I mean just about all of them. "Your mission: To scrub dirty floors. To replace burned-out light bulbs. To clean out latrines. To boldly go where no man has swept the floor!" Space Quest: The Sarien Encounter saw simultaneous releases on multiple 16-bit platforms in 1986, including the Atari ST. Mark Crowe and Scott Murphy programmed what would turn out to be the first in a series of six goofy science-fiction adventure games that sent up *Star Wars*, *Star Trek*, and a variety of pop-culture totems from the Energizer Bunny to Radio Shack (some of which attracted the attention of lawyers).

The game featured the same pseudo-3D environment that powered King's Quest. You could move Roger Wilco behind, in front of, and into objects, as the box copy put it, in addition to moving screen by screen to explore the game world. The game contained the same parser as King's Quest, part of Sierra's Adventure Game Interpreter engine, though here it was used to much more comic effect. You started the game on board the spaceship Arcada. You woke up from a nap in a broom closet to discover aliens had boarded the ship and killed some members of the crew. You immediately had to figure out how to get off the ship, which then propelled the storyline onto a barren wasteland planet with underground caves and new adventures to look forward to. As you solved puzzles, your score slowly increased to a maximum of 202 when you finished the game.

Space Quest seemed to take inspiration from Infocom's Planetfall text adventure. But in a 2015 interview, both Crowe and Murphy said they didn't know about Planetfall until they were already working on Space Quest II, and that they each had a distinct "aw, crap" moment (as they put it) when they saw the Planetfall box.[2] Both King's Quest and Space Quest did well enough on the ST to immediately merit sequels, and both served as useful demonstrations of the ST platform's power—and as a signal mouse control would also change computer gaming forever.

Computer Role-Playing Games (CRPGs)

Aside from pure twitch games found in the golden age of arcades, my *other* favorite genre of game will always be CRPGs. And as I mentioned in my first book about the Atari 8-bit computer lineup, I was sad certain key titles such as the Wizardry series never made it to the platform. Others, such as Origin Systems' Ultima IV: Quest of the Avatar, showed up a bit late and were missing key elements thanks to memory constraints (in this case, the in-game music). The ST gave CRPG fans like me *much* more to sink their teeth into.

Phantasie (SSI, 1986)

SSI made its name on bringing classic tabletop wargaming to the computer screen. But arguably more effective were its attempts at simulating Dungeons & Dragons–like role-playing games. The first SSI game we'll discuss for the ST was one of its best CRPGs. It set the tone both for what we should expect from both SSI and 16-bit platforms going forward.

Phantasie ended up being the first of three installments. Programmer Winston Douglas Wood developed the game on an Apple II; SSI then ported it to a number of other platforms, including as a graphically enhanced and more colorful version for the ST. I still love hearing the theme song with its trills in the melody. In Phantasie, you started the game on the medieval isle of Gelnor with a party of six adventurers, selected from a whopping 15 races and six character classes. You had to find the Nine Rings and use them to destroy the Dark Lord Nikademus and his Black Knights. The game featured a passive skill system Wood said was derived from RuneQuest and D&D.[3]

The towns in the game let you form parties, save games, buy and sell equipment, and store your money in a bank. The land spanned wilderness, mountainous regions, and of course, dungeons, populated with all kinds of treasure and 80 different monster types. In combat, the game showed detailed drawings of each player and monster. You queued up your commands and executed them all at once, and then the combat system played out that turn of the battle so you could see what happened before you made your next set of moves. Watching enemies get destroyed one by one was quite satisfying.

One of Phantasie's best features was it mapped itself. The "fog of war" was cleared as you explored and then stayed persistent. That meant you didn't need a pen and graph paper to map it by hand. The game even saved the state of a dungeon after you left it, which was unusual. And when you arrived back at a town, you chose how many shares of experience points you'd earned to allot to each character, another innovative difference from other CRPGs.

Phantasie first came out for several 8-bit systems in 1985. The ST port that arrived a year later was considerably sharper and more colorful, and supported the ST's mouse-based GUI. In an April 1987 review of Phantasie in *Dragon* #120, Hartley and Patrick Lesser wrote the ST port "incorporates far more sophisticated graphics and sound, and has almost become a new game because of the ST's environment. Windows now accomplish a great many of the keyboard commands, such as combat, spell-casting, and earning levels…In the ST version, you simply click on the Guild's doors with the mouse, and a pull-down menu at the top of the screen displays your choices…This same convenience is found throughout Phantasie, no matter where you are adventuring…The Atari ST version presents us with a far more graphically enjoyable and aurally pleasing format than previous releases of this game."

Figure 4.3: One of the best original CRPGs of its day, SSI's Phantasie delivered a massive world to explore and plenty of challenges for your party of six adventurers.

There was no in-game music, but that was one of the game's few faults. To this day I hear the game's distinct "bleep" alert sound in my head. Phantasie delivered hours of in-depth RPG goodness, and it was the start of a superb trilogy as well. Remember it would be at least a year before The Bard's Tale and an Ultima IV conversion showed up, much less Ultima V and VI. For a time, Phantasie was the most hard-core CRPG available for the ST.

The second installment, Phantasie II, came shortly after. It had a new town screen and, of course, all new maps to explore and monsters to fight, including new terrain features such as molten lava, mist, and Dark Voids. Otherwise, the game stuck to the original's mechanics, which, as the blog World 1-1 points out today, was commonplace with Ultima, Wizardry, and other popular RPG series.[4] This time around, Nikademus has created an orb he used to curse the people of the island of Ferronrah. Your goal was to find and destroy the orb. There was one new skill called Toss Rock, which any of the six characters could perform in combat at any time. You could import your party from the first game to play the second one, though you lost most of their accumulated gold and experience in the process. Together, the two games could well add up to more than 100 hours of play.

Rogue (Epyx, 1986)

The dungeon crawler Rogue was originally written for UNIX-powered mainframes in 1980 as a kind of graphical iteration of earlier text adventures (even though "graphics" in this case meant simple ASCII text characters). But Rogue came into its own on the Atari ST thanks to a colorful port from Epyx. Your goal was to retrieve the Amulet of Yendor from the Dungeon Lord. After entering your name at the trademark title screen with the red serpent, you began each game with a mace, a suit of armor, a bow, and some arrows. Along the way, you encountered hobgoblins, bats, winged kestrals, and a host of other monsters, 26 in all. Traverse each level of the underground maze and you'd find pots of gold, suits of armor, new weapons, food, wands, and scrolls that let you cast magic spells—some of it potentially cursed.

As you fought monsters, you gained experience points and levels. If you lost all your hit points, you were greeted with a death screen, complete with a three-dimensional tombstone and custom inscription containing your name. If you started another game, you had to begin at the top of the dungeon once more, and the layout was randomized each time, so you never played the same game twice.

Figure 4.4: The dungeon dive Rogue benefited considerably on the ST with a huge graphics upgrade, including a zoomed-in view and liberal use of color.

The main view consisted of three windows. The largest displayed the dungeon, while the right side showed your current inventory. You could control your character with the mouse, but it was clumsy; I always found it much easier to just use the keyboard cursor keys, or the ST's numeric keypad to move in eight directions instead of four. You attacked by moving "into" a monster, and picked up items simply by moving over them. The bottom of the screen provided a rolling text update of in-game action, such as "You have defeated the orc," or "The kestral has scored an excellent hit on you." As you played, you had to keep an eye on the bar graphs, which showed you how many hit points you had left, your current strength level, and how strong your armor was. After combat, it was important to rest to restore hit points.

The Atari ST port of the seminal CRPG contained a beautiful zoomed-in view, which featured colorful graphics and attractively drawn character and monster icons. You could also play the game zoomed out—it was still more attractive this way than old-school ASCII characters—or switch between the two views during the game by pressing the Enter key. Other keys let you equip or remove weapons or armor; at some point your pack would fill up, so you'd have to let go of some items if you wanted to pick up new ones.

Every interaction with monsters was also randomized to some extent, just like in Dungeons & Dragons, and weighted in some way based on the power of the monster you were attacking and your character's current strength and armor. Sometimes secret passages let you get to rooms ordinarily not visible. The lack of a multiple save-game feature made it extremely tough to get to the deepest of the 26 levels in order to claim the Amulet of Yendor. You could save your progress and go eat dinner, but once you were dead, you were dead and the save would be gone.

If I had to pick just one Atari ST game to play today, despite its lack of overall depth (no pun intended), it would be Rogue. It's tough to overstate the significance of this game, as it gave birth to an entire genre of solo-adventure turn-based and "action" RPGs such as Diablo and Torchlight, not to mention the proliferation of "roguelikes" that dot the gaming landscape today across consoles, Steam, and phones. I like to think a good portion of that influence came specifically from the Atari ST port of Rogue.

Temple of Apshai Trilogy (Epyx, 1986)

A refreshingly different interpretation of the common CRPG, the original Temple of Apshai appeared in 1979 and spawned many variants, sometimes collectively known as Dunjonquest. Temple of Apshai Trilogy was notable for its improved graphical elements, mouse-driven interface, and memorable title soundtrack on the ST. This package included upgraded versions of the original game and its two direct add-ons, Upper Reaches of Apshai and Curse of Ra.

In this game you controlled a single adventurer who explored a dungeon, fought monsters, and collected treasure and magic items. The GEM interface, although appreciated, still felt a little bit like a prototype here—sometimes moving your character in a room took multiple tries, and you still needed the keyboard if you had any hope of beating monsters quickly.

Temple of Apshai originally stood out for being one of the earliest CRPGs with graphics. It may also well be the first game that included paragraph-length room descriptions, as columnist Scorpia pointed out in an expansive survey of all the CRPGs released by the middle of 1991.[5] The descriptions were printed in the manual, and you matched them by number to the room you were currently in. These gave the game a similar feel to playing Dungeons & Dragons around a table with a real dungeon master. The ST contained enough power to contain and display these descriptions as part of the game, though.

My favorite Apshai game to this day remains Gateway to Apshai on the Atari 8-bit. But Temple of Apshai Trilogy occupied me for many hours on the ST, and I did appreciate the graphics upgrade. Reviewers were somewhat less kind. Gregg Pearlman noted several interface-related deficiencies in the May 1987 issue of *Antic* and said although many of the game's elements were interesting and imaginative, "Apshai probably should have actually been souped up a bit more for the ST, though, instead of just looking that way."

Alternate Reality: The City (Datasoft, 1986)

Next, let's talk about a port of an existing 8-bit title that serves as a good window into what the ST brought and didn't bring to the table. Philip Price's Alternate Reality series, sadly left unfinished after just two of the planned seven installments, quickly made its way from the Atari 8-bit line to the ST. Price didn't program the ST port; that task was handled by Rick Mirsky and Jim Ratcliff, with Steve Hofmann doing the graphics.

As before, you were kidnapped from a quiet life by an alien space-ship and transported to a room with one exit. You first created a character by walking through a colorful portal, which would randomly freeze a group of spinning counters to score your various attributes (Strength, Dexterity, and so on). You emerged at the other side of the portal in the City of Xebec's Demise. Once in the city proper, your goal was to build up your character by exploring the various passageways, fighting enemies, buying equipment, eating at taverns, and otherwise gathering clues to try to figure out how to return to Earth.

The ST port came with a Quick Reference card that explained the need for a blank Character disk, which you had to create before getting started, as well as the following instructions that encapsulated early life on the ST platform:

> 1. If you have a machine with ROM-based GEM (the operating system is always in the computer), just insert Side 1 of The City into Drive A and turn on the computer. The game loads automatically.

> 2. If your machine has RAM-based GEM (you use a system disk to boot the machine), insert the GEM disk into Drive A and turn on the computer. Once GEM is loaded, remove the disk and insert Side 1 of The City into Drive A. Double-click on the Drive A icon, then open the Auto folder. Double-click the AR file and the game loads.

The game itself contained numerous innovations, such as changing weather, night and day cycles, hidden character attributes that affected your well-being in various ways, a complete alignment system that responded to your in-game actions, a sophisticated combat system featuring the ability to charm or trick your enemies, and even an in-game economy where you could earn money at various jobs and invest it in banks.

The ST version added support for joining guilds of various disciplines, which brought another nice dimension to character development. Dedicated fans may have noticed significant changes to the arrangement of Gary Gilbertson's memorable music. It acquired more of a rhythmic staccato quality on the ST, likely as compensation for the Yamaha chip's three-voice configuration instead of POKEY's four-voice polyphony on the 8-bit platform.

Six more games were planned in the series. The City was meant to be a kind of home base for the other games once you've built up your character. Only one other game (The Dungeon) was released, itself just a split of what was supposed to be part of The City in the first place, so unfortunately there wasn't a whole lot to do beyond exploring and building up your character. Plus, the game was unbelievably difficult, with copper, shops, and experience points hard to come by. And whenever you died, you were gone forever and had to start from the beginning unless you had made an extra copy of your character disk. Even the song it played at your death was worthy of distinction, with on-screen lyrics and a bouncing ball just like the title sequence: "Now that you're gone…some will grieve on, on, and on…" It was this plodding, minor key imperial march thing that sounded like when Mozart was making fun of Salieri in the movie *Amadeus*. (What? You expected me to make *current* pop culture references?)

Time hasn't been kind to Alternate Reality's impressive technical achievements, either. The view of the game world through the interface was small and the 3D animation somewhat sluggish. And as with most games of this era, you needed to map it out on paper (though Datasoft thoughtfully provided you with graph paper and a head start in the manual). Ultimately, Alternate Reality proved too ambitious for its time, but it set the stage for modern, open-world, persistent CRPGs such as those in The Elder Scrolls series and World of Warcraft. (Note: This is a tricky one to emulate, as it seems particularly sensitive to the TOS version and needs an early hardware configuration. To get it working in Hatari, use TOS 1.00, uncheck Fast Floppy Access, check MMU emulation, and uncheck the Patch Timer-D box.)

Ultima III: Exodus (Origin Systems, 1986)

Ultima creator Richard Garriott founded Origin Systems in Houston in 1983 along with his brother, father, and Chuck Bueche (Chuckles, of Ultima fame). The group had grown sick of trying to collect payments from other companies that had published Garriott's games. Origin released numerous key games on the ST throughout the platform's life. One of my favorite RPGs on the Atari 8-bit platform was Ultima III: Exodus. Its arrival on the ST, refreshed with a new graphical user interface, gave me reason to play and solve it again.

As before, the game was the first in the series to let you play a party of characters (in this case, four) in an effort to save Sosaria from the evil Exodus. You had to build up your adventurers by fighting monsters, getting treasure, and gaining experience points and levels. The goal was to discover the secrets of the mysterious moongates and find the four marks that let you enter Exodus's lair.

The graphics were much improved on the ST—not necessarily sharper, but with 16 colors instead of four, and without requiring artifacting to display them. This meant you could easily see real differences in each character's appearance and outfits, and you didn't have to rely on, say, one character holding a cross and the other holding a staff to tell the cleric from the wizard. The game also ran quite a bit faster, which made it easier to move across Sosaria and explore the towns. Another key difference between the Atari 8-bit and ST versions, and not necessarily for the better, was the music. All of the tracks in-game were the same, but on the ST, they were pitched an octave higher. I never figured out why this was the case and I had always found it annoying. (Your tastes may vary.)

A May 1987 review in *Antic* complained there was still plenty of disk access, which was a problem then but not so much now if you're playing off an SD card or in an emulator. It also had the by-then standard issue combination mouse-and-keyboard interface; the mouse control helped, but you still needed the keyboard for a lot of tasks and the two together didn't necessarily make the game easier to control. Nonetheless, the game was enjoyable and is arguably the best period-correct iteration to play now (notwithstanding later MS-DOS upgrade patches and LairWare's 1995 640-by-480-pixel remake on the Mac).

Sports

The ST quickly became a solid platform for sports games. Some of the best were titles equally popular on other platforms, such as Accolade's Hardball!. Others weren't remarkable, such as Gamestar's GBA Championship Basketball Two-on-Two and On-Field (American) Football. Rather than survey the entire field, I'll instead focus on some titles that specifically shone on the ST. One of the biggest game studios of the 1980s, Accolade grew big fast, and had a hand in distributing some of the decade's most important titles. Let's start with one that practically revolutionized the way video games would model it for the foreseeable future.

Mean 18 (Accolade, 1986)

Mean 18 was the first golf game to deliver gameplay from the golfer's perspective. The game was also one of the first, if not the first, to use a three-click control scheme. The first click began the swing, the second set how hard you hit, and the last set the draw or fade of your swing. It truly felt realistic, if that was at all possible with a computer game, and the giant meter to the left made it satisfying to get your swing just right.

The game modeled four courses: Bush Hill CC, St. Andrews, Pebble Beach, and Augusta National. An expert mode made the correct swing tougher to achieve, while a beginner mode offered a caddy to help you select the right club for each turn. A practice green helped get you acquainted. Another then-unique feature was a course editor, which let you add bunkers, a creek, or a lake, and draw the green just the way you wanted it. The game technically supported one to four players, but because you were all taking turns it didn't necessarily matter. In 1988, *Compute!* praised Mean 18's "superb graphics and digitized sound," as well as the way it simulated everything from club selection to green breaks.

Access Software's Links on the PC in 1990 would push the bar further, with its 256-color VGA graphics and sampled digitized sound that played through the PC speaker. Years before Links, Mean 18 set the course for the genre. I've never been a big fan of golf, so for me to become addicted to Mean 18 meant something.

International Karate (Epyx, 1986)

Most of the world knew this game as International Karate, but in the US it was sold as World Karate Championship. Two martial arts experts—either one against the computer, or human versus human—faced off against each other in a deliberate, strategic, cerebral fight. Each time someone scored a hit, you started back at the original position and then fought again. It was precise and mathematical—more of a Karate Champ clone, rather than a game where you're punching and kicking your opponent repeatedly until his health falls to zero and he drops to the ground.

There were 11 different moves you could make with the joystick. You could score either a half point or a full point with each move. The first combatant to score two points won that round. There were some mini bonus games in between, where you'd break bricks or jump or dodge obstacles such as bouncing balls. In the single-player game, you started as a white belt and gradually worked your way through different opponents until you were fighting at the top level as a black belt.

The nice background graphics shifted and animated as you played, making the game feel more like it was taking place in real life, instead of on some abstract level. This occurred on a level not seen in competing games. The main sprites were large and detailed, and moved with a fluidity that foreshadowed what we'd see in 1991's Street Fighter II in the arcade. The graphics featured beautiful 16-color renderings of the Alps, New York City's Brooklyn Bridge, and Tokyo among the eight various scenes.

The Karate Kid Part II: The Computer Game (Microdeal, 1986)

In the mid 1980s you couldn't walk 10 feet without hearing a Mr. Miyagi reference. If you weren't on the ST platform for the release of this game, it may seem ridiculous to even cover it. Most blockbuster movie tie-ins weren't worth the floppy disks they came on. But this title had two tremendous things going for it: It arrived when there were still precious few games available for the ST, and it was actually good.

In this game you played Daniel, who wore white. You had to win fight after fight using a variety of movies to score hits on your opponent's body each time. The game started with one-on-one karate, but gradually increased the number of enemies you faced at any one time. The backdrops were beautiful and the sampled digital sound effects were straight out of karate movies. Breaking up the game were a series of full-size animated screens where you tried to score bonus points catching a fly with chopsticks (as Mr. Miyagi himself) or breaking ice with your bare hands. In the last battle of the game, you faced Chozen in the Castle of King Shohash; you had to defeat him to win the game and learn the secret of the drum that appeared at the top-right corner of the screen.

What made the game work were its fluid animation and precise control. I always liked the way a fighter, after a hard hit, sat up on the floor and scratched his head before fully getting up and rejoining combat. You'd think a joystick with a single button would be limiting in an age of Street Fighter V and Soul Calibur 6, but it turned out there were a variety of moves you could pull off—16 in total (eight directions, with the Fire button either pressed or not). The moves varied in speed, impact, and recovery time, and became second nature after just a few games. A two-player mode let another person control an enemy fighter facing Daniel; the goal was to win three bouts before the other person did.

For the record, I tried to catch a fly with chopsticks in real life recently. It didn't go well. I'm also not planning on practicing for 40 years like Mr. Miyagi, so I suppose it's all for the best.

ST Karate (Eidersoft, 1986)

If you've ever seen or played this game, you'd recognize the menu screen instantly. It featured six karate warriors bowing in a sped-up "wave" pattern. During each game, and like the other karate games we've discussed, ST Karate featured a series of attractive backdrops. These were a big deal in 1986. On each screen, you had to defeat the other player (either computer- or human-controlled). Both fighters had an energy bar at the top of the screen; this bar reset every round. The trickiest aspect of the game was you didn't automatically turn to face your opponent. You had to hold the button and push in the opposite direction to turn around.

I spent many hours playing this game. I found the little ninja stars that periodically flew out to be incredibly annoying, and the same went for trying to kick or punch apart all the vases on the bonus screen. The action wasn't precise—I think the game would have benefited from just a bit more attention to collision detection and the frames of animation for each fighter.

ST Karate is flawed in ways that the Atari 8-bit would have handled better. The game illustrates the ST's sheer speed, beautiful color, and sharp resolution at the expense of the Atari 8-bit's smoother sprites and fuller-sounding POKEY chip. Perhaps the closest analog on the 8-bit would have been Chop Suey, which came out the year before. Chop Suey was another karate game with large sprites, and it played better, even if the graphics were more pedestrian and the fighting was set in an ultrasimple, pseudo-3D rectangle of a stage (albeit in front of three rows of crowd participants).

Championship Wrestling (Epyx, 1986)

American wrestling became absolutely huge in the 1980s, its breakout decade with the WWF, so it was little surprise to find video games offering to bring the action home. It was a bigger surprise to play a game like Epyx's Championship Wrestling, which was good enough even a non-wrestling fan such as me wanted to play it all the time. The game was much more fun than Nintendo's Wrestling cartridge for the NES. Even though the NES was an 8-bit system, its various hardware enhancements were better suited to action gaming, so it was a nice surprise to see the ST excel at something with two oversize characters on screen in a two-player environment.

Championship Wrestling put you in control of one of eight wrestlers, a real cast of characters with names such as K.C. Colossus, Colonel Rooski, and Purple Hays. Each one had a signature move, plus a standard array of 25 others, including spin kicks, body slams, leg drops, and airplane spins, which you could use to dispatch your opponent. The crowd would join in on the fun, cheering or booing depending on how well you were doing. You could even throw your opponent out of the ring.

As you fought, you had to watch your strength level, as certain moves took more strength than others; your strength would then slowly rise back up after each move. The joystick control and collision detection were pretty much spot-on, and the game played at a good enough clip to keep you glued to the action. A Practice mode let you get used to a wrestler's moves in the ring. You had the most fun when playing with a friend, although you could also play against the computer in a series for the Championship Wrestling Belt. In Competition mode, you and up to seven friends took turns battling each other in a giant tournament.

Strategy

The ST's library overflowed with sophisticated strategy games, many of which offered more detail and more involved experiences than you'd get on 8-bit platforms. Even early in the ST's life span, we saw some tentative steps into new genres that weren't possible before.

Little Computer People (Activision, 1986)

Long before The Sims and even several years before SimCity, Little Computer People simulated real life in surprising and fun ways. In this program, designed by David Crane and Rich Gold, there were, well, Little Computer People (LCPs) inside your Atari ST. And now because of this special Activision software, you got to meet one of them and watch him go about his life. Your LCP, in his "house on a disk," spent his days eating, sleeping, playing organ (literally every review and site I found talking about this game called it a piano; it's an organ, wake up people), watching TV, enjoying his turntable, and working on his own (even littler) computer. You had to care for him. That meant feeding him and giving him water, talking to him (by typing words), playing games with him, or giving him presents. The parser had a vocabulary in excess of 100 words.

Once you started a new game with a new house, your LCP would spend a little time working up the courage to enter the house and then getting familiar with everything. Then he'd go get his suitcase and unpack for the duration. You could also wake him up in the morning with his alarm clock and feed the dog. More importantly, you needed to attend to his moods to keep him happy and emotionally fulfilled with friendship. It helped to play games with him, give him activities to perform, and especially be nice to him, such as saying please and thank you. Together, you could play poker, blackjack, Card War, anagrams, and word puzzles. The game also came with a Deed of Ownership for your "house" you were supposed to fill out and mail to Activision. I wouldn't recommend doing this today.

Compared with a broader, more in-depth game such as The Sims, Little Computer People was lacking. The graphics were sharp and detailed, but there was less animation than you would expect. A January 1987 review in *Computer + Video Games* pointed out numerous ways the Commodore 64 port was better, if not as attractive looking. Inexplicably, in all versions, you could only play a male character with a dog.

But perhaps the program's biggest quirk was related to the above: Although you only received one house, you also only received one LCP. It was always the same one. If you wanted a different LCP, you had to buy another copy of the program. A March 1987 review in *Compute!* highlighted the game's educational appeal for children to learn how to take care of his or her own LCP. With regard to the one LCP-per-disk thing, the reviewer found it initially disappointing, but then realized it's in keeping with the rest of the design: "You *can't* change LCPs, because you have made a commitment to caring for the one you already have. The LCP simulates a little person inside the computer, one which the child must take care of even if he would like to have somebody else." The reviewer went on to say as a design decision it was unusual, but it was "one worth considerable praise."

Figure 4.5: Who knew there were little people inside your Atari ST? If anyone picks up their monitor, turns it upside down, and shakes it while playing Little Computer People, write in and let me know what falls out.

Little Computer People went on to win numerous magazine awards for its innovative design. From a historical perspective it's worth looking at the game as a prototype example of computer-controlled simulated people. In a CNN online chat in January 2000, a reader asked Will Wright if he had ever played Little Computer People. He responded, "Yes, a long time ago. I've since gotten to know several people who were involved with that project, and many of them gave valuable feedback on The Sims, especially Rich Gold."

Perhaps the most interesting thing about this game today is how every single copy had a different LCP. A 2004 post by member fiath in AtariAge's ST forum said the only thing different on each copy was a serial number used to seed a random number generator, which in turn shaped the LCP's personality and appearance in the same way each time. This also means everyone who downloads the same ROM on a website today (not advocating for or against, as per the usual legal gray area) is always getting the same LCP.

Shanghai (Activision, 1986)

Activision's Shanghai worked the same as Mahjong in real life. There were 144 tiles, arranged in various four-level patterns and facing up. You had to match open pairs of identical tiles in order to remove them from the board and reveal new tiles underneath. "Open" tiles were those that could move left or right freely; if you clicked on a closed tile, the computer beeped and said it was an invalid move. The three higher layers of tiles were marked with colors (green, yellow, and purple) to help you distinguish what was open. If you matched two tiles and double-clicked, the game removed them from the board and decreased the tiles-remaining counter by two. You could play in one of four modes: Solitaire, Team Play, Tournament, or Challenge.

This probably doesn't seem like a big deal today. But now, we're completely used to the ubiquity of mouse-controlled card and puzzle games. We didn't even get free Solitaire and Minesweeper in Microsoft Windows until 1990, with version 3.0. Minesweeper was first part of an option pack; it wasn't included with the base operating system until Windows 3.1 in 1992. Although Shanghai was packaged retail software for the Atari ST, playing it was still novel. Thanks to the ST's high-resolution color graphics, the tiles were easy to distinguish and looked quite realistic. The title screen dragon even breathed animated flames as the game loaded.

The game came with a rule book, a strategy booklet, and a guide to the seven different classes of tiles (Winds, Seasons, Dragons, and so on). All of these things were accessible from the Help drop-down menu. You could also "peek" under tiles or instruct the computer to show all possible moves. Both functioned as miniature cheat modes. When I received Shanghai for the ST I had yet to ever play Mahjong solitaire before. I became addicted quickly.

Silent Service (MicroProse, 1986)

Another top software developer of the 1980s and 1990s, MicroProse released a number of critically acclaimed titles for the ST platform. The company was known for developing realistic simulations with just enough action elements to make them addictive. The first we'll discuss,

Silent Service, offered the kind of in-depth gameplay ST owners wanted. A submarine simulation set in the Pacific Ocean during World War II, Silent Service evoked the feel of movies such as *Das Boot* and *The Hunt for Red October*. It offered five war patrol scenarios and seven convoy action scenarios. Your goal in each was to vanquish the enemy while surviving and maintaining your own submarine and crew.

Silent Service's sound design came in for special mention. In an April 1987 review in *Antic*, Rick Teverbaugh wrote, "Silent Service provides a you-are-there feeling in so many ways, but the most striking feature is its sound." Teverbaugh went on to describe the ping when an enemy destroyer located your ship on sonar, the splash of a depth charge drop, a whistling explosion indicating you'd been hit by a destroyer's shell, and a metallic grinding sound from scraping your sub on the bottom of the ocean or (worse) colliding with an enemy ship. An 8-bit port of this game would have had synthesized sound effects, not digital samples, so this was new and different.

The submarine simulation was one of the more popular game genres of the 1980s. Silent Service did a fine job of balancing the more realistic aspects of simulation and the fun of an action video game. I always enjoyed playing it, and I never considered myself a submarine or even wargame enthusiast. Back when it wasn't the norm, Silent Service had a way of pulling you in and convincing you that you were on a submarine.

Daleks (Bloom County Software, 1986)

As the ST community grew online, plenty of people began programming little utilities, games, and other desk accessories, the same way it always happened with a new computer platform people cared about and wanted to contribute to. I'm going to call out just one of these now, because it still sticks out in my mind as the most memorable. Daleks was a simple, downloadable shareware game that occupied my time probably far longer than it should have. I remember it primarily as a game that helped me get used to the ST's mouse. I also appreciated that this windowed game changed the background color from neon green to light gray.

Because this game wasn't sold at retail or online, but was simply a free download, it's difficult to find out much about it today. You were Doctor Who, and the rules of the game were simple. During each turn, you could move in one of eight directions, designated by arrows surrounding your character. Each time you moved a space, all of the Daleks on the screen would also move one space closer to you. Your job was to move in such a way that all of the Daleks collided with each other—either alive, or one at a time into heaps of metal left by previously destroyed Daleks—until there were none left, in which case you won the level, or until you were exterminated, in which case you were dead.

Options at the top of the screen let you turn the sound off, start again, or view the high score table. The Command drop-down menu was more interesting; it let you do things like teleport randomly on the board, use your sonic screwdriver to zap everyone immediately surrounding you, or hit L for Last Stand to automate the rest of the possible moves and assume you're going to stand still until all the Daleks are dead. (Hopefully that's what happened and you didn't get obliterated because of poor planning.)

That's all it was. The bottom of the screen contained your name, score, current level, and high score. It looked sharper in monochrome, but I always played it in medium resolution on a color monitor, because that's what I had. The game was free to play, but the programmer Brian McClendon asked for $10 if you liked it or were addicted to it. I should find him and send him a check.

For gaming and otherwise, by the end of 1986 the ST had established itself as the premier 16-bit personal computer mere mortals could afford. The Amiga was quite slow in getting off the ground, and the Macintosh remained way too expensive for most consumers. Even Apple's new Macintosh Plus, with 1MB of memory and an integrated 9-inch monochrome display and floppy drive, stickered at a whopping $2,599. ST sales steadily increased and Atari Corporation became larger and more profitable again.[6] The aggressive cost cutting and improved net profit grabbed the attention of Wall Street, and Tramiel took Atari Corporation public in November. By the middle of the following year, the stock would triple its IPO price.[7]

5 | Mega

In the late 1980s, Atari began to advertise the ST on television more heavily in the US and UK. One popular Atari commercial purported to tell viewers "how the computer business works." The ad showed how Atari, IBM, and Apple all buy chips, circuitry, and plastic, but IBM and Apple have these "special attachments that add to their price." The commercial then cut to a shot of small plastic IBM and Apple company logos. It claimed the ST has more power than the Mac SE and more features than the IBM PS/2 Model 50 at about one-third the price.

I don't remember seeing any ST commercials on TV in America, but I was following the computer closely in various magazines. The excitement was hard to miss. The ST platform was already in full swing for home consumers. Soon, Atari would have the business hardware the company needed to go after IBM and the Mac in earnest.

Mega 2 and 4

Atari's biggest computer-related introduction of 1987 took place at the Winter CES in January. The Mega 2 and Mega 4 ST machines featured new form factors along with some important hardware upgrades. The Mega STs consisted of low-profile CPU enclosures that housed a double-sided 3.5-inch floppy drive. The enclosures were sized such that they'd stack neatly with the company's hard drive and removable tape drive. They were also intended to act as strong stands for monitors, a necessity given Atari's inexplicable reluctance to include a stand with its ST displays.

The keyboards had an improved feel, thanks to new rubber cups under the keys instead of weak springs. Underneath the keyboard on one side were the mouse and joystick ports in recessed areas, with a path to run the cabling. The keyboard also had legs, so you could prop it up at a slight angle toward you if desired. A coiled cable connected the keyboard to the Mega's CPU enclosure right next to the cartridge port.

Figure 5.1: Atari made an ST for business with the Mega, a model that could support more memory and stack on top of a hard drive.

The biggest change inside was the available RAM. Atari sold the Mega in 2MB and 4MB versions (hence the model designations). A 4MB ST instantly catapulted the platform into the higher-end business realms normally occupied by PC-compatibles and the Mac. Atari designed the Mega STs as "open-architecture" computers that could accept a faster CPU and a math coprocessor. The internal architecture was similar otherwise, though; the machine still had a 68000 CPU that ran at 8MHz, it remained fully compatible with earlier ST machines, and all of the original ports were still present. The Mega STs were also the first Atari machines to come with a PLCC socket for the blitter chip for faster graphics, although some early models reportedly left the socket unfilled from the factory. The Mega STs added a battery-backed clock and calendar powered by two AA batteries, and there was a small, quiet fan inside with an accompanying exhaust vent on the back panel.

To coincide with the Mega's release, Atari refreshed its SH204 drive to better fit with the new lineup. At first, Atari simply incremented the model name and called it SH205, but quickly renamed it the Megafile 20. The new enclosure was the same size as the Mega computer, so you could stack one on top of the other. It usually made sense to put the hard drive on the bottom as a base stand so you could more easily access the floppy drive in the main computer. Atari also released an upgraded Megafile 30 model with 30MB of storage. Third-party manufacturers quickly began to release iterations of their peripherals for the Mega line as well. One notable vendor here was Supra Corporation, which introduced the MegaDrive ST, a 40MB drive upgrade that installed inside the Mega's case, connected to the internal DMA port on the motherboard, and took power from the Mega's own supply.

The Mega STs were designed to work (and be sold) with Atari's new SLM804 laser printer, which Atari positioned as a direct, lower-cost competitor to Apple's groundbreaking LaserWriter. The computer was often photographed in Atari marketing materials with the SM124 monochrome monitor, emphasizing its business chops over any improvements in gaming from the blitter chip. Atari achieved a lower price with its laser printer by omitting a processor and memory, opting instead for the Mega to render pages internally and then control the printer through its DMA port and companion SLMC804 controller interface.

The Mega STs gave Atari the stronger product it needed for business markets, most notably in the UK. They didn't move the needle all that much in total sales, and Atari was still vulnerable to a sharp challenge from the Amiga on the low end. Atari also wasn't providing an internal hard drive as you'd find on a 286 PC or a Mac SE in 1987. The ST was still largely operating as a floppy-disk-only platform, as hard drives were extra and expensive as peripherals went, putting the total cost of a model so equipped within shouting distance of something from an IBM clone manufacturer.

With the introduction of the new Mega STs, Atari also saw fit to upgrade TOS. The new version 1.02 came baked into ROM on the new machines. The first change was to add support for the Mega's new blitter chip—and it was done in a transparent way so software didn't have to be rewritten, assuming it was written well in the first place. The good news was if your favorite program wasn't compatible, you could turn the blitter off in TOS with a simple software switch.

TOS 1.02 also included numerous smaller upgrades, including a rewritten RS-232 handler, support for the battery backed clock, and (finally) the ability to hold down a mouse button so that it sent repeated "clicks" to the OS. This way, you could hold down a scroll bar button in a window and not have to press it a bunch of times.[1] There were also dozens of bug fixes inside the OS. As time bore out, TOS 1.02 introduced few compatibility issues with older software, and was stable and solid in daily use.

Atari SX212

The SX212 ($99.95) promised what until then Atari had been unable to deliver: a proper Hayes-compatible 300/1,200bps modem that could auto-answer and upload and download files. For the ST, the SX212 was plug-and-play; it connected to the ST's RS-232 modem port and worked fine with basic VT-52 emulators.

The SX212's gray plastic housing looked the same as the XEP80 Atari made available to bring 80-column support to its 8-bit XE line. The front panel contained many of the same status lights that you'd find on common (and much more expensive) Hayes modems, including a high-speed indicator for 1,200bps use and whether auto-answer was enabled. The *Antic* reviewer had no problem setting up a FoReM-ST-powered BBS and then running it with the SX212.

For the Atari 8-bit line, the SX212 was a different story. It only offered auto-answer and download capabilities if you connected it via an RS-232 interface, meaning through an Atari 850 interface. If you connected it to an Atari computer using an SIO cable, you'd no longer be able to use many of the software packages that enabled those features. And confusingly, the SX212 also hit the market without software of its own, as a June 1988 review in *Antic* pointed out, although it still worked with freebies such as AMODEM on the Atari 8-bit platform.

It's a shame the SX212 didn't arrive a few years sooner, though I suppose we could say that about lots of Atari computer products. The problem was as Atari finally released its 1,200bps modem, Hayes, Supra, and others were already selling 2,400bps models (albeit at higher prices). The best part is people are still using the SX212 and other modems with their ST systems today to connect to BBSes.

New Applications

Software manufacturers continued to develop improved applications for the ST lineup, now that there was something of an installed base to sell to. Some developers even found ways to push the hardware past what Atari engineers had originally intended, or even thought possible.

Cyber Paint (Antic Publishing, 1987)

Cyber Paint was a comprehensive 2D computer animation package published by *Antic* magazine and developed by Jim Kent, the same person who was behind Aegis Animator the year before. This new software worked as a kind of hybrid between paint software and an animation studio, letting you essentially paint many frames and then animate them together. It offered comprehensive creation and editing tools, including flood fills, Airbrush, Stipple, tweening operations, and a flexible, broadcast-like editing mode that updated in real time with the current frame number at the bottom of the screen.

Cyber Paint included titling facilities within the program, and you could operate on individual areas of the frame. This means you could, for example, grab a title and rotate it as an object, and then the program would then generate the intermediate frames necessary to complete the rotation. "The main advantage over a Mac is it's in color, and it's cheap," Kent said in a 1989 interview on *The Computer Chronicles*. He demonstrated several animations, including a robot emerging from water, a bee flapping its wings, and a merged animation containing both. "The major benefit over an Amiga is it tends to be a lot more reliable. I've lost so many floppy disks on an Amiga that I've sort of gotten depressed over it." Cyber Paint was one of the first programs that let you paint across time in a compressed digital format.[2]

Spectrum 512 (Trio Engineering, 1987)

NEOchrome and Degas Elite both did a nice job of bringing visual arts to the ST's display, so how do you top it? By writing a program that could display the computer's entire 512-color palette simultaneously—up to and including 48 colors on a single scan line. Boris Tsikanovsky's Spectrum 512 did this with a perfect static image, with no flicker or other visual tricks. Trio Engineering, the company Tsikanovsky started to sell Spectrum 512 and other products, explained its engineers hooked an oscilloscope to the ST's MMU chip and reverse-engineered the timers. This way, they could add more colors into extra simulated bit planes before the signal traveled to the Shifter chip.[3]

Also included was a then-groundbreaking technique called anti-aliasing, which you may be familiar with from today's graphics cards. Anti-aliasing smooths out the lines and curves on the screen so they look sharper than they would otherwise, reducing or eliminating the "pixelated" look. In Spectrum 512, it worked by shading a jagged line with darker pixels of the same color to make it look smoother than it was before.[4] The program included freehand, rubber line, and French curve tools, along with 20 patterns (plus room for 20 defined by the user) and 38 brush shapes. There was also an airbrush tool, a blur tool, and an undo buffer, plus a 1MB 12-screen cut-and-paste buffer. A Gradient Fill mode let you create a beautifully shaded transition from one color to another automatically.

A two-page magazine ad that ran for Spectrum 512 boldly took the Degas bumblebee image and recreated it with a 512-color version that was more dynamic and, well, sparkly. The only issue with Spectrum 512 didn't affect its beautiful output: the interface. It was complex enough that you needed some time to adjust in a way you didn't with NEOchrome or Degas. A review in the August 1988 issue of *ST-Log* gave an example of the right mouse button, which did three different things based on where the cursor was currently located. The program even imported 4,096-color Amiga images, using a dithering technique and 3,000 simulated colors from the ST's palette to interpolate the image in the best way possible.

ViewTouch (ViewTouch, 1987)

Vertical applications were no one's idea of a good time, but it's worth calling out this one. ViewTouch was the first touch-screen point-of-sale system. Entrepreneur Gene Mosher first began working on restaurant point-of-sale systems in 1979, when his electronic cash register's motherboard failed and he had to replace it with his Apple II. Soon it became apparent you would need some kind of graphical touch interface for this to be practical on a larger scale.

"In 1986, I hired Nick Colley to do the C programming to complement and bring to life the color bitmapped touch-screen GUI that I was developing," Mosher said. "The result was the world's first color-graphic, touch-screen, point-of-sale computer. We used the revolutionary Atari 520ST, the only computer up to the job at the time…[it] was the first consumer computer with the power and integration of a workstation."[5] He installed his first ST system, with first-generation touch-screen POS software, in a restaurant of his in Springfield, Oregon, and demoed it at the 1986 Fall COMDEX.

Mosher went on to sell the system beginning in 1987. The ViewTouch was a $4,999 package that included a Mega 2, a special color monitor with glass touch-screen hardware, a 40-column receipt printer, software, and a cash drawer.[6] The software employed dozens of menu pages made in NEOchrome. "To order a hamburger customers simply touch a hamburger icon. The Mega adds up the items, figures the tax, and prints out a receipt," all without needing the keyboard.

Today, point-of-sale systems are absolutely everywhere and have largely replaced the lowly cash register, especially thanks to the availability of inexpensive iPads and other tablets. Wildly, the original ViewTouch still exists today as free point-of-sale software, licensed under the GNU public license version 3. It works on a Raspberry Pi coupled with any inexpensive touch-enabled desktop monitor or Android tablet. You can download a copy yourself from GitHub.[7]

Zoomracks II (Quickview, 1987)

A small but important development in the history of computing was the little-remembered Zoomracks, a database management system developed by Paul Heckel and first unveiled in 1985. It pioneered a version of the cards-and-stacks metaphor most commonly attributed to Apple's HyperCard, which is widely regarded as the inspiration for Tim Berners-Lee's first web browser proposal in 1989. Heckel's card-based system used Rolodex-like racks to hold cards that could be "inserted, removed, and moved into other slots in the same or different racks."[8]

Zoomracks II was available for both the ST and the PC. It let you view up to nine files at once in a rack at the side of the screen. It gave you the ability to mark where you were working in one file, go to another one, and then return to your mark in the first, a capability known as "back to."[9] A 1987 *InfoWorld* review panned the PC version of the product's performance, saying it was "much faster" on the ST, and overall called it a "highly innovative but also eccentric, slow, and somewhat buggy flat-file database system that might be interesting for those who like to experiment."

Despite a three-page feature in the Winter 1987 issue of *STart,* Zoomracks never gained traction. Heckel sued Apple, IBM, and others over his patent in 1988, a controversial move that resulted in Apple making a one-time payment to Heckel, but not the royalties he had sued for.[10] The suit helped relegate Zoomracks to the dustbin of history.

With software, the metaphor had to be simple, Heckel said:

> A spreadsheet is a good example. It gives people a base that is independent of the program. In word processing, the scroll is the basic metaphor. In Zoomracks, you have the time card rack, just like a time card rack at work. You take a card out of the rack and zoom in on it and see what's on the card.[11]

Regardless of the program's failure in the marketplace, it's hard to argue with the concept.

ChessBase (Saitek, 1987)

Little-known then but hugely influential in retrospect, ChessBase upended everything we knew about computer chess. On screen, the program wasn't impressive—it looked like any number of two-dimensional chess games you'd find on the personal computers of the day. But the simple 2D board on screen hid what it was: a competition-level chess game and an interactive, graphic database for storing and reviewing some 1,000 chess games. With that database you could analyze the moves from world champions playing international tournaments, your own opponents, or even yourself, right on the computer screen instead of in books. You could select groups of games to review based on the opening variation, from a certain player, and more. Then it was a matter of using the arrow keys on the keyboard to step back and forth through the moves. You could also save the current position so you could move the pieces around yourself before continuing where you left off.[12]

Chess champion Garry Kasparov was an enthusiastic supporter of ChessBase. In 1986, he first signed a sponsorship deal with Atari, netting him 50 new systems he used to form a youth computer club in Moscow, making it the first in the Soviet Union.[13] He and two friends, Frederic Friedel and Matthias Wüllenweber, built ChessBase, the first professional chess program that could compete on a world-class level. Kasparov said in a 2017 interview he even used a version of the program (a diskette labeled "00001") to review his real-life opponent's previous games in hours, "a process that would have taken weeks without a computer."[14] He said the preparation with the program helped him win the next tournament 7-1. Soon not just Kasparov but other Grandmasters began to use laptops to prepare for tournaments.

"There's no way to prove causation, but I'm certain that the rapid decline of many veteran players in the 1989-1995 span, when Chess-Base became standard, had much to do with their inability to adjust to the new technology," Kasparov said.[15]

The company sold the program for $229.95, a demo version for $49.75, additional opening classifications for $19, and a one-year subscription to an accompanying ChessBase magazine with six disks for $89. Stunningly, ChessBase is still going some 30 years later. The latest PC version at the time of this writing, ChessBase 15, was released on November 15, 2018. It includes a new training mode, a 7.6-million-game historical database, more than 70,000 master analyses, and a new ray tracing engine for 64-bit CPUs that works at 4K (3,840-by-2,160) resolution. "While they may have shortened the careers of a few older players, computers also enabled younger players to rise more quickly," the company stated. "Not just playing the games, but because of how PC database programs allowed elastic young brains to be plugged into the fire hose of information that was suddenly available."[16]

STOS The Game Creator (Terrific Software, 1987)

Creating your own games started out relatively straightforward on 8-bit computers, but quickly became more complex as you added more graphics, sound, and animation to your programs. The ST was another jump in complexity, thanks to its 16-bit processor and ability to program in C and other higher-end languages. But what if you just want to make a simple game quickly? That's where STOS The Game Creator came in—and it was honestly much more powerful than you would have expected.

This program gave you an entire suite of tools for creating arcade games, including its own BASIC, a sprite editor, a character set editor, a music editor, a room designer, and even an optional compiler. It came with three example games in the box: a horizontal-scrolling train game, a vertical space shooter, and a Breakout clone. You could work with up to 15 sprites and 16 scrolling areas, and add stock sounds effects, import and compress Degas or NEOchrome images, and create drop-down menus and windows and files that stored in-game data.

If your only exposure to prepackaged "game creators" included level designers and construction sets, STOS The Game Creator was on another level. You didn't need BASIC programming knowledge to get started, but it helped. A September 1989 review in *STart* called out the manual for being "roughly the size of a Dostoyevsky novel," but that the manual was tutorial in nature, and that STOS BASIC was friendly even with its error messages and powerful trace routine for debugging your program.

Other game creation software included STAC, The ST Adventure Creator from the same company (capable of creating Infocom- or The Pawn–style interactive fiction), and TaleSpin (from MichTron/Microdeal) for rolling your own point-and-click adventure games that played like primitive LucasArts titles. One of the 47 or 48 projects I want to do after finishing this book is go back and try creating a game with one of these programs.

CRPGs

The year 1987 saw some more excellent CPRGs arrive on the ST, and we'll get to those, but they were all overshadowed by a single title, one that would come to define an entire subgenre and become the biggest-selling title on the Atari ST platform.

Dungeon Master (FTL, 1987)

Faster Than Light, the developer behind SunDog: Frozen Legacy, spent the next two years hard at work on its next game. The result was incredible. If you had to pick just one title that embodied the ST, the platform's true killer app, Dungeon Master would be it. This is despite how the title was essentially a hard-core, real-time CRPG with what would normally be a distinctly narrow audience. The game's box promised to "put you *inside* [emphasis in the original] the most detailed dungeon ever created in software," and it completely succeeded.

Your goal in this seminal title by Doug Bell and Dennis Walker was to penetrate the depths of a foreboding dungeon to recover the Firestaff and save the world from succumbing to Lord Chaos. Even the way you assembled your party was unusual and groundbreaking. You started the game at the beginning of the dungeon in the Hall of Champions, a series of corridors with framed mirrors on the walls. The mirrors contained imprisoned "champions" you could free to join your party. You could choose a total of four; clicking on a mirror displayed the champion's attributes and possessions, as well as their skills (Fighter, Wizard, Ninja, or Priest). You could either resurrect a champion as they were before imprisonment or reincarnate them as something else. You also needed to choose one champion as the party leader, who would open doors and pick up objects. During the game, you constantly had to make sure each champion had enough food and water, not to mention a supply of torches to light the way. Some creatures you killed could be eaten as food.

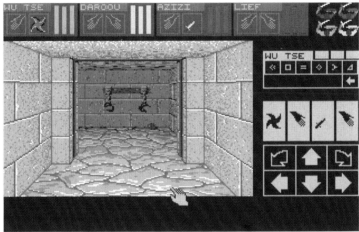

Figure 5.2: Perhaps the killer app for the Atari ST platform, the groundbreaking Dungeon Master brought an immersive dungeon delve to your computer screen.

What was truly innovative was the level of environmental interaction; you could pick up any object and unlock doors with keys, all by using the mouse. The dungeon was full of levers, platforms, and switches you could manipulate, and often that you'd only notice in the first place if you looked closely. You could manage each champion's inventory with the mouse as well. When you clicked an object, the pointer cursor would then turn into that object to show you were currently moving it. You examined an object by placing it on the eye icon, equipped it with the hands, and ingested it (if possible) by clicking it onto the mouth. This "paper doll"-style interface, with graphic representations of each of the four characters and individual sprites for pieces of gear, soon became the standard for dungeon crawlers.

The game's real-time engine added to the challenge, and was a completely novel concept at its introduction. It meant you had to equip and prepare your characters before you ventured into unknown territory; otherwise monsters could surprise your party and then start attacking you while you figured out where you put everyone's weapons. The real-time system even affected mapping; it was helpful to do on paper as with many other CRPGs, but in this case you could be drawing as a group of monsters wandered down the corridor and attacked your party. And the maps themselves were a wonder, almost works of art. The game was chock-full of intricate level designs and sophisticated puzzles.

The stunning graphics and dynamic lighting sucked you into the game to begin with, but the sound came in for special mention. There was no in-game soundtrack, something that usually bothered me a lot. But in this case it was easy to make an exception. The silence only heightened the drama of wondering what's around the next dark corner, and the digitally sampled sound effects for opening gates, getting injured ("oowah!"), and fighting sounded realistic if sparsely deployed. Most importantly, you could tell how close a monster, closing gate, or triggered floor platform was by how loud the sound effect was; combine this with the light sourcing and the creepy-atmosphere factor was off the charts.

The sophisticated magic system required learning not just spells, as with other CRPGs, but the syllables you had to recite to cast them (assuming you had enough Mana). You had to practice reciting and casting spells; this improved how quickly and how reliably (!) your wizards and priests could employ them. The same went for fighters and ninjas practicing combat with specific weapons; the more your characters battled the denizens of the deep, the better they became at it. This dynamic skill system replaced the usual "gain experience points and levels" system found in most CRPGs, and only added to the sense of visceral engagement with your party of characters. To help get you started, Dungeon Master came with two thick booklets: a manual that laid out the detailed backstory and in-game controls, and *Secrets of Dungeon Mastery,* which offered tips on everything from forming your party to exploring the dungeon, attack tactics, and improving your magic ability.

FTL immediately planned a sequel. Chaos Strikes Back, released in 1989, was more of the same dungeon-crawler goodness, albeit significantly harder. The dungeon map was more convoluted and the puzzles much more difficult. There wasn't much reason to play this one until you solved Dungeon Master, but if you were ready for a massive challenge, it helped to set aside the next few…weeks.

All told, Dungeon Master served as inspiration for an entire genre of three-dimensional dungeon crawls. It introduced a new level of mouse control and environmental interaction that quickly became standard for first-person CRPGs. SSI extended the formula with its Eye of the Beholder series for the PC later on, virtual clones of Dungeon Master but set in the Advanced Dungeons & Dragons Forgotten Realms world. Any dungeon crawl with real-time elements, from the Ultima Underworld series in the early 1990s through three-quarter-perspective games like Diablo, Torchlight, the fabled Baldur's Gate series, and massive current-day CRPGs like The Elder Scrolls: Skyrim all owe something to Dungeon Master, and fan-made games like Legend of Grimrock paid direct homage to it as well. There's no way to overstate Dungeon Master's influence, on role-playing games, on first-person games in general, and on the ST's profile in the personal computer market. The release of this game was a key moment in computing history. An event of this magnitude wouldn't be duplicated on the ST. But for a time, the platform truly shone in the spotlight.

The Bard's Tale (Interplay, 1987)

"The denizens of this mystic place assault you without warning. You see three Barbarians. Will your stalwart band choose to Fight or Run?" Programmed by Michael Cranford and one of the best role-playing games of its time, The Bard's Tale put you in control of a party of six adventurers in the fabled city of Skara Brae. Your goal was to rid the land of an evil mage named Mangar by fighting your way through his minions and mazes. Along the way, your party would build up experience, collect gold, increase in level, and grow more powerful.

The Bard's Tale contained all of the key components of a classic CRPG, including a combat system, a magic system based on spell points, character development, and the ability to explore (and map by hand) new places. The game came with a map of Skara Brae itself on the inside of the album-cover-style packaging, along with a few tips to get started building a party in the Adventurers' Guild, outfitting your characters at Garth's Equipment Shoppe, and setting off for the first mysterious places on the map. The game was notoriously super-hard in the beginning; you could well be offed on your way to Garth's before you even bought some equipment.

Some notable differences from other CRPGs included the Bard character class, which made magic by playing music; four classes of magic-user (Conjurers, Magicians, Sorcerors, and Wizards), plus the ability to master them all and become an Archmage; and a day/night system that passed time even if you didn't press a key, and where magic-users only regenerated spell points during the day. Otherwise, the game hewed closely to typical first-edition Advanced Dungeons & Dragons rules. It contained six races, 10 character classes, five ability scores that ranged from 3-18, and a full item and equipment system. There were plenty of dungeons and above-ground mazes to explore, complete with traps; "Magic Mouths" that offered hints; and plenty of magic items and spell regeneration zones. There wasn't much to the story, though; it was mostly a hack-and-slash game.

The main interface was broken into three distinct zones. There was a three-dimensional view of what your party saw in front of it on the top-left corner of the screen; the in-game graphics were well drawn and colorful. To the right was a text window that told you what was happening (be it exploration, combat, or other in-game information). Along the bottom third of the screen were your party's main stats, most importantly each character's armor class (AC), maximum hit points, condition (current hit points), and spell points. You could control the game with the mouse, but I preferred the keyboard. And as with many titles of this era, even saving your game didn't necessarily preserve your characters if you died, so you had to make manual backup copies of your character disks.

This port of The Bard's Tale was perhaps the best one available, with its colorful high-resolution graphics exceeding anything the Apple II or Commodore 64 were capable of. As much as I enjoyed Pool of Radiance and its greater depth on the PC three years later, I couldn't help but notice the graphics in that game didn't compare well with The Bard's Tale's on the ST. The same went for sound; Pool of Radiance didn't support sound boards on the PC, whereas the tunes that played in The Bard's Tale on the ST were memorable and added character to what could have been a garden-variety dungeon romp. The game even let you import beloved characters from Ultima III or Wizardry, assuming you played either or both of those games first.

Even today, The Bard's Tale is worth playing (and replaying, and replaying, until at least you get a party of characters strong enough that won't die every 30 seconds). Joking aside, it's all I could do to finish the book. Every time I go back to a game like this, I want to play it for hours and relive the times when I'd get lost in it for days on end.

Phantasie III: The Wrath of Nikademus (Westwood/SSI, 1987)

Phantasie III was a significant leap over its two predecessors. This final installment featured improved graphics, sound, and play mechanics, although it was a smaller and shorter game overall. The Dark Lord Nikademus gave up on controlling islands, and instead wanted to take over the entire world. Once again you had to assemble a party of six adventures, this time to explore not just the continent but the Astral Planes of Light and Darkness.

The combat system received some nice upgrades. This time around, you could position each character at the front, middle, or back, and aim spells at specific ranks of targets. Most significantly, an extensive damage system targeted specific body areas and levels of injury, adding compelling depth to combat. Otherwise, Phantasie III was still based around the same AD&D-like rules as the first two games. As before, you could import your earlier characters into the latest version, which is what I did when I was 14, or you could create new ones.

With its more detailed graphics and smoother trading system, Phantasie III felt like more of a natural fit on the ST than the first two games, even though those also had GUI-related elements grafted on. Especially once you were out in the wilderness for the first time, you'd see the clear upgrade in graphics, although the view out to the landscape was smaller. I immensely enjoyed playing this game. Even though some criticized it for its shorter campaign, and what was by then rapidly becoming standard-fare CRPG mechanics (aside from the body area system), I still thought—and think today, after some replay—it was a well-balanced example of RPG goodness on the Atari ST.

Rings of Zilfin (SSI, 1987)

In Rings of Zilfin, your goal was to defeat Lord Dragos, a necromancer who wrested control of the town of Batiniq from the wizards who had been maintaining peace. The game, which came on three floppy disks, played more similar to a Sierra adventure than a traditional turn-based RPG. You controlled Reis, a two-dimensional character who walked from place to place on scrolling screens. You encountered many of the usual denizens found in RPGs, including goblins, demons, dragons, elves, and kings. Your character had innate magic ability you developed throughout the game as well.

The graphics on the ST were a nice upgrade from the 8-bit ports and were the showcase screenshots on the box—always good for bragging rights back in the day. Each location had its own graphics, unlike in the Phantasie series where all towns looked the same within each game. You could set the difficulty level right at the beginning, from 0 (hardest) to 9 (easiest). I remember being quite frustrated at how long it took to walk through forests, where you had to pick mushrooms and nip some wandering monsters along the way. Even the theme song was unusual, and sounded like a cross between medieval orchestral music and "Flight of the Bumblebee."

In the April 1989 issue of *ST-Log*, reviewer Kevin Peck wrote he "especially recommend[s] this game to those getting started on the road to adventuring because of its logical menu setup, logical and multiple goal obtaining and well-done graphics." That first bit about menu setup is key here. Rings of Zilfin was more accessible than many other RPGs primarily because of the ST's GUI—though I'd also throw in having to control just one character, rather than a party, and the fact that you just didn't die often as additional contributing factors.

Ultima IV: Quest of the Avatar (Origin, 1987)

If not the best, then one of the top three CRPGs ever created, Ultima IV: Quest of the Avatar revolutionized what had become a tired good-defeats-evil formula. In this game, you were judged not by how many monsters you killed, how powerful you became, or whether you were able to vanquish some newfound evil in the world, but instead, how closely you hewed to eight key virtues in order to become a leader and example to the people of Britannia before going on a final quest to find and read the Codex of Ultimate Wisdom. While the game's top-down interface and tile-based graphics resembled earlier titles in the series, Ultima IV's world and your quest were both much larger, with a more intricate storyline and more complex interactions with the people of the world.

A late arrival to the ST platform, Ultima IV included several notable additions. The most significant was the in-game music, which was extremely well done and memorable and notably missing from the earlier Atari 8-bit port. I didn't know this then, but this version also supported MIDI for the music, so you could hook up an external MIDI synthesizer or sound module for a more-realistic soundtrack. Other upgrades included a refreshed color palette that improved considerably on the 8-bit's four-color artifacting setup, and nicer stills during the famous character creation sequence with the gypsy fortune teller. As with earlier ST Ultima conversions, there was mouse support; you could control your party by clicking on the map. But you still needed the keyboard for too many in-game tasks to make mouse control worthwhile.

Figure 5.3: Richard Garriott's magnum opus that transcended traditional hack-and-slash dungeon crawls, Ultima IV received some nice upgrades on the way to the ST, including 16-color graphics and a full soundtrack.

Otherwise, the game was as wondrous and groundbreaking as before. Although 1987 was a bit late to play Ultima IV—the fifth installment in the series was to arrive on other machines early the following year—for ST fans it was worth the wait. I distinctly remember being home sick for a week in eighth grade and playing this version of the game morning, noon, and evening (except for when I was told to eat, get off the computer and go to bed, and so on).

As with Ultima III, this is the best period-correct port of the game. You'll have to move up to upgrading the MS-DOS port with recent patches (they do things such as add 256-color graphics and the missing music) in order to beat this one. And in case you need me to tell you what you should already know, Ultima IV is worth playing, even now, and again even if you've already played and solved it years ago. When *Computer Gaming World* created its Hall of Fame scored by reader input, Ultima IV was one of the first and immediate additions. There's still nothing quite like it.

Strategy Games

The ST had no shortage of good strategy games, but those in this next group broke some ground in their respective subgenres. Let's start with a famous action hybrid that brought more than a little a cinematic flair to the ST.

Defender of the Crown (Cinemaware, 1987)

Cinemaware games billed themselves as interactive movies. "Cine-maware is ADULT entertainment," it read on the game boxes (and without the seedier implication of that term), "a revolutionary new genre that pulls you emotionally into the story and characters. It's more similar to being in a movie than playing a computer game. Popcorn not included." The box graphics depicted people buying movie tickets at a theater counter, complete with screenshots that read "Now Playing" below them.

The company's first game, distributed in the US by Mindscape, grabbed everyone's attention for its realism and graphics. Defender of the Crown really lived up to its billing as an interactive movie. The game was set in 12th-century medieval England. King Richard was murdered, and there was civil war as the throne lay vacant. Six different lords battled for supremacy—three Saxons, and three Normans—in an epic conflict that evoked the spirt, if not the plot, of old Robin Hood movies.

You started the game by choosing one of four possible Saxon lords: Wilfred of Ivanhoe, Cedric of Rotherwood, Geoffrey Long-sword, or Wolfric the Wild. Each had different leadership, jousting, and swordplay attributes. A map of England served as the main game board. You had to build up an army for conquest as well as spend re-sources on defense. You could build new castles as you gained income by joining the enemy in battle and conquering more territories that generated revenue. When your Saxon lord captured all three Norman castles, you won.

The toughest decisions often involved whether you should hold the line and spend your income growing your army (and in what way? Would you save up for catapults and knights, or buy more infantry?), or seek conquest earlier. Whether you chose wisely would come down to the battle scenes, where you could stand and fight, try and outflank or charge the enemy, or retreat in shame. The battles were turn-based but with an advancing clock, so if you didn't decide quickly, the computer took its turn anyway.

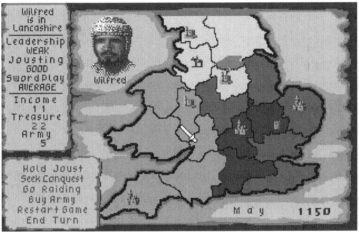

Figure 5.4: The first (and possibly finest) example of interactive cinema, Defender of the Crown put you inside a Robin Hood flick in a battle for medieval England, complete with castle sieges, jousting, swordplay, romance—the works.

In addition to the main strategic portion, there were a couple dozen interstitial dialogs explaining what was happening in the game along with several action sequences that added to the drama. One sequence put you on a horse in a jousting tournament with a computer-controlled opponent. You could fight for either territory or leadership. During each round, you had to aim carefully and time the thrust of your lance just right. If you both missed, you'd have to do another go-around. Worse, if you took a hit, you'd get knocked off your horse and lose the tournament.

Another sequence occurred whenever you attempted to attack or defend a territory. The game put you behind a catapult you could use to destroy enemy castle walls, either with boulders, Greek fire, or a cauldron of diseased meat (yuck). In perhaps the most memorable action sequence, you had to rescue a captured princess. To do so, you fought castle guards in a courtyard with your sword; an occasional meteor would streak across the sky. Inside, you had to fight more guards; there, the interplay of candlelight with your fighter's oversize shadow on the wall added to the cinematic feel. If you won the second battle, you would be treated to a portrait of one of several different princesses.

All told, Defender of the Crown featured top-notch graphics, sound, and music for the time, but was kind of light on strategy and gameplay. Reviews generally alternated between being blown away by the presentation and level of sophistication, and disappointed with the meat of the game itself. Some of the impact is diluted 30 years on, now that 16-bit graphics and what was then a cinematic approach to the music and pacing don't excite so much. What's left is a mixed bag. You could squint and say it's a rather simplistic, stilted strategy game with several frustrating minigames included. Whatever you think of the gameplay, Defender of the Crown remains a showcase for the ST platform and was hugely influential in its day. It was one of the earliest successful games that did in fact seem as if you were "playing" a movie rather than just watching one.

Airball (Microdeal, 1987)

One of the best action puzzle-style games to grace the Atari ST platform, Airball featured fantastic graphics, sound, and music, not to mention a thoroughly engaging play dynamic. In this game, an evil wizard turned you into a ball and stuck you in a mazelike underworld with 150 different rooms. (Jerk.) Figure out how to get to the end of the maze and you would find a spell book that, once you returned to the first room of the maze, you could use to turn back into a human. The catch: Your ball had a slow leak, and if it fully depleted, you would lose a life. Inflation stations were scattered around the underworld; these quickly pumped you back up, but it was also easy to overfill and lose a life. A bar at the bottom of the screen showed your current air level. You started the game literally on top of one of the air pumps, so you had to be ready to leap off within a few seconds.

You could move in any of eight directions; pressing the joystick button jumped, which was also necessary for climbing stairs. You picked up or dropped items using the space bar. If you were masochistic, you could choose keyboard or even mouse controls. But trust me, the game was plenty tough using a joystick. (Emulation tip: When the game loads, it will start playing by itself. Press F1 to cycle between joystick, keyboard, and mouse control, and then press the space bar to start the game.)

The map wasn't linear, either. You'd find dozens intersections to navigate and explore throughout the underworld, as you avoided the hundreds of spears sticking out of the ground, electrified floor tiles, and other dangerous situations. The wizard left useful special objects throughout the underworld, including statues, food, crosses, and crates, the last of which you could use to get past certain obstacles.

Airball's isometric graphics were superb throughout, fully conveying the sense of an underworld maze with a unique style. The game's butter-smooth animation belied the lack of hardware sprites, and because each screen of the underworld didn't scroll, there was no evidence of choppy movement anywhere in the game. The music in Airball deserves special mention, with catchy, arpeggiated synth riffs that intertwine with each other over a gritty drum beat. The Yamaha sound chip's polyphony limitations became apparent whenever you picked up an item or accidentally popped your balloon and lost a life; a sound channel would cut out, and you'd only hear the melody channel while the sound effect played. Even the noisy percussion track disappeared momentarily.

Figure 5.5: Airball's sweet graphics, memorable music score, and unforgiving action made this one tough puzzle game to solve.

Three people were credited for Airball: Ed Scio, the main program-mer; Paul Shields, for the music; and Pete Scott, for the level design. The game originally came out for the TRS-80 Color Computer and the Dragon 32/64, before being ported to the ST with enhanced graphics and sound, including music in the game and not just on the title screen. The August 1987 issue of *Computer + Video Games* declared the ST port of Airball an "impeccably coded and highly playable game that sets a high standard other companies will have to beat...Airball is the first isometric arcade adventure, written specifically for the ST, and has hit written all over it!" All told, Airball was unforgettable. Even if you didn't ultimately take to the game's unforgiving collision detection, it was worth playing Airball just to see it and hear it run. There was noth-ing else like it.

Balance of Power (Electronic Arts, 1987)

Electronic Arts developed its reputation on 8-bit computers with titles such as Archon, The Seven Cities of Gold, and M.U.L.E. By the time the ST came out, EA was already a large, well-known publisher of top-quality games, as famous for the album-style packaging as well as the quality of its products. The ST didn't get those first titles, but it did start to get ports of the some of the best and more sophisticated ones that came in the late 1980s and early 1990s. The first significant one was quite literally a game-changer. Possibly game designer Chris Craw-ford's magnum opus, Balance of Power brought the realities of 1980s geopolitics and foreign policy—specifically, the Cold War—to your computer screen. You played as either the US or the USSR, against the computer or a friend. Your goal was to boost your superpower's pres-tige while balancing your opponent's geopolitical interests and, ulti-mately, avoiding a nuclear war. There were four levels of difficultly: Beginner, Intermediate, Expert, and appropriately enough, Nightmare.

The game took place between 1986 and 1994. Each year, the game presented you with incidents and crises in the world, and you had to respond to each one in some way, be it sending aid, moving troops, or doing nothing; your opponent would then respond in kind. Under the hood, the game combined a comprehensive database, artificial intelli-gence, and a sophisticated model of the world that covered attributes such as available resources, civilian well-being, political and civil rights, and accounts for major events, revolutions, and insurgencies as well as the expected focus on diplomatic relations and signing treaties. If you were too much of an isolationist, your opponent could end up as the dominant superpower; if you went too far in the other direction, your brinkmanship might well trigger a civilization-ending nuclear war. If the worst occurred, the screen turned black and displayed: "You have ignited a nuclear war. And no, there is no animated display of a mushroom cloud with parts of bodies flying through the air. We do not reward failure."

Crawford developed the game for the Macintosh, but it was the PC port that rocketed the game into the stratosphere in sales, thanks to the platform's already-significant dominance of personal computer sales by 1986. The ST port preserved the Mac version's sharp graphics and added a full-color mode. Crawford's companion book covered the politics, statistical formulas, and development history of the game. Balance of Power went on to win rave reviews, including one in *The New York Times Magazine* by David Aaron, Jimmy Carter's Deputy Assistant to the President of National Security Affairs, where he called it "about as close as one might get to the cut-and-thrust of international politics without going through confirmation by the Senate."[17]

Barbarian (Psygnosis, 1987)

When I first played Barbarian as a teenager, it blew me away with its detailed graphics. Even the title screen and the following beautiful scene, with the bright red dragon that was a rendering of the box art, were enough to make me just want to stare at the monitor. (I had a good amount of time to do this, too, because loading this game from floppy disk took quite a while.) Famed album cover artist Roger Dean did the artwork for Barbarian, which was programmed on the ST before being ported to other platforms.

As the dragon-slaying barbarian Hegor, your goal was to enter the underground realm Durgan inside a volcano and destroy the lair of the evil wizard Necron. You accomplished this by locating and destroying a special crystal that gave Necron his power. Once you did this, the volcano started to erupt, just as you would expect it to. You had to then reach the surface as quickly as possible before it blew.

You started the game standing around in the marsh. Hegor came equipped with a sword and a bow. The controls were complex; although you could move left and right, as well as up and down stairs and ladders, you could also jump, run, attack, defend, or flee, as well as get, use, and put down objects. (Because I was 14, I loved "fleeing" repeatedly and watching the Barbarian run, wide-eyed, yelling "Help!") Because all of this was too much for a joystick, you were given a strip of oversize icons across the bottom of the screen that you could choose with the mouse; pressing the right mouse button revealed additional control icons plus some that appeared only for specific scenes. You could also stack up a series of commands as Hegor performed actions. Playing this way was as difficult as it sounds; I used to play with the mouse, but I've since learned keyboard control was the best bet.

As you played the game, you encountered falling platforms, collapsing bridges, and a variety of monsters. Adding to the complexity of the controls were the restrictions. For example, if you were going up or down stairs, you couldn't stop in the middle and change your mind. You just watched helplessly as you walked right into a monster and were killed. Plus, the controls were context-sensitive; the same commands would perform different actions depending on what was happening on screen. You couldn't manually switch between the sword and bow, for example.

The graphics and digitally sampled sound effects lent a classy, high-end feel to Barbarian that looked state of the art in 1987. Although *STart* magazine praised the game's "incredibly realistic" character animation for Hegor, including his "fluid motion" and the way his "eyes bug out momentarily" when he walks into a wall, today it just looks sluggish.[18] The lack of in-game music and aforementioned stiff control scheme also date the title, and unbelievably it didn't have a way to save the game in progress. (Today, playing in an emulator helps with the last issue.)

But overall, Barbarian was a solid improvement over Brataccas and another clear example of a game that wouldn't look as good on an 8-bit platform. The next year, Psygnosis released Obliterator, a game set on an alien spaceship with a similar control scheme, similarly nice graphics, and an in-game soundtrack by David Whittaker. The developers also wisely added a save-game feature to that one.

The Chessmaster 2000 (The Software Toolworks, 1987)

"The Software Toolworks presents…The Chessmaster 2000." Sampled speech was still a relative rarity in 1987, even though the ST could produce it (at least in software) since the beginning. Nonetheless, this talking introduction and the speech throughout the game grabbed your attention as they welcomed you to an ancient pastime. Chess games with three-dimensional boards have been a dime a dozen for several decades, but The Chessmaster 2000 on the Atari ST was the first time I had seen one. The game took advantage of the ST's crisper resolution and higher color count over 8-bit machines.

As a chess program for the layman, as opposed to the high-end ChessBase, The Chessmaster 2000 excelled. It offered both 2D and 3D board views, a full GUI for in-game control, 12 different levels of play, the ability to switch to an easier mode during a game, a hint mode, and a teaching mode that showed all possible legal moves for each turn. You could switch sides, rotate the board 90 degrees, save a game in progress, and replay it from scratch. The game also included many tournament-level features, such as a chess clock, the ability to read all three chess notation schemes, and a library of classic games you could load up and study. All of this sounds fairly pedestrian for a chess game now, but was positively cutting-edge then. The Chessmaster 2000 delivered many advantages over the standalone electronic chess computers popular in the 1970s and 1980s. Programs like this were a key reason why that category of product fell out of favor.

Electronic Arts distributed The Chessmaster 2000 for The Software Toolworks in the company's famous album-cover format. And that cover, showing an elder chess player with a long, gray beard looming over a chess board near the end of a game and about to move a piece, seems iconic to me today. The image was practically everywhere in magazines and on retail shelves for years. It's still the game I think of whenever I play chess on a computer, regardless of the platform or the specific piece of software.

Prime Time (First Row Software, 1987)

One of the most novel and distinct titles I've ever played, this offbeat game put you in charge of a television network. You would control the programming, come up with new ideas for shows, yell at your employees, and cancel underperforming flops. Your goal was to ensure your network made the most money against two others that were either computer- or human-controlled.

The game contained 175 canned shows with ridiculous titles such as *Miami Mice*, *Wheel of Torture*, and the public fundraiser *Beg-a-Thon*. Each show had its own length, genre (action, comedy, variety, and so on), blurb, and demographic targets. One play-through consisted of one season, from September to July, and you were judged against not only the money you raked in but the ratings your shows achieved.

Each turn, you bid for shows against other networks, including important ones such as the World Series and Emmy Awards. The interface during bidding wars was reminiscent of playing M.U.L.E. on 8-bit computers. You also would create and develop your own shows with the help of five studios. In your office, your desk came equipped with a Rolodex, a desk blotter for doodling, and a phone. The Programming closet let you set up the evening's shows using graphical representations of cans of film.

The game was amusing throughout, from the rolling opening credits to the sampled digital sound effects to the "commercials" that sometimes showed up in the middle of play. Each turn, a fictional newspaper gave you insight on what was trending as well as anything that had an impact on your current performance, such as getting a larger budget due to your slick maneuvers. You could also chat with the other two network heads, who were always named Fred Silverfish, to do lunch and get the latest gossip. It all sounds quite ridiculous now that I'm writing it out, but I remember the game as well balanced and I kept coming back to it, at least until I played through whatever scenarios it was capable of throwing at me.

Roadwar 2000 (Westwood/SSI, 1987)

Demand for car-based, post-apocalyptic strategy games like this was strong, as was evidenced by the run of *Mad Max*–style movies doing battle at the box office in the 1980s. In Roadwar 2000, a turn-based take on Origin's Autoduel with a larger game world, the story went that biological warfare had decimated America, with major cities now run by rival gangs. You led one such road gang in an effort to locate eight missing scientists on behalf of the government and bring them back to a secret underground lab to develop a vaccine.

Along the way, you crossed different kinds of terrain and fought mutants, cannibals, and rival gangs. You had to stock up on food, gas, and ammo, as well as court new recruits. Your job was to put together a group that included warriors and vehicles, plus other characters such as a doctor and politician, to explore and take control of multiple cities across the continent. The roads between cities were essentially battle zones. The game's combat system worked two ways: Either you controlled the fighting unit by unit, man by man, and order by order (Tactical), or you let the computer resolve battles for you (Abstract). There were tons of detailed rules about cities, cargo capacity, the nearly 20 different kinds of vehicles, food and firearm caches, and the skill levels of gang members.

Figure 5.6: Essentially SSI's take on Autoduel, the turn-based Roadwar 2000 put you in a post-apocalyptic United States controlled by rival gangs.

The left side of the screen showed the map view, while the right listed your group's statistics. The drop-down menus at the top of the screen offered the rest of the in-game options. The graphics received a significant boost in resolution and color over 8-bit machines, as was typically the case, and looked closer to a game like the first Civilization (which wouldn't debut on the ST until 1992) than an RPG.

"If all this sounds like a lot, rest assured it is—and that's why the game is so good," Steve Panak wrote in the June 1988 issue of *ST-Log*. "The ease of play keeps you in high gear. You quickly learn the operation of the pulldown menus, and choices are made effortlessly with the mouse." The mouse comes up again and again, along with issues such as copy protection (this game didn't have any, which was a plus) and how much disk swapping you had to do during play (none aside from your saved game disk, in this case). Later that same year, SSI released

Roadwar Europa, a sequel that took place in Europe (obviously), and that largely kept all of the same mechanics in place.

Star Trek: The Rebel Universe (Simon & Schuster Interactive, 1987)

By 1987 it was already becoming obvious *Star Trek*–themed games would always be a running theme, given how many computer enthusiasts cut their teeth watching the original series, four blockbuster motion pictures (by that point), and the soon-to-be-launched *The Next Generation* on television. Unfortunately, most games based on the show were mediocre; aside from some fun type-in programs running on mainframes and appearing in computer magazines, we had yet to see a great *Star Trek* video game.

Star Trek: The Rebel Universe may have well been the first. This epic, polished, and memorable title was originally developed for the ST. In it, you faced legions of rebel Federation starships, plus Klingon and Romulan battle cruisers, in an effort to quell a tremendous rebellion in the dangerous Klein sphere. The main interface showed the Enterprise bridge and crew in the top left, with smaller boxes along the bottom and right containing thumbnails of seven secondary screens. Each of the main characters was responsible for an individual system on the ship; if you clicked on one with the cursor (shaped like a Starfleet badge), you would see a control view for their station, which either provided information, offered further functions, or a combination of both. No matter what was happening in the game—say, if the view shifted to navigation or ship combat—the bridge always remained in at least one box somewhere on the screen so you could easily return to it.

In addition to exciting space combat, you also travelled to alien planets, where you could beam down a landing party to explore the surface and collect items that were key to completing the mission. The manual was well written and detailed, and made the game that much more immersive. It's worth comparing this game with top Atari 8-bit computer titles such as Rescue on Fractalus! and Koronis Rift, games that pushed the envelope on those machines and even in some cases exceeded the animation capability of the ST, but that couldn't match Star Trek: The Rebel Universe's overall sophistication and finer graphics resolution.

I enjoyed playing this one in the 1980s and had honestly forgotten all about it in my initial dive to return to classics such as Starglider,

Phantasie, and Dungeon Master in preparation for this book (and it was hard work, let me tell you). Hopefully you're finding some things in this book that bring back pleasant memories, too. In fact, I'm going to go play this one again right now. Be right back.

While Atari pushed the ST as its flagship computer, it continued to sell its popular 65XE and 130XE home computers at much lower price points. These latter machines remained compelling, as had the benefit of a mature, wide-ranging software lineup that comprised thousands of applications, utilities, and of course games.

But one place Atari continued to falter was with its game consoles. After launching its breakthrough Home Pong in 1975 and dozens of variants, and its world-changing 2600 Video Computer System in 1977, Atari lost the plot. The 5200 SuperSystem, a repackaged Atari 400 with analog controllers and some lightly tweaked cartridge versions of popular 8-bit games, was a middling seller after its 1982 launch, and was history by 1984. The 7800, which Atari Inc. had initially shelved after the market crash, only for the new Atari Corporation to hurriedly dust it off and shove it out into the marketplace in 1986 to fight the Nintendo Entertainment System, became another sales disappointment.

For whatever reason, Atari Corporation tried one more time with its then-ancient 8-bit computer hardware. The 1987 XE Game System was essentially the 5200 SuperSystem, except in a freshened, significantly smaller, light gray plastic design with pastel-colored buttons. The new model came with a light gun just like the NES. The company released some new cartridges for this machine, most of which were (once again) repackaged versions of older games, and of course older Atari 8-bit cartridges from the 400/800 and XL eras also worked.

Consumers didn't bite. All Atari hardware related to the original 400 and 800 was solid on its own, and the XE was no exception. But by this point, there was no getting around the system's age, not to mention Atari Corporation's cynical repackaging of it. It's like those record labels that incessantly milk the catalogs of aging rock bands to release "new" greatest-hits collections every few years. Nothing with an 8-bit processor would ever catch the NES; it would take 16-bit machines such as the ST and the Amiga (for home computers) and the upcoming Sega Genesis (for consoles) to surpass the NES and its already-stellar lineup of cartridges.

6 | Arcade

Somewhat under the radar were the ST's exceptional arcade game chops. From space shoot-em-ups to racers, the ST had what it took to deliver console-style gaming and finally deliver on the promise of bringing the arcade home. First, let's take a look at some original ST titles. We'll start with a game that proved the ST could demonstrate beautiful playfield scrolling—perfect, in fact—without a blitter chip or any other additional coprocessors.

Goldrunner (Microdeal, 1987)

For the first couple of years, the ST was starved for space shooters. "It's about time someone wrote this game," wrote D.F. Scott in his May 1988 review of Goldrunner in *ST-Log*. "The ST game player withstood nearly two years of not having one decent Galaga-style game."

This top-down, vertical-scrolling shooter offered fast action and sharp graphics. The story went that the Earth was dying, and humans had to migrate to the New World to survive. In between were the hostile Ring Worlds of Triton, an advanced civilization that wouldn't let anyone pass through. As the Goldrunner, a lone fighter, you had to take them on. Each ring was filled with enemies; you had to destroy whatever you could, reducing the ring's energy each time until it reached zero. Once that happened, you could exit the ring and move on to the next. The levels were like "rings" in that if you kept flying in the same direction, you would eventually end up back where you started. You could fly through (over?) enemies, but you still had to avoid the land mines and the taller buildings.

The game worked with keyboard, mouse, or joystick control. I usually played with the mouse, because that was a novel thing in a world of console and Atari 800 joysticks, but the joystick probably made the most sense for accuracy. What made Goldrunner tricky, aside from the speed of the game and the number of enemies to shoot, was you didn't fly in one direction at one speed the way you did in arcade games such as Vanguard or Xevious. In Goldrunner, you accelerated or decelerated over a wide range of speeds, and could even flip and reverse direction to accelerate the other way.

The gorgeous, colorful sprites and fluid animation made it a joy to play. The game also featured digitally sampled voices saying things such as "Welcome to Goldrunner," "Get ready," and "Watch out." The memorable in-game music, composed by Rob Hubbard, could be turned off if you wanted. I never minded it repeating, although the way it would drop a voice of polyphony out to play sound effects always bothered me. When I was 15, I even learned to play the Goldrunner theme song on my Casio CZ-5000 synthesizer, and made a good sound patch to mimic the warbling lead synth that carried the melody.

Even after repeated play, it was tough to tell what you could destroy and what you couldn't in Goldrunner. You might as well just shoot at everything, as a May 1988 review in *ST Action* suggested. In *ST-Log*, Scott wrote, "the spectacular fine-scrolling routine Bak and Lyon have conceived is what makes Goldrunner work…if they use it in another game, it too will succeed. This is yet another instance where two programmers have created code that outperforms [Digital Research's, which created the ST's GEM desktop], and they are to be commended." Whatever they did, I wish other programmers had figured it out earlier; it would have helped some of the choppier (if still great) titles on the ST such as Major Motion and Time Bandit.

Goldrunner could stand up to anything on a home console such as the Nintendo Entertainment System or Sega Master System, a more natural comparison for Goldrunner's gameplay than competing computer titles. Its vertical scrolling was fast and effortless. I couldn't stand the enemy missiles; they looked like tiny "x" characters, and they inevitably drifted right toward your ship no matter how slow or how fast you flew over the landscape. All told, Goldrunner was another solid title from Microdeal, and one I played all the time back in the day.

Oids (FTL, 1987)

The excellent Oids began life as an Atari ST exclusive developed by Dan Hewitt and was later ported just to the Macintosh. This space shooter was inertia- and gravity-based, similar to the arcade hit Asteroids. In Oids, you had to rescue android slaves (the Oids) Choplifter-style from their terrible lives underneath the evil Biocretes, while maneuvering your craft to avoid crashing into the mountainous landscape. There was a built-in level editor, an unusual bonus for games of its era, complete with a play-testing mode.

Figure 6.1: One of the ST's best overall games, Oids resembled Asteroids for its control scheme and inertia-based movement, but brought a search-and-rescue element and a bonus level editor to the proceedings.

You rotated your V-wing fighter by pushing the joystick left or right. Pushing up activated the forward thruster, and you had to account for the inertia when changing direction. Gravity also tugged at your fighter at all times, which added to the challenge. Pulling back activated a shield (hey, some home variations of Asteroids had shields instead of hyperspace). Periodically you needed to recharge your shield, which you could do with the space bar. The button fired your pellet gun, and a fast double-press activated one of your precious few NovaBombs.

To rescue the Oids, you had to first destroy the Biocrete factories where the Oids were forced to work, taking care not to shoot the Oids in the process. Then you landed on a flat spot of ground and waited for the Oids to run to your ship. Once you had eight on board, or you picked up the last one on that planet, the mothership appeared and dropped a probe to collect all eight at once. The mothership also refueled your fighter each time, though you could also refuel by landing near a Biocrete fuel base. The top of the screen showed your current shield status, fuel level, how many ships you had remaining, and how many Oids you were currently carrying on your ship.

Nice touches abounded, such as the bouncing dot over the I on the title screen, and the little animation of the ship rescuing the tiny running man at the bottom of the Select a Galaxy to Defend screen. This was one of the best action games ever released for the ST.

MIDI Maze (Hybrid Arts, 1987)

One of the most innovative titles ever to hit the ST platform—and relatively unknown until the retro gaming press picked up on it recently—was MIDI Maze. It was a proto-first-person-shooter game designed exclusively for the ST by CAD-3D designer Tom Hudson. The game harnessed the MIDI protocol as a local area network. Thanks to the built-in MIDI ports, 16 people could play at once through their connected STs. And as the packaging indicated, everyone in the maze looked like a smiley Pac-Man, with each a different color. You shot balls at each other, because of course.

The game worked on any ST with a color or monochrome monitor. There was also a single-player "campaign," though I'm using that term loosely; basically you fought up to 15 other computer droids, and there were three levels of difficulty to choose from. You could combine some human players with some droids in any one game. The game came with a maze designer so you could create your own, and there was a tournament-style scoring setup for running your own competitions. The game's simple, filled-polygon graphics and limited movement—you could only turn 90 degrees at a time—may seem primitive today, but the game still holds up.

MIDI Maze is now remembered for introducing the concept of a deathmatch in first-person shooters. A prototype for 8-bit Atari computers was discovered more recently. Because the 8-bits didn't have built-in MIDI, the game worked on those machines via Atari's XM301 or SX212 modems, or the ancient Atari 850 interface, as well as the third-party MIDIMate MIDI interface. The game still lives, too; at VCF East

2019 in Wall, New Jersey, ST enthusiast Peter Fletcher set up numerous STs so attendees could play MIDI Maze together in real time.

Figure 6.2: The first computer game ever to use MIDI as a local area network, MIDI Maze was a comical 16-person deathmatch game that arrived back when the term "deathmatch" didn't exist yet. Shown here is an impromptu MIDI Maze tournament at VCF 2019. Credit: Peter Fletcher

10th Frame (Access Software, 1987)

A sports sim miles beyond earlier efforts such as Bowling on the 2600, 10th Frame delivered mouse-controlled, overhead-perspective action. The game depicted a real bowling alley, with neighboring lanes and sets of pins, clearly delineated gutters, and an electronic scoreboard. You used the right mouse button to position the player and mark; you'd do this by moving the mouse cursor to each object and then holding the right button while you dragged the mouse left or right. Once you set both, you would press and hold the left button once to start the throw, release it to set the speed as the left indicator graph rose into the Speed Zone, and then press it once more to set the hook as the right graph fell into the Hook Zone. These three moves, along with your initial player and mark positions, set the path of the throw.

The game included both open bowling and a league mode; each accommodated up to eight players. League play consisted of up to four teams playing from one to three games, whereas Open Bowling (no teams, just alternating players) allowed for up to five. There were three difficulty levels you could set for each player. Kids (designed for ages 4-8) automatically set the speed of the ball and disabled the hook so the ball always tracked straight. Amateur (the real Beginner level) enabled varying speed and the hook feature. Professional reduced the margin for error on the speed and hook indicators, and made the game much tougher and more of a simulation of real bowling.

10th Frame's sound on the ST came in for special mention. It was made up of digital samples, including the sound of the ball rolling down the alley, the explosion from hitting the pins, falling into the gutter, and the "cleanup" the automated alley did after each round. Digitally sampled music played at the beginning of the game on the title screen as well. At the end of a game, you could send a hard copy of your score sheet to the printer if desired. The original game employed a hardware dongle that plugged into the joystick port not used by the mouse. Not everyone knew this, thanks to the proliferation of software piracy. Nonetheless, 10th Frame offered just the right amount of fun and difficulty to keep you coming back for more.

Test Drive (Accolade, 1987)

Test Drive put you behind the wheel of five supercars. The roster included a Porsche 911 Carrera, a Ferrari Testarossa, a Lamborghini Countach, a Lotus Esprit Turbo, and a Chevrolet Corvette—all in their 1980s glory, and complete with specification and performance cards. The 3D view displayed proper dashboards for each car, including the Vette's digital readouts and the Testarossa's trademark orange gauge font, and a functioning rear-view mirror. Each game consisted of a race along mountain roads, with pit stops for gas along the way at various roadside attractions. Your goal was to complete each section of the course in the fastest time possible, without crashing into the mountain on your right or driving off the cliff on your left. You also had to avoid the fuzz, or you'd get a speeding ticket; a radar detector clipped to your car's sun visor helped in this endeavor, although you could also try your luck at outrunning the police car. Whatever you did, you could never crash into the cop car. Whenever you screwed something up, the windshield cracked and you had to start again.

During acceleration behind the wheel, the game managed to simulate a manual transmission even just with the single Atari joystick; you pushed the button down and then moved a pop-up visual representation of the shifter into the proper gear. You also got a real sense of each engine's torque curve. Different engine sounds were beyond the scope of the YM2149 sound chip, but the maximum RPM of each engine was enough to at least signal some difference in the drivetrains between cars.

I received this game for Christmas when I was 14 and it changed my life. Okay, that's a slight exaggeration. But after years of arcade-style racing games, this was my first exposure to something that could properly be called a simulation, even a lightweight one—and one involving real production cars and real roads at that. It was the perfect game for a teenager who was already into cars and car magazines. I still remember the Countach topped out at 173mph and the Testarossa at 185.

The realistic dashboards were probably the biggest thing for me. Until Test Drive, every racing game I had ever played either had no dashboard at all (with various stats such as current speed floating over the gameplay) or a generic dashboard that looked nothing like the real one for that given car. This one displayed not only a dashboard with working gauges but even the right steering wheel design for each car. Test Drive was the first title to show me the in-car, first-person, cockpit-simulating future of racing games.

Coin-Op Conversions

As the ST platform matured, we began to see a slew of arcade conversions that, like Joust, took full advantage of the machine's graphics, sound, and animation capabilities to deliver as real a coin-op experience as possible at home. Early ST interpretations of coin-ops such as Spy Hunter (Major Motion) gave rise to full-on licensed versions of popular titles, and Atari converted many from its former coin-op division catalog. In addition, many of these conversions ran in both high-resolution mono and low-resolution color, giving the significant installed base of SM124 owners action games to play in addition to CRPGs and strategy games.

Even beyond coin-op favorites, there were plenty of new ST- and computer-specific action games still to come. Nonetheless, many of these arcade conversions were superb and helped fill out the ST gamer's library, in many cases with a polish never seen before in the home.

Crystal Castles (Atari, 1986)

Crystal Castles put you in control of Bentley Bear, who had to clear maze after enchanted maze full of sparkling gems and pots of honey. The mazes were also filled with enemies, including Nasty Trees, Gem Eaters, bee swarms, ghosts, skeletons, and more. Various elevators, stairways, and dark alleys impeded your progress. Most of all, you had to avoid the Witch and her bubbling cauldron. A special Magic Hat made you temporarily invulnerable.

If you're unfamiliar with the arcade game, Crystal Castles was set up as a series of isometric boards with a three-quarter view of the playfield for a quasi-three-dimensional look. You had to clear all of the gems on each board before you could progress to the next. You had three lives, and every 70,000 points you received another. The game contained a total of 37 castles on 10 levels; clear the only level 10 castle and you'd win the game. A hidden warp system let you skip some levels.

Hungary's Andromeda Software programmed the ST version of the game, and it was well done. This conversion was significantly different from the 8-bit one, with more colorful graphics, well-drawn characters, and many of the details that were missing in the 8-bit port. Movement wasn't quite as smooth, though, for both the in-game characters and the scrolling boards themselves, though it didn't get in the way of gameplay. You also had the option of playing with the mouse instead of the joystick.

Gauntlet (Atari, 1987)

One of the best arcade games of the mid 1980s was Gauntlet, the four-player real-time dungeon crawl that pit you against swarms of all manner of evil beings. The Atari ST port was badass, with near-arcade-level accuracy throughout the game. This port came thanks to US Gold and two freelance programmers named Graham Lilley and Teoman Irmak. Atari Games didn't give them a whole lot of help. "It wasn't as if they gave us source code or even maps to start with," Lilley said. "It was more a case of, here's a machine, now go do the conversion!"[1]

Gauntlet fans know how the game worked, but in short, each player could choose one of four characters: Thor, the Warrior; Thyra, the Valkyrie; Questor; the Elf; and Merlin, the Wizard. Any one player claimed a character, so the other player couldn't also be the same one.

Each character had its own benefit: Thor was good at close combat with his axe, Thyra was better at long-range attacks with her bow and arrow, Questor was the fastest, and Merlin shot magical fireballs. You had to collect as much treasure as possible while killing hordes of ghosts, grunts, sorcerers, and other enemies, and then finding the exit to the next level. The scariest threats were the black "Death" characters that drained your health quickly and were exceedingly tough to kill. You had to pick up food and healing potions along the way.

Figure 6.3: Perhaps the hottest arcade game of 1985, Gauntlet made its way to the ST largely intact, save for some stuttering during gameplay and a limit of two simultaneous players instead of four.

The developers even built in some of the same minor bugs found in the arcade, such as when generators overlapped in a few spots, and when the heads of characters accidentally became superimposed on a generator if you moved too close to it. "The coin-op uses 32 colors and we only had 16, five of which make up the floors and 11 for the walls and characters," Irmak said. "Their sprites are all eight color, but each one can be any eight colors while ours all have to be created from a single, unchanging palette."[2] Other differences included a slightly smaller viewable playfield, a smaller collection of sound samples, and a maximum of two players instead of four.

There was one big issue: As you maneuvered around each level, horizontal scrolling was noticeably choppier than vertical scrolling. There was talk as early as 1986 the Atari ST would see the blitter chip upgrade, which would resolve the scrolling issues, although the chip only appeared on later versions of the ST, as I mentioned earlier. "If the blitter had been standard in all Ataris," Lilley said, "we would have written the program differently to take full advantage of it…As it is, we've written our own software blitting routines instead." Aside from the scrolling issues—and a later STE patch fixed a lot of the problem, as we'll get to in chapter 11—the ST put up a solid game of Gauntlet. The sequel, Gauntlet II, was even better on the ST, with improved frame rates and support for four players via a joystick adapter.

Arkanoid (Taito, 1987)

Arkanoid's slick gameplay and colorful graphics delivered the Breakout upgrade players wanted for more than a decade. Taito described Arkanoid as a space game and a battle for survival: "After the mothership Arkanoid was destroyed, a spaceship Vaus scrambled away, only to be trapped in the void…" You had to fight your way through 32 levels and then confront the Dimension Changer; destroy it and you'd reverse time and resurrect the original Arkanoid mothership. To control the Vaus paddle on screen, you moved the mouse left or right. As with most Breakout clones, the further to the edge the bolt (ball) landed each time, the sharper the angle it would travel back up the screen. The graphics offered a level of depth to the bricks, complete with a three-dimensional look and colorful backgrounds for each board, and the bricks themselves came in multiple varieties. Some of the bricks required more than one shot to be destroyed, while others were impregnable.

As you destroyed bricks, some of them would turn out to contain energy capsules, which then rolled down the screen. Move the Vaus to collect a capsule and you'd gain special powers, such as the ability to catch and release the bolt, slow it down, shoot lasers from your paddle, "disrupt" the bolt into three separate ones simultaneously, and more. The left mouse button shot lasers and released the bolt when appropriate. Grab a rare "P" capsule and you'd score an extra life.

The original coin-op machine had a paddle, similar to Breakout, but I couldn't imagine playing this game with anything other than a mouse thanks to the ST. *Computer + Video Games* called the ST conversion "absolutely faultless…Every moving element of the game glides across the screen as if floating on air and the superior graphics are identical, in almost every detail, to the original arcade version." A sequel called Arkanoid: Revenge of Doh added Warp Gates that appeared on the sides and gave you different versions of the next level, along with new kinds of bricks, power-ups, and enemies. You also had to fight a miniboss part of the way through, in addition to an end boss.

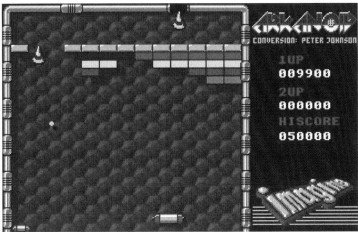

Figure 6.4: The best Breakout game since Breakout itself, Arkanoid made a flawless leap from the arcade to the ST.

Rampage (Activision, 1987)

It didn't get much more fun than this. In Rampage, you were of three gargantuan B-movie monsters terrorizing a city. You had to climb and demolish buildings, eat the frightened human inhabitants for food, and beat (or just beat up) the other two monsters in the process. Various guards poked their heads out of building windows to try and shoot all three of you down, but you were free to eat them, too. Police cars on the ground and helicopters in the air also took shots at you.

The controls were exceedingly simple—you would move the joy-stick up or down to scale buildings, or left and right to aim your punches or walk. Press the Fire button repeatedly and you'd either punch or eat things, or if you were just walking along, you could use the Fire button to jump. The more you punched a building, the more damage it took on—and it was satisfying to do so. Destroy enough of the building's facade and it would come tumbling down in a tremendous cloud of smoke; you had to leap away from it before you were caught in the resulting demolition.

Once you destroyed all the buildings on one board (referred to as a "city") three times, you'd move onto the next one. There were a total of 50 cities and 150 levels. When you lost all your energy, you reverted back to human form and walked off the screen in shame. The game supported up to three players, two on joysticks and one using the keyboard; otherwise the other monster (or two) were computer-controlled. This ST conversion of the popular arcade coin-op looked and played well. The graphics didn't quite match the arcade, but they were a huge leap past all the 8-bit systems, with oversize, multicolored sprites being the most obvious difference. The teenager in me still loves this game.

Super Sprint (Electric Dreams Software, 1987)

This super-fun, top-down racing game, a conversion of Atari's 1986 coin-op, let up to three players compete with each other. Atari developed Super Sprint as a contemporary, full-color installment of its classic Gran Trak 10 and Sprint 2 black-and-white coin-op machines from the mid 1970s, and for those of you playing at home, the Atari 2600's Indy 500 cartridge that came with two infinitely rotating Driving controllers. As with those games, Super Sprint's screen stayed fixed. The entire track was displayed at once.

The game contained eight tracks, and you could choose one of four levels of difficulty. During each race, you upgraded your car by collecting wrenches you could trade in for faster acceleration, higher top speeds, or more traction. The first racer to complete three laps won and then advanced to the next circuit. Later races included obstacles such as oil spills and even miniature tornadoes that caused your car to spin out of control. You controlled your car with the joystick, steering left and right with the stick and holding the button down for acceleration.

The only real complaint I had against the game was that the controls were a little tough. Unlike Indy 500, where you could slide the rear end of your car out around sharp turns (known as oversteer), in Super Sprint the dominant handling trait was understeer. That meant if you entered a turn too fast, you would shoot wide of the mark unless you slowed down considerably. That, plus overly fast turn-in, meant it took a deft and not necessarily realistic touch to drive the car around the track smoothly. Nonetheless, it was an arcade game, not a simulation. There's something that will always be tremendously fun about playing these go-kart-like video games on a computer screen.

Road Runner (US Gold, 1987)

In this solid conversion of the Atari coin-op machine, you controlled the famous Road Runner as he dodged Wile E. Coyote and many other hazards. Part of the challenge was that you were moving from right to left, and you remained close to the left edge of the screen the whole time. This meant you didn't have much warning as to what was coming next. The game scrolled as you moved left, eating as much seed as you could, and the scrolling stopped when you went back the other way to the right. But you couldn't go back far enough to scroll the board in the other direction. You had to constantly advance to the left. Miss five seed piles and you'd lose a life.

Just as you would expect, Wile E. Coyote chased the Road Runner the entire time. The first level was a simple, mostly straight road, but later levels introduced many more twists, turns, and other obstacles. On the second board, Wile E. Coyote would light a fuse on his red rocket and shoot back and forth across the screen trying to grab you and take you for a ride. Starting on level five, the levels would repeat but with the added fun of land mines. The graphics, bright colors, smooth (and often hilarious) animation, and spot-on sound effects conveyed the atmosphere of the cartoon. I was thrilled to play a game that looked this good.

Arcade conversions for the ST continued to appear throughout the platform's time on the market. Some of the best later on included a pitch-perfect Star Wars: The Arcade Game, as well as Robotron: 2084, Bubble Bobble, Missile Command, and Marble Madness. The ST also saw abbreviated but beautiful versions of the Cinematronics laserdisc games Dragon's Lair and Space Ace. Sega churned out hit after hit from its own arcade catalog including Out Run, Space Harrier, Afterburner, and Golden Axe. Ports of Irem's classic space shooters R-Type and R-Type II also made it over to the ST (although they were not as good as they were on the Amiga).

Atari released a very playable Paperboy conversion late (1989-ish). The fiendishly difficult Ghosts 'n' Goblins and sequel Ghouls 'n' Ghosts arrived on the ST with all of their maddening challenge intact. The ST also received a solid conversion of the 1989 racing game Super Monaco GP, courtesy of US Gold in 1991. Way late, in 1993, Sinister Developments put up intense, graphically enhanced versions of Centipede,

Asteroids, Space Invaders, and Galaxian. None of these were arcade-accurate by design, but all four were seriously worth playing.

In many ways, the ST came closer than any other system in bringing the arcade home. That may no longer have been as important for home computers of this era. But for anyone who cut their teeth on a 2600 or even a ColecoVision, only to be disappointed at having something less than the perfect arcade translation, the ST was a godsend. It was the arcade platform gamers had wanted all along. The only problem was it arrived too late. The rest of the industry moved on, as those gamers gravitated to the NES, the Sega Genesis, and other popular home consoles.

Arcade conversions aside, the year 1987 served as a kind of golden age for the ST thanks to its enviable array of new software and attractive hardware pricing. Some of the best software had yet to arrive, and we would soon see more powerful iterations of the machine and a couple of 32-bit variations, which I'll get to later in this book. But I'd argue 1987 and 1988 are what brought us the heart and soul of the ST platform in the US, at a time where the PC had yet to catch up and the Mac had yet to drop enough in price.

Still, challenges were brewing. Commodore unveiled the breakthrough Amiga 500, the first low-end Amiga, which muscled right into the ST's pricing turf at just $699 in America. Overseas, the ARM-based Acorn Archimedes also competed with the ST, though it stayed mostly within the UK home and educational markets and never captured significant market share. As we'll soon see, Atari would be too slow to respond. Shiraz Shivji had begun working on an enhanced ST to better compete with the Amiga and Mac, but he left Atari in 1987, dealing the project a significant setback.

Atari could have recovered from Shivji's loss quickly, but something else was sucking up all the oxygen in the room. If there was one key disaster you could point to, a moment where Atari's fortunes turned once again, it would be in its acquisition of Federated Group, a chain of 65 electronics stores located in California, Arizona, Texas, and Kansas. Atari was still having trouble getting dealers on board selling its products—in part because retailers remembered being stiffed when Atari's video game business collapsed in 1983 and 1984, but also in part because of Tramiel's notorious reputation for ruthless cost cutting during his reign at Commodore.[3] Against anyone's better judgment, Atari decided to hedge its bets and buy its own dealer network. On

August 24, 1987, Atari announced it was acquiring the Federated Group for $67 million.[4] This was something I was oblivious to then, because I lived on the East Coast and there were no stores in our area. I know now there were articles about it in the various ST magazines, but I probably blew past them looking for all the new product reviews, not knowing what Federated Group was or why I should care.

It soon didn't matter, because one year later, the whole thing was already toast. Other dealers located near Federated Stores complained incessantly of unfair competition, and nationwide, many existing dealers said Federated Stores would receive stock of Atari products first, as *ST-Log* columnist Clayton Walnum detailed in the November 1988 issue. *ST-Log* called a couple of stores to look into Atari executive Neil Harris's claim that the stores weren't exceptionally aggressive in pricing, only to find those dealers saying straight out they'd match or beat any other dealer's price, and that they had tons of 1040STs in stock ostensibly because they were relatively unknown to consumers as Atari dealers.

It got worse on the financial side as well. Atari sued Federated's founder and former CEO, saying he overstated the company's assets, and that Atari wouldn't have bought the chain if it had known what it later learned.[5] By November 1989, Atari was looking for a way out altogether. "Within months of [Atari's] acquisition, the operation soured and Atari was beset with losses," the *Los Angeles Times* reported. "Last March, after announcing a loss of nearly $85 million because of the continuing poor performance of the retailing unit, Atari put Federation on the auction block." About 25 of the 65 stores had already closed. Analysts said Federated's own poor marketing efforts, limited product selection, aggressive competition from Circuit City and other retailers, and an absence of attractive new gadgets did the stores in.

It was a mess.

7 | Studio

Before the ST, most people making music on a professional level were still renting out recording studios on an hourly or daily basis, rather than doing it themselves. Home studios, and even the smaller "project studios" of the 1980s, were often based around multitrack cassette recording, and usually could only deliver "demo" audio quality. In this environment, the new MIDI standard began to rise in popularity as an easy way to synchronize multiple synthesizers and realize full compositions without live instruments.

Tape still played a key role, even on the higher end with reel-to-reel and the first digital tape systems, because you couldn't use MIDI to record vocals, electric guitars, violins, or other acoustic instruments. Still, the seeds were planted for a revolution in low-cost recording. MIDI sequencers let you record and play back multiple instrument tracks, and then edit them to your heart's content. Sequencers made it easy to mock up new songs, and in many cases deliver finished instrumental compositions. With MIDI, you could change the notes after the fact, try different sounds for the same part, and endlessly rework your music, similar to what the word processor had done for writing. No matter how much you edited a song or added tracks, you'd never degrade its sound quality, which wasn't true with tape. Synthesizer manufacturers were beginning to catch on to this phenomenon and began to build rudimentary, pattern-based scratchpad-style sequencers into their instruments as well.

But there was still one huge limitation, regardless of whether you were using an external sequencer or one built into a synthesizer keyboard: memory. For example, the Korg M1, a popular synthesizer of the late 1980s I owned and the one that introduced the concept of the "keyboard workstation," had an internal memory that allowed for just 4,400 notes to be stored in total, *shared across 10 songs*. This, to put it mildly, was not enough. Hi-hats on the drums alone could eat up a couple hundred of the 440 you'd have on average per song. You were given the option to reformat the internal memory such that you could store 7,700 notes, but at the painful expense of half the included sounds. To expand the M1's available memory in a genuine fashion, you had to buy expensive, proprietary memory cards. Because I couldn't afford these, I was constantly deleting hundreds of hours of hard work on songs I had made or covered—I loved early Phil Collins—just so I could start again with fresh new memory for new songs.

The Atari ST eliminated this problem. Inexpensive floppy disks contained essentially unlimited free space for MIDI recordings, because the song files were small even by the standards of the time. Having the ST also meant you could hook up numerous synthesizers without internal sequencers and control them all from a single point. By connecting them to an analog mixing board, you could hear all of them play together. The ST also delivered full graphical editing of your songs in a variety of ways, including MIDI "event lists," piano-roll-style editing, and full musical notation with treble and bass clefs.

The impact all of this had on music recording was on the order of what word processors did to the typewriter. Computer-based recording made creating, editing, and producing new music much, much faster, both for pros on the clock and for amateurs who couldn't afford the hourly rates of real studios, or even just for those who couldn't play an instrument well enough to record it live. The ST's importance also became clear by the number of famous musicians who bought and began working with one. Soon, early ST programs like Pro-24 gave way to hundreds of music software packages large and small. Three of these programs in particular turned out to have historic impact, and set the design and tone of music software for decades to come.

Notator (C-Lab, 1988)

C-Lab got its start making MIDI sequencers for the Commodore 64 and ST. In 1987, C-Lab released the landmark Creator, a pattern-based music sequencer that offered 64 tracks split up into four "players" across 16 MIDI channels. Rather than Pro 24's timeline-based approach, Creator adopted what now seems old-school: the drum-machine-style method of breaking tracks into "patterns" that you then strung together to form "songs." The user interface contained an arrangement section on the left, an area for basic pattern recording and editing in the middle, and a transport and locator display on the right for recording, rewinding, and punching in to make edits on the fly.

In 1988, C-Lab built on the Creator platform and released Notator, which was the same program base with a full musical staff and scoring notation module grafted onto it. This made much more sense for any classically trained composer, or even just someone who knew how to read music on a basic level, and it took full advantage of the mouse-based GEM interface to depict accurate notation on screen. The result was a more musical and less mathematical approach to recording.

Notator became incredibly popular for music sequencing, thanks to its full feature set and the ST's tight MIDI timing, and Notator and Creator quickly evolved into one package. Soon, the programmers would move to create their own company separate from C-Lab called Emagic in 1992 in order to sell an upgraded product called Notator Logic, and then, Logic. Many musicians relied on Notator and Logic throughout the 1990s. Eventually, Apple purchased Emagic in 2002 and discontinued the PC version of Logic. Today, we know the program as Logic Pro X on the Mac.

Master Tracks Pro (Passport, 1987)

Master Tracks Pro began life on the Apple II and Commodore 64, but it was the ST that catapulted the program into the mainstream (or at least, the mainstream for music studios and project studio owners). Master Tracks Pro cut through some of the complexity of Notator and presented the information in a more easily digestible fashion. The program broke the interface into several pieces. The left side held a track sheet, showing you which instruments corresponded to which tracks. The right side included a piano-roll-style step editor, a song editor for arrangements, and a transport and beat clock at the bottom-right corner of the screen.

In 1988, Passport released a lower-cost version of the program called Master Tracks Junior. It left out the grid-based step editor, MIDI controller editing, and SysEx-based editor-librarian features, but retained 64-track recording and a precise 240 clocks per quarter note resolution. The program still let you record multiple MIDI channels at the same time. You could also filter out recorded MIDI data so it didn't pick up aftertouch, pitch bend, modulation, patch changes, or even notes if you wanted to add the other stuff on the second pass.

An ST paired with Master Tracks Pro and a couple of well-chosen synthesizers or rack-mount modules, perhaps synced with an eight-track and a mixing board, made for a powerful MIDI studio at a cost within reach of many independent musicians and producers. Although Master Tracks Pro didn't survive for the long haul, it remained a popular and exceptionally easy-to-grasp sequencer for many years.

Cubase (Steinberg, 1989)

Steinberg's Pro 24 sequencer had gained a considerable following with recording musicians. After a few years' worth of updates, Steinberg released Pro 24's successor Cubase, which quickly became one of the most famous music recording packages of all time—especially in Europe, but still used today the world over on Macs and PCs. Steinberg initially priced Cubase in the UK at a whopping £500, as *ST Format* reported in its September 1989 review. That put the program squarely on the professional end and out of the reach of many home enthusiasts.

Let's quickly go over why Cubase was such a revelation compared with all the earlier ST sequencers and MIDI editors. Steinberg packed in many of the best features from C-Lab Creator/Notator and Passport's Master Tracks Pro, and also ensured it remained fully compatible with Pro 24. When you clicked Play, the horizontal timeline display updated in real time, so you could see your music going by track by track. The program showed a tape-deck-like transport at the bottom of the screen along with easy-to-read locators, plus buttons to activate the metronome and whether you were syncing to an external source. Another key innovation was the Arrange page. It supported up to 64 tracks, with 16 visible at any one time in a vertical list; each track displayed the instrument, track name, plus mixing console-style solo and mute buttons. You could record at a resolution of up to 192 parts per quarter note. The program offered groove-based parameters and non-destructive quantization to make your music feel more natural.

Once you had recorded something, editing it was super-easy. Cubase included score, grid, drum, and key views. These gave you access to your recorded data and let you lay down new notes if you didn't want to play them live on a synthesizer keyboard. You could draw a box around multiple music events and then cut, move, or paste them all at once. Below each editing window was a view of MIDI controller data for things such as sustain pedals and the pitch bend and modulation wheels; there you could even draw curves using the mouse, rather than inputting and editing numbers from 0 to 127 all day long on a MIDI event list.

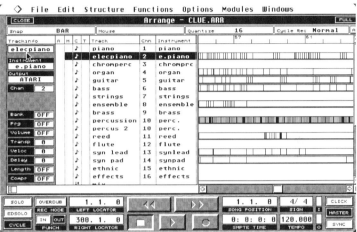

Figure 7.1: The famed MIDI sequencer Cubase launched on the ST platform, and has since blossomed into a tremendously capable and popular digital audio workstation on Macs and PCs. (Credit: Atari74user via atari-forum.com)

Computers wouldn't begin recording digital multitrack audio—meaning voice, acoustic guitar, and other live instruments in the room—until the late 1990s. The same would be true for virtual instrument plug-ins, where synthesized or sampled sounds played "in the box" (meaning the computer) instead of via external hardware keyboards and rack-mounted sound modules. But this first Cubase looked so much like Pro Tools, Logic Pro X, and other major sequencers do *today*. I remember when Cubase debuted on the ST and I still can't get over how much of the "foundation" of modern music recording was laid down in this program. Cubase was an earth-shaking release in the music world and it all happened on the Atari ST.

Dr. T's Music Software

Numerous other vendors released quality music software for the ST as well. A few stood out for their large user bases and, well, large numbers of magazine advertisements for products from the likes of Hybrid Arts and Nilford Labs. You may remember Dr. T's music software because you've owned it and used it, or you may just remember the ads: "The Dr…Developing Amazing ST Software." Either way, Dr. T's programs were ever-present for us ST fans, as the company focused on the ST platform—and, specifically, programs for working musicians. Dr. T's was founded by synthesizer fan Emile Tobenfeld in 1984. He first developed a MIDI sequencer called KCS (an acronym for Keyboard Controlled Sequencer) for the Commodore 64 and then another one called Omega for the ST, and then grew the business from there.

One popular package was The Copyist, which transcribed MIDI data for up to 24 tracks to virtual sheet music. You could then print your scores on dot matrix or laser printers. This program began life on MS-DOS machines, so the ST port's interface was unnecessarily convoluted, according to a Summer 1988 *STart* review. Other ads proffered editor-librarians for many popular synthesizers of the time, such as the Yamaha DX7, the Casio CZ-101, the Ensoniq Mirage sampler, and the Roland MT-32. These programs let you make new sounds or edit existing sounds for these synthesizers using the ST's high-resolution display, rather than squinting at a tiny two-line, 32-character LCD and paging through cramped menus to adjust obscure parameters. Editor-librarians were extremely popular programs, and only began to fade once synthesizers began to appear as software plug-ins (in which case you would just save new sounds to your computer's hard drive).

Other Dr. T's programs came in for occasional criticism for their number-focused interfaces as well. But thanks to low pricing and the company casting a wide net for releasing different kinds of music software, it was popular throughout the ST's tenure. Dr. T's also released software for the Amiga and Macintosh—neither machine had built-in MIDI ports, but MIDI interfaces eventually became widely available, especially for the Mac.

Computer Music Research

As the Atari ST platform matured, plenty of other developers began to create music recording and composition applications. I definitely don't have space to cover them all—there were hundreds—but I want to touch on a few that were unusually innovative and, in some cases, positively groundbreaking. The first would be Dr. T's Tunesmith, a

1988 algorithmic phrase generator program and an extremely early example of a computer composing music on its own. Tunesmith's arranger page was a pile of obscure attributes and numbers, but if you looked a little closer the fog began to clear. The program offered a series of theme and variation parameters, such as the phrase's length, what the first note was, the desired range of note values, and the weighting and probability of rests, longer notes, and shorter notes. You could set up an accompaniment with six voices that you could then play another instrument over, and those voices could have different rhythmic and harmonic qualities, along with a drum track you could fix so that the notes didn't get accidentally transposed, which would wreak havoc on the sound samples triggered.[1]

Another sophisticated composition system was Presto, a program based on mathematical transformations that arrived in 1989 and saw a major update a few years later. The program was developed by Dr. Guerino Mazzola on the Atari ST, which one computational music science textbook has called "at the time one of the leading platforms used for computer music composition and research, not least because it supported MIDI natively."[2] Presto let you compose music by manipulating graphics on screen, without needing to know how to read music or play an instrument. It could analyze an existing piece of music and manipulate or rearrange it; feed it a Led Zeppelin score and you could add an orchestral section, for example, or give it Mozart and it would play the melody in a different scale and with a variety of instruments.[3] This program lives on as $10 shareware for the ST today.

A third program still around is Intelligent Music's M, an interactive composition program developed in 1987 for the Mac and quickly ported to the ST. The software let you compose and shape music as it unfolded. You would first record some patterns of notes and chords, and then M would start playing back possibilities, which you could then shape further in real time using the mouse. You could do things like loop a line of music and then, as it played, change the length of the notes or the key of the piece. In another example, you could program complex African drum rhythms by setting the software to play multiple phrases by reading each one backward or forward, and set to different "time bases" that still lock onto the beat.[4] The program still exists today for Macs and is maintained by Cycling 74, which at the time of this writing was selling M for exactly $74.

MT-32 Multi-Timbre Sound Module (Roland, 1987)

By the late 1980s, the music synthesizer was already 20 years old. It begat a mature industry full of established brands such as Moog, ARP, Yamaha, Korg, Roland, Sequential Circuits, Emu, and Ensoniq. The big sea change in the 1980s was the move from fat-sounding analog synthesis, as popularized on keyboards like the Minimoog, the Roland JUNO-106, and the Sequential Circuits Prophet 5, to the more crystalline digital sounds found in the Yamaha DX7 and the Roland D-50. Another key development around the same time was the "multi-timbral" module, which could simultaneously play many sounds, often digitally sampled versions of acoustic instruments, on different MIDI channels.

One of the biggest sellers in the latter category was the Roland MT-32. This sleek black MIDI sound module and synthesizer could play up to eight instruments and one drum or percussion kit at the same time. It featured what Roland called an LA synthesis engine, which combined short PCM-based samples with synthesized sound waves. The MT-32 also began to show up in the support notes for ST games over the next few years. Soon, the MT-32 would become the standard for top-notch game audio.

Let's take a closer look at the hardware. The module came preset with 128 synth and 30 rhythm sounds. The unit also had a built-in reverb effect, and an oversize volume knob sat on the right side of the front panel. A two-row green LCD on the left indicated the current sound selected, and if you were a masochist, you could even edit sounds in a pinch using the display and the 10 buttons on the front panel. You could connect the MT-32 to the ST with standard 5-pin MIDI cables, unlike the PC that required an ISA card installed and an external expander module such as the Roland MPU-401 or the MPU-IPC-T. The MT-32 was priced at around $400 on the street, which was on the low end for professional synthesizers but high for a computer accessory.

Many ST games had support for MIDI, and specifically the MT-32 beginning around 1989 or so. Any Sierra game running the SCI interpreter (meaning various games from series such as King's Quest, Space Quest, Police Quest, Hero's Quest/Quest for Glory, and Leisure Suit Larry, plus outliers like Conquests of Camelot), along with many other titles (Marble Madness, Pirates!, ST Karate, and Ultimas III through V, just to cite a few examples), would play music through the MIDI ports and either work with any sound module from the period or support the MT-32 directly.[5] If you had an MT-32 setup, you were treated to soaring orchestral scores and pulsing electronic music nearly indistinguishable from contemporary professional recordings. Sierra spearheaded the MT-32's adoption in computer games and even distributed the MT-32 itself for a while; that's where I had ordered mine from in 1989. Many games, especially those from Sierra, would employ custom MT-32 patches for an even fuller sound.

The MT-32 went on to live a long and distinguished life, with newer variations from Roland repackaged as dedicated computer modules (such as the CM-32L) and ISA sound cards for desktop PCs (such as the LAPC-1). Roland eventually discontinued the MT-32 in 1991 in favor of the more advanced, 16-part-multitimbral Sound Canvas line, which began with the SC-55 module and SCC-1 PC sound card, which succeeded the MT-32 and LAPC-1, respectively. These Sound Canvas modules contained the first popular support for the new General MIDI standard, which was essentially a refined iteration of the MT-32's default sound set.

Desktop Publishing

Desktop publishing began with word processors on personal computers such as the Apple II and the Atari 800 in the late 1970s. It evolved into covering all aspects of laying out a page, including design, graphics, typography, and printing, enabling the owner of a desktop publishing system to "self-publish" work that was indistinguishable from the product of a traditional printing business. The Macintosh is usually credited first as the platform that brought desktop publishing to the masses. But the Atari ST enabled much of the same user interface design and ability to work with fonts and graphics that the Mac had. And this proved especially irresistible overseas, where exchange rates worked against many computer buyers and the ST offered the most value by a significant margin.

Although applications such as Publishing Partner brought desktop publishing to the ST, the biggest player on this scene was Calamus. The German software manufacturer Ditek International released Calamus on July 1, 1987. Sometime in late 1988, a company called ISD Marketing distributed Calamus in the US with a rewritten user manual and new fonts. Calamus included enough features to prove solid competition for the two big players, Aldus PageMaker and Ventura Publisher (neither of which made it to the ST), while costing just $299 at retail. The recommended configuration to run Calamus was a Mega 4 ST, a monochrome monitor, and an SLM804 laser printer, a package that cost $3,995 at launch—and, as an episode of *The Computer Chronicles* noted, that was a good value because the same money usually bought a laser printer by itself.[6]

Calamus used its own vector font format with what the company called Intelligent Kerning. The GEM-based interface provided WYSIWYG output, but you didn't see the real beauty of the fonts on screen; it showed in laser output, as a May 1989 review in *STart* pointed out. The program was split into four main modes: Page Setup, for basic layouts and documents; Frames, for individual components on the page; Text, for editing; and Graphics, though only for import at launch, with vector and raster graphics creation coming later. Many of the features overlapped in more than one mode as well.

STart dubbed Calamus "the most daring entry into the desktop publishing market in years," and said it was "a powerful program that incorporates all of the best features of existing publishing products into a fast, easy-to-use product." The review called out Calamus's ability to rotate text, group frames, and save objects to clipboards (all of which PageMaker couldn't do), and its ability to resize fonts while conserving memory and disk space. It also refreshed the screen quickly and offered many zoom levels, unlike the competing Ventura Publisher.

In testing, the review claimed Aldus PageMaker and Ventura Publisher both took more than 30 minutes to print each page, and that Calamus could print a page in 30 to 45 seconds in comparison. This seems suspect to me now, but as you may have noticed then, there was a bit of a "root for the home team" thing going on with Atari-focused magazines, even if they weren't straight-up house organs such as *Atari Explorer* or *Atari Age*.

Other competing desktop publishing programs on the ST included Fleet Street Publisher and Timeworks Desktop Publisher (the latter of which I owned a boxed copy of in the late 1980s, but never used much). Publishing Partner evolved into PageStream, a more flexible program that ran on Windows, Linux, the Macintosh, and the Amiga. Today, when people discuss the ST, they often mention its success in the German desktop publishing and business markets. Calamus was the single biggest reason for that success. Calamus lived on past the Atari ST with its PC version, beginning with Windows 95. The last owner of Calamus, invers Software, finally closed its doors in 2018. Not a bad run.

Computer-Aided Design

The ST also established itself as a key platform for the CAD market. The combination of a 16-bit 68000 processor, 1MB or more of memory, and a graphical user interface with a mouse made the ST a natural choice for CAD, and at a much lower cost than competing UNIX or MS-DOS–powered workstations.

One of the best-known CAD software packages on the ST was Cyber Studio CAD-3D, which was codeveloped by Tom Hudson and Gary Yost (of Degas and Degas Elite fame). CAD-3D let you assemble scenes out of geometric, custom, or lathed objects, and you could adjust the lighting and camera positioning. You could then render still images, or beginning with v2.0, animated sequences.[7] Hudson's "open-architecture" interface meant you could extend CAD-32 with plug-ins—most notably for a desk accessory that enabled delta-compressed animation, which meant you would start with a picture and then only store the parts that changed for each subsequent frame to conserve data.

A 2002 feature article by Martin Doudoroff detailed the process in full, along with CAD's connection to the hit ST game Starglider:

> By this point, everybody in the business had noticed a new computer game called Starglider (for the Atari ST and Amiga) created by the British game designer and programmer Jez San. Starglider featured highly responsive 3D graphics for the time, so Tom and Gary contacted Jez and purchased some useful routines from him that helped speed the redrawing of CAD-3D's viewports. The most dramatic way this new technology manifested itself in CAD-3D 2.0 was that the user could now use the mouse to rotate the perspective camera's view "in real time" while in wire frame mode.[8]

CAD-3D later grew into the industry-standard 3D Studio, 3D Studio Max, and Autodesk 3DS Max packages.

Another popular package was DynaCADD, which also billed itself as a fully three-dimensional design program intended for electrical, mechanical, architectural, and civil engineering applications. The program boasted more than 350 features, including multiple 3D views, 256 layers, vector-based fonts, and sophisticated plotter output support. DynaCADD could also send draft or final versions to laser printers, and it integrated with desktop publishing systems like Calamus. One two-page ad spread showed the program running on a Mega 2 ST system and interfacing with a slick Roland DG DXY-990 wide-format pen plotter. Later, Atari would release an even more powerful system and monitor combination for CAD work, which we'll get to later.

StereoTek 3D Glasses (LC Technologies, 1987)

CAD-3D's open architecture also enabled a new kind of accessory for genuine 3D viewing. Several decades before movie theaters resurrected the idea of 3D, and television manufacturers tried (and failed) to turn 3D into a home theater craze, there was a serious effort to bring three-dimensional viewing to the ST. LC Technologies promised "true stereoscopic 3D graphics for your Atari ST," saying its StereoTek glasses would deliver a real sensation of depth. When wearing them, the viewer could watch objects fly out of the CRT, view the real structure of a molecular model, or weave their way "through an infinite geometric universe."

The design was a kind of proto version of the active shutter 3D glasses that work with some of today's flat-panel televisions. The StereoTek product consisted of electronic liquid crystal shutter glasses and plugged into the interface unit in the cartridge port. It worked in both color and monochrome modes, and you could plug in a second pair of glasses at the same time. The frames contained optical shutters that opened and closed in time to the ST's screen refresh, which meant either 60Hz in color or 70Hz in mono. In turn, the monitor displayed alternating right- and left-eye views that synchronized with the shutters. The package also came with a desk accessory that enabled the glasses to work in Degas Elite, along with a simple CAD program and a "stereo slide show" developed by Tom Hudson. A $149.95 package contained the glasses, cable, and cartridge port interface; $99.95 bought a second pair of glasses for the second port in the interface.

Practical Solutions

There were all kinds of accessories and gadgets available for the ST, and it would be impossible to cover them all. Instead, I'll highlight a few important ones from Practical Solutions, which developed numerous products for the ST. Three were highly desirable, and still are today if you have a real ST (or, ahem, several of them) in the house.

The VideoKey solved a pervasive problem on the ST for video enthusiasts: It added a composite video output. This simple RGB converter peripheral meant you could take the output from any ST and record any 3D animations or other projects onto a VHS tape, as well as view them (or anything) on a big-screen television. The VideoKey was a small gray box that measured about 5 by 4 by 1.5 inches (HWD). The right side contained a hardwired composite cable. The back panel held a feed-through monitor port for the ST, audio output and video composite jacks, a channel 2/3 selector, and a TV jack. There was no power switch; the unit powered up as soon as it detected an ST in color mode, and you would know it was working because of the power LED. Your original monitor stayed on when the VideoKey was in use. The unit also contained an RF modulator, though the composite output looked better. A review in the December 1988 issue of *STart* pointed out the unit wasn't designed to project an 80-column medium- or high-resolution display, but that it was designed for use in low-resolution mode for games or animation—and "if the game [had] an intensely blue display, like Typhoon Thompson from Broderbund, the TV display [was] just a bit too muddy to use."

The Monitor Master let you switch between two monitors with the same computer attached, as well as a third monitor if your ST included composite video support. With the ST, the ability to run multiple monitors was paramount, because choosing between a monochrome monitor at high resolution (for work-related tasks) and a color monitor at low or medium resolution (for graphics, animation, and of course gaming) was always one of the platform's sticking points. The Monitor Master also included a separate RCA audio output. The Mouse Master did the same thing, but for computer mice as the name suggested. It let you keep a mouse and a joystick plugged into the same port and switch between them whenever you needed the second joystick for something. As *ANALOG Computing* pointed out in a November 1989 gift guide, it was also perfect if you had an Atari 1040ST and didn't want to deal with lifting the machine off the desk just to get at the joystick and mouse ports.[9]

New Games for 1988

As the ST platform matured for professional work, game developers continued to exercise the platform and learn its secrets. Another banner year for ST games, 1988 brought its share of groundbreaking, fun, and just plain addictive titles. Here's a roundup of some of the best, along with one genuine flop I have still not have recovered from mentally. Let's start with the wonderful brains at Psygnosis, who continued to flex their programing muscles.

Baal (Psygnosis, 1988)

This side-scrolling platform shooter made you the leader of the Time Warriors. Your mission was to save Earth from Baal, a demon with an army of undead that stole a War Machine. You had to invade all three of Baal's domains and collect all pieces of the War Machine in each one. The game's packaging lacked the company's trademark Roger Dean artwork, but it still looked good. The manual set the mood with a short story introducing the characters.

The controls were slightly tricky, but became second nature with practice. You moved the joystick left or right to run, or up and down to climb or descend ladders. Press the Fire button and move the stick right or left and you would fire your weapon. Push up with the button pressed and you'd jump; push diagonally up and you'd do a somersault. This setup was a bit more complex than, say, Contra on the NES, which offered nearly all of the same actions but used the button only for firing.

Your laser had four stages you could employ, three of which needed cartridges, and you had to periodically refuel. The same went for your energy shield. The game did a convincing impersonation of something you'd play on a Sega Genesis, if not in an arcade. Scrolling was surprisingly stable, and your warrior moved fluidly throughout. The color scheme and background graphics were especially sharp, and struck a good balance between futuristic space station and demonic lair.

Baal isn't the first title to come to many people's minds when they think of Psygnosis, or the Atari ST for that matter. But it is well worth playing today and a good example of a second-generation ST game that shows what happened when programmers began to hit their stride with the platform.

Bubble Ghost (Accolade, 1988)

This original and fun title delivered hours of nonstop puzzle action (yes, that was a thing). You played a ghost that floated from room to room in an old haunted castle, guiding a bubble containing his soul safely past various obstacles and traps. To do this, you blew on the bubble to give it a speed boost. You could also blow on a switch to turn it on or off, or blow out a candle to extinguish its flame.

Pressing the left mouse button would rotate the way the ghost was facing, through eight different angles. By doing this and blowing on the bubble with the right mouse button, you could move it around the board in any direction you wanted. The bubble had a tendency to slowly drift into a wall or another obstacle, which would cause it to pop. This made the ghost mad at you. Blow the bubble from one side to the other so it floated through the exit, and you would successfully complete one hall. There were 35 halls in the castle.

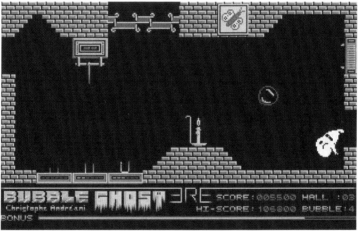

Figure 7.2: This humorous puzzle game put you, a ghost, in charge of blowing a delicate bubble through 35 obstacle-filled halls in an old haunted castle.

French developer Christophe Andréani designed and programmed the game on an Atari 1040ST using Megamax C and 68000 assembly language, and then used Degas Elite for the graphics, as he confirmed in an e-mail.[10] "In [those] years, a lot of the game was entirely designed by one person only," Andréani told me. "It was very interesting to do programming, graphics (sprites, background, animations), music (synthetic, first sampling), work on game control and game design...The games were small enough for one person be able to do all that stuff."

Bubble Ghost later saw ports to other platforms. The game was nicely animated, with humorous sound effects. And if you could handle the frustration factor—which was considerable, because you weren't controlling the bubble—Bubble Ghost was a satisfying challenge and rewarded repeated play. I remember getting a full weekend out of this game when I was 15, and enough time has passed that I was able to enjoy another go-around while writing this book.

Captain Blood (Infogrames, 1988)

Captain Blood, created by Philippe Ulrich, was an incredibly innovative space adventure simulator. You were the cyborg Captain Blood, whose life force was slowly being drained by five clones scattered among 32,768 planets. You had to find and quickly assimilate the clones, before your ship permanently assimilated *you* into its bionic structure. The stunning graphics were dominated by your spaceship's organic and bizarre control panel. During the game, you would warp to different sectors, fly over craggy landscapes of alien planets, and communicate with aliens in different tongues using a sophisticated and often incomprehensible language parser.

Figure 7.3: Jean-Michel Jarre's avant-garde soundtrack offered the finishing touch on the revolutionary Captain Blood, a universe-spanning adventure that combined space exploration with a sophisticated alien language parser.

You controlled the game with the mouse, which moved your cyborg hand cursor and let you press buttons with the on-screen finger. The more you played, the more vitals you lost and the more uncontrollable your on-screen hand became. The time limit of the game worked out to about two and a half hours before your arm would become too shaky to control. If you found one of the clones and absorbed its fluid, you would be able to play another couple of hours.

Obviously, you didn't have enough time in the game to explore the whole galaxy. To narrow down the search, you would warp to different sectors, looking for worlds inhabited by any of 12 different races of alien. If you found some, you had to attempt to communicate with them in order to gather clues about where the clones were located.

The usual order of events was that you needed to choose a destination likely to have aliens, successfully activate hyperspace, survive the jump, navigate your ship carefully to a new planet, send out an OORXX reconnaissance orbiter (you had as many of those as you needed), and land it on the rocky landscape full of valleys and canyons. From there, you employed the game's icon-based Universal Protocol of Communication to talk to any aliens you found.[11] You had to figure out what interested that alien and what he or she wanted, and possibly use a bribe or threat to get what you wanted. It helped to take notes, as you never knew what you would learn. Assembling the right syllable icons to speak in the correct order was tricky, given there were 120 of them in total.

The graphics were stunning then and still look good today. The game was ported to many 8- and 16-bit platforms, but was developed for the 16-bit ST first and it showed. This game played better on the ST than on the Amiga, mainly thanks to better-rendered graphics, clearer-sounding music, and digitized alien voice samples that were missing from the Amiga. When you landed on a planet, it looked like the result of someone taking all those fractal graphics demos that were everywhere in the 1980s and folding them into a computer game.

One of the best things about Captain Blood was its soundtrack, which was derived from Jean-Michel Jarre's 1984 track "Ethnicolor." As with Starglider, it was digitized, so it had no polyphony or MIDI-based limitations. If you listened carefully, though, you would notice that as the music changed chords, it also slowed down or sped up. It seems like the game only contained a few short sampled clips from "Ethnicolor," and then played them back at different speeds to act as chord changes. Programmers pulled off all sorts of tricks like this to conserve memory in those days.

What you thought of Captain Blood may depend on what you were looking for in a space-exploration sim. If you wanted to trade with alien nations, colonize planets, and battle enemy ships, this was the wrong game to play and could well disappoint. It also had a serious learning curve. But there was nothing like this game before or even since. It was one of the defining pieces of software for the Atari ST.

Postscript: In a weird twist of fate, through several complex acquisitions between 1996 and 2003, Infogrames would end up owning all of Atari's IP outright. That's a conclusion even 120 different icons couldn't have convinced me of 30 years ago, no matter what order they were in.

Carrier Command (Rainbird, 1988)

One of the most influential games of the late 1980s, Rainbird's Carrier Command combined elements of simulation and real-time strategy. Its solid-fill polygon engine rendered the world in three dimensions. Your job in this game was to pilot a futuristic robotic aircraft carrier and colonize an archipelago of 64 newly risen islands, which contained vital energy elements and materials that had run out on the rest of the planet. The carrier was one of two developed by research scientists; the other one, which was more powerful, fell into the hands of terrorists. You had to use the less-advanced model to defeat the better one.

When you first loaded Carrier Command, you had to choose between starting a strategy game or an action game. During play, you flew aircraft and drove tanks into combat, and you could customize your vehicles with an array of weapons. You could play with either the mouse or a joystick. In-game, you switched between Pointer mode, which let you move the cursor around the screen, and Direct Control mode, which meant you were controlling whatever craft you were in at the moment (aircraft, tank, the carrier, and so on). The soundtrack, by Dave Lowe, only played if you had a double-sided disk drive (either an SF314 hooked up to a 520ST, or a 1040ST onward).

The Games Machine magazine said it was "destined to change the state of software...almost certainly the game of the year,"[12] while *Computer Gaming World* called it an improvement over Starglider and praised its gameplay.[13] "[Carrier Command] is the most complicated simulation I've ever played. It's also the best," reviewer Scot Tumlin wrote in the

November 1988 issue of *STart*. While it may feel dated now, Carrier Command was a good example of the then-state-of-the-art in 3D gaming, years before the first accelerated graphics cards arrived on the PC platform. In a testament to its enduring popularity, Carrier Command remains one of the most viewed ST games on Atarimania.

Elite (Rainbird, 1988)

Many gamers speak of Elite with reverence, and with good reason. Developed by Ian Bell and David Braben and first released in 1984 for the BBC Micro, the open-world Elite combined elements of space trading, simulation, combat, and soaring adventure into a single fantastic game. It was one of the first to incorporate wireframe 3D graphics on the 8-bit platforms. Elite took its sweet time arriving on both the ST and the Amiga, and with good reason: Rob Nicholson, who did those two ports and the MSX, said in 2013 he had to "write them blind, i.e. it was a visual copy of the game as I didn't have access to the source code…All I had was the wireframe shapes plus the code for the planet name generation."[14]

In Elite, you had to make as much money ("credits") as possible using a variety of methods: trade, bounty hunting, military missions, asteroid mining, and straight-up piracy. Every star you travelled to had a planet and an orbiting space station; periodically, you had to fight off Thargoid aliens in spaceship combat. The most lucrative trading was in illegal goods, but that brought its own risks. As you collected credits, you could upgrade your ship's weapons, cargo capacity, energy stores, or even add an automatic docking system. The game deliberately recalled *2001: A Space Odyssey* by playing "The Blue Danube" whenever you activated the docking sequence.

The ST port came in for some criticism, with *The One* magazine saying in November 1988 it could have used some kind of parallax starfield. I'd probably pin the result as a distinct lack of the sensation you were flying through space. Even just some type of low-level engine whirr (as in the 8KB Star Raiders on the Atari 400/800!) would have helped. That's the thing about so much time passing; Elite was a tremendous achievement and infinitely more complex than Star Raiders, but today Star Raiders is praised for its realistic sensation of flying through space because it still holds up. It's easy to see this kind of difference with the benefit of hindsight.

Virus (Rainbird, 1988)

This breakthrough game was also programmed by David Braben, and originally released on the Acorn Archimedes in 1987 under the title Zarch in the UK. Rainbird's Jez San (of Starglider fame) ported Zarch to the ST in 1988 for release in the US under the name Virus. It was an early key example of a game with solid 3D polygons and light sourcing. Virus foreshadowed the kinds of three-dimensional space games we'd see in the next several decades, and as with Carrier Command, it was another example of the state of the art in 3D gaming then and holds up much better now.

In Virus, seeder vessels spread virus spores on Earth. You had to find and destroy the seeders by flying your hoverplane across the 3D-contoured landscape, shooting down enemy fighters with your laser cannons and heat-seeking missiles. Meanwhile, when the virus spores landed, they would poison the ground and turn it brown and red, which caused the trees to mutate.

Basically, the game was kind of a 3D upgrade of Defender, but it was more difficult to control the ship. You did it primarily with the mouse, but with much smaller inputs than you may have expected at first (crashing 10 or 20 times would drive the point home). The problem was, your ship only had a downward-firing thruster, so to move in a certain direction, you had to tilt the ship with the mouse. Worse, you couldn't bank left or right; you could only dip the front end or lift it (pitch and yaw), and if you did it wrong you would end up upside down in a split second.

Control issues aside, the game played well. Even on 8MHz STs, the frame rate was more than acceptable. There was more than a little sense of impending doom during the periods of silence in between encountering enemy fighters, with their creepy wobbling engine sounds. Reviewers were largely thrilled with the game. *ST Action* said "the smoothness of the graphics is absolutely incredible; the filled terrain scrolls smoothly…you even reduce trees to charred stumps if you collide."

Most reviewers called out the diabolical control scheme. I'm not sure the scheme was even necessary—this could have been a more accessible game than it was—but if you persisted, you were amply rewarded with one of the best titles on the ST platform. It's still pretty amazing to see this game in action now and realize it came out so long ago.

Goldrunner II (Microdeal, 1988)

The highly anticipated sequel to the top-selling Goldrunner, Goldrunner II brought a more complex game (now on two floppy disks) and even more arcade-like graphics. Goldrunner II was set 50 years after the first game. Along the way, humans apparently decided they liked the Ring Worlds of Triton better than whatever the "New World" was, so they stayed put. The robot fighters the humans created to defend their new home did fine until pirates, plotting an ultimate attack on the human race, arrived and captured the robots. Your mission was to take up the cause of your grandfather and fly a gold one-man ship to each of 16 space research platforms to recover as many of the robots as you could.

The left two-thirds of the screen showed the current playfield. Immediately to the right was a vertical radar that showed your location within the context of the entire board, along with your score and two additional gauges. On each board, you shot transporter cars, which then released captive robots. You had to collect the robots and deposit them into teleport zones for safe return. At the same time, green-and-yellow recovery ships attempted to catch the freed robots before you could save them. If one succeeded, it would turn red and yellow, and you had to shoot it to free the robot once more. Some of the recovery ships mutated into magnet fighters or mines you had to steer clear of. Later levels featured deadly Noumenon Missiles, Fighter-2s, and a Fighter-1 Carrier that released Fighter-1 enemies to attack you. Once you collected all the robots on that level, the Mother-ship returned and you would move onto the next board. Two additional scenery disks at $14.95 a pop offered new levels once you played through all 16 that came with the game. (We older folk used to call in-app purchases "expansion disks.")

Thankfully, Goldrunner II featured the same lightning-fast scrolling and reverse-direction ability as the original. But another key difference was that enemy fire couldn't penetrate your ship's armor; instead, the bullets caused your ship to ricochet in the opposite direction. The game had a different lineup on the Credits list, but it was clearly cut from the same cloth and is just as addictive, with similar gameplay if different goals.

Heroes of the Lance (SSI, 1988)

Oh, the disappointment. I can still feel it. Even the silver box looked sharp, complete with artwork I already knew and loved from Advanced

Dungeons & Dragons. SSI's Heroes of the Lance game was based on the first Dragonlance module DL1, called Dragons of Despair. I had many of the Dragonlance modules, but I became a fan of this world through the *Dragonlance Chronicles*, an excellent trilogy of books written by Margaret Weis and Tracy Hickman.

This real-time computer game adaptation put you in control of eight companions in a quest to retrieve the Disks of Mishakal from the temple Xak Tsaroth in the world of Krynn. You had to fight off the dreaded Draconians in close combat, as well as undead, giant spiders, and Gully Dwarves to find Khisanth, an ancient black dragon that guarded the disks. Along the way, you explored the temple, fought monsters, collected treasure, and found magic items and new weapons and armor.

The game depicted the view from the side, with a CRPG-like window below showing a compass and eight character portraits you could click on. I say "CRPG-like" because this game was different from the turn-based Phantasie series or The Bard's Tale. Instead, you played it with a joystick, and called up additional commands by pressing the space bar. Although the game was based on first-edition AD&D rules, the mechanics (ability scores, tables, and die rolls) were all hidden. Heroes of the Lance wasn't an action RPG, either. It was really a fighting game in disguise, except with stilted, stubborn controls, a high difficulty level, and no save-game feature to help you along. Although the eight characters had different abilities, they mainly served as extra lives, as you could only have one character in play at a time.

Some reviews praised the game's visuals and sound (the graphics were quite nice), although the NES version came in for almost universal criticism. I didn't like the ST game, although I may have been in the minority, since I was expecting more RPG elements. Done correctly, Heroes of the Lance could have pointed the way forward for action RPGs such as Diablo, Baldur's Gate: Dark Alliance on the PlayStation 2, and the Dragon Age series. Instead, it served as a warning beacon: Not all genres mix.

Pinball Wizard (Accolade, 1988)

Macadam Bumper delivered fast-paced pinball and a full table construction set, all in a single mouse-driven program. The original game was released in 1986 in Europe, and I know some pirated copies made their way to the US rather quickly because of reasons I won't disclose. Accolade officially distributed the game in the US in 1988 under the name Pinball Wizard, which I also had a boxed copy of. (I'm serious; I can't remember why I bought it even though I already had the other one, but I found it listed in an old for-sale post on the internet I had made in 1994, so I definitely had it.)

The best feature of Pinball Wizard was the "Parts Box," which gave you dozens of pieces you could use to make your own tables. It also included a Paint Pot section that let you create Decorations—marquees and other details that then went on the table and that your ball passed over—or you could design Obstacles the ball collided with. The Paint Pot included a paint can, a brush, a pencil, a fill tool, a variety of line tools, two erasers, and 15 different colors. You could also set the score and bonus (but not sound effect) for each part; adjust the slope, tilt, speed, and elasticity of the table; and set the number of balls per game and whether there was a "Stroboscope," which let you decide if the ball ever became invisible and, if so, how often.

Pinball Wizard supported one to four players, featured a Tilt mode, and also required you to insert virtual "coins" before you could press the Start button and pull back the plunger to launch the first ball. Pinball Wizard was a more attractive game than Microdeal's Pinball Factory, which also offered a table construction set. Between the two games, pinball fans were well served on the ST.

Starglider II (Argonaut Software/Rainbird, 1988)

After considerable hype, Starglider II arrived on the Atari ST as well as on the Amiga, MS-DOS, Mac, and ZX Spectrum. As with the original, Starglider II was a 3D space combat game that took place in an open world setting. But unlike the first game, in this one you could also fly to other planets. This game also borrowed liberally from *Star Wars*, with the inclusion of giant enemy walkers that looked more than a little like AT-ATs from the ice planet Hoth.

The story was set two years later, after the Egrons failed in their Novenia invasion, with Starglider wreckage scattered across the now-ruined planet. Now the Egrons were trying again, this time with a giant beam projector situated around another planet and aimed at Novenia. You had to pilot a new Icarus prototype craft in a mission to build a neutron bomb, which could destroy the beam projector's various components before the Egrons completed its assembly.

The Icarus's cockpit was even more futuristic looking this time around, with holographic projections emerging from the control panel (we'd probably call that augmented reality today). The best way to control your ship was still with the mouse; you pushed it around to bank left or right, or climb or lose altitude. The left button shot the currently selected weapon, while holding the right button and pushing forward or back would increase or decrease velocity.

The biggest visual change between the original game and Starglider II was the second one displayed filled-in, flat-shaded polygons instead of wireframe graphics. It looked sharp in 1988, though I'll break with the majority and say that while the sequel may well have been a better game, I can't imagine Starglider without the original title's trademark wireframe look and feel. Maybe it's because Star Wars: The Arcade Game is one of my favorite games ever. Nonetheless, Starglider II's graphics were widely praised.

The sound, or rather the lack of it, came in for criticism. The Amiga port had a soundtrack and digitally sampled effects, while the ST version lacked music and all the effects came synthesized from the YM2149 chip. A December 1988 review in *Computer Gaming World* said the reason for the missing music is the ST port was developed for single-sided drives, even though double-sided drives such as the SF314 and the one built into the 1040ST were becoming commonplace.

Typhoon Thompson (Brøderbund Software, 1988)

Not many people remember it now, but Typhoon Thompson was easily of the most imaginative and finely crafted titles to come out for the ST. It was programmed by Dan Gorlin, of Choplifter fame. In this title you flew a Jet-Sled rescue craft—basically a glorified inner tube—above and below the surface of the sea. Your mission was to find a helpless Sea Child, the lone survivor among wreckage from an ill-fated flight over the uncharted ocean planet of Aguar. Sea Sprites had adopted the child and, with the help of flying machines, killed off prior search parties.

Your goal was to find four artifacts that together would help you free the child. You would do this by shooting flying machines and collecting the Sea Sprites they released. Spirit Guardians helped you along the way by giving you special weapons to fight the Sea Sprites. At the start of each game, you received five lives and four sleds. You controlled the Jet-Sled with the mouse; the movement felt natural in all directions. The thrusters let you turn around sharply, or if you pushed the mouse forward, they enabled you to dive underwater. Pull back and you would launch right out of the water again. Whee!

Figure 7.4: An utterly original action game, Typhoon Thompson took place on a faraway planet's ocean, with pitch-perfect animation and beautiful little touches throughout.

You could shoot as much as you wanted, and as you played you would acquire special weapons such as Scatter Bombs and Sprite Magnets, depending on the leg of the mission you were currently on and which artifact you were searching for. In the water you'd find things such as bumpers, which were just in the way, and Forcers, which pushed you away as you approached. More troubling were the Spitters, which dissolved your craft, and Suckers, which, well, sucked you and your Jet-Sled right up.

The graphics, sound effects, and music were all well done—especially David Bunnett's sprite animation, which was clever and nicely detailed. For example, right at the beginning of each game, a UFO delivered you to your Jet-Sled. You would walk out, look down at it in the water, and immediately run back inside, frightened. Then someone would take you out, wriggling around, and do one of several amusing things like bonk you on the head (it's different each time) before throwing you overboard into the Jet-Sled. The whole game was like this. It was wonderful to play.

Xenon (Arcadia Software/Mastertronic, 1988)

Captain Xod was in trouble—you know because you saw him in one of those "help, we're dying!"–style staticky TV feeds that are always the mark of a good sci-fi show. The first title developed by the famed Bitmap Brothers for the Atari ST, Xenon was a quality vertical-scrolling shooter with satisfying explosions (always important) and detailed gameplay. It wasn't as fast as Goldrunner or Goldrunner II, but it was easier to get into and understand, and you blew up a lot more things in the same amount of time. (This was also important.)

As the only other nearby ship from the Federation, you had to try and save Captain Xod by fighting through 16 zones and collecting the necessary supplies. Each zone had an end boss. During play, you could switch between controlling a ground-based saucer and a fighter jet, depending on which one you thought would be most effective in each part of the game. Periodically, vaporizing enemies released power-ups that improved your weapons capability.

ST Action magazine called Xenon "the first home computer game that has been able to be described as arcade quality," saying, "the game's graphics are superbly drawn." The game was ported to other platforms such as the Amiga and MS-DOS, and even the 8-bit Commodore 64, which was still going strong in the late 1980s. David Whittaker's soundtrack was also solid. Interestingly, Mastertronic also later released an arcade coin-op of the game. But Xenon gained fame as an ST exclusive first, and was especially popular overseas, where it was featured in a UK television show called *Get Fresh* as a play-by-phone game, similar to what we had in the New York area in the early 1980s with WPIX and Atari 2600 and Intellivision games.

Xenon didn't see much play in the US market, but if you missed it the first time around, it's seriously worth playing now. The sequel, Xenon 2: Megablast, featured nicer, more *Alien*-esque graphics and another good soundtrack. Gameplay in that one was set up as a more traditional vertical-scrolling shooter and at a slower pace.

By this point the MIDI sequencer space was beginning to take shape. A GUI made recording and editing tracks much easier than the tiny LCDs often found in hardware keyboard workstations and standalone sequencers, though the hardware would persist for another couple of decades. There was no denying it even then, though—the future recording studio would be computer-based, and in the late 1980s the ST was leading the charge.

Otherwise, as 1988 drew to a close, the ST platform was still a bit of a mixed bag. It was selling "phenomenally well" in Europe, especially in the UK and Germany for the desktop publishing, CAD, and general business markets, but it wasn't seeing the same success at home in the US.[15] The new Mega line, while impressive with its accompanying laser printer and hard drive, didn't do much for the company's profits either.[16]

"There are several reasons [why]," Leonard Tramiel said in a summer 1988 interview in *Antic*:

> One is that the United States has this terrible disease called IBM-itis, and the IBM PC had gotten a good stranglehold on business here. Plus, Apple had never gotten its stranglehold on Europe. What you wound up with in Europe was the PC, Mac, and ST all arriving at just about the same time. People had a fair, uniform comparison. 'Which of these machines do you want?' and they looked at the price and performance and people bought STs. In the US, we had to fight an I-don't-know-how-many-hundred-million-dollar propaganda campaign from Apple, and we didn't have hundreds of millions of dollars to spend on propaganda. Finally, the phrase, 'No one was ever fired for buying an IBM' I don't believe has ever been translated into German.[17]

Atari also had to work on its developer relations, including boosting the documentation available and formalizing the support mechanism with a tracking database for bugs and feature requests, the same story indicated. This would do well to help beef up the ST's still relatively spartan software catalog, a good portion of which was ports that didn't showcase the ST's native capabilities.[18]

By this point Atari had already made many missteps, with the ill-fated acquisition of Federated Group the crowning achievement. For a short time, even Atari tried selling a variety of PC-compatible computers, including the cult-favorite Portfolio palmtop, to diversify its lineup. But Atari Corporation itself remained relatively whole. The launch of both the ST and the revised XE lineup, while not perfect by any means, went reasonably well. The ST was fast finding various niches, not just in gaming, but in music production, desktop publishing, and CAD. The trick, at this point, would be rescuing the US market before it was too late.

8 | Enhanced

As the ST platform flourished, much more software had become available. This included games, as we have already well seen. It had become the primary gaming computer for me. I spent many a summer afternoon biking about a mile from my house in Sheepshead Bay, a neighborhood at the south end of Brooklyn, across East 19th Street to Avenue U, a local strip of small businesses and storefronts. My favorite computer store was A&R Computer World, a shop that at the time of this writing in 2019 still exists in the same spot that it did in 1988—quite a feat given its small size and the comings (and goings) of the Best Buys and CompUSAs of the world. It was in this shop I bought a lot of Atari ST games.

Another local store a bit farther away on Kings Highway, called Computer Software Plus, also had a good selection of ST software. Both stores were increasingly expanding their PC sections by this point as well. Neither carried anything for the Mac or Amiga, if memory serves, though it's possible those sections of the stores were there but simply didn't exist in my 15-year-old, Atari-soaked mind. Regardless, it was so much fun to browse the shelves of big-box ST games, looking for changes, new arrivals, and newly marked-down bargains.

Once in a while, I'd buy a game (Heroes of the Lance) only to find out I hated it. Because there were no return policies then, those were expensive mistakes. I remember *Antic, STart,* and *Dragon* magazines together didn't have quite enough ST software reviews to head this off at the pass (or if they did, I didn't see the review in time). I wish I had known about *Computer Gaming World* or *Compute!,* magazines that had existed for years but that I didn't come across until a bit later. None-theless, it's a time I look back on fondly, especially because for what-ever reason I had the money to buy games on a semi-regular basis. I remember stuffing the bills into a small red pouch on the back of the bicycle right before I headed out each time.

In the last few years of the 1980s, there were several serious attempts to bring to the ST big-name DOS programs that used up a lot of ink in computer magazines. These conversions often ended with either mixed results or downright failure. Arguably the most popular word processor of the MS-DOS world, at least before Word for Windows passed it, was WordPerfect. The long-anticipated ST port finally arrived after numer-ous delays and was indeed stuffed with high-end features. It was also sluggish, bug-ridden, and not well integrated with GEM. This was to be expected in some sense, given WordPerfect's MS-DOS and keyboard roots. But even just for document compatibility's sake, WordPerfect on the ST should have been better than it was. For a while, we also thought we'd see some variant of the then-new Microsoft Word on the ST as well. Instead, we received Microsoft Write, which I thought would be a port of the word processor I liked on the Mac SEs we had in our high-school lab. It wasn't that, though. Instead, this was a stripped-down iter-ation of an already-basic application that came bundled with Windows. It was a huge disappointment. The ST Microsoft Write brought little of the expected ease of use, and therefore, little reason to switch to it from Word Writer ST or even ST Writer.

There was still plenty of awesome stuff to come. Atari would fi-nally address some deficiencies the ST platform had had since its in-ception. But the market was changing, and even infringing on the ST's turf. The Mac was already good at music, but the PC was also gaining more abilities for MIDI music production. Even clunky DOS-based sequencers were still easier to use and more powerful than hardware boxes and the ones built into synthesizer keyboard workstations as we've covered. Then there was the Amiga 500, the powerful home computer that landed in 1987 and quickly became a tremendous threat to the ST's existence. The competition was fierce. Fortunately, after several years of delays, Atari had its long-awaited, next-generation ST ready. First, though, let's look at another system that was at least as significant, and that came earlier in the year.

Figure 8.1: The STacy, Atari's first portable computer, still weighed 15 pounds, but it gave you an entire 1040ST setup and a high-resolution monitor on the go, and in some configurations even with more memory. (Credit: Perfect Circuit Audio)

Atari STacy (1989)

At the Spring COMDEX in Chicago in 1989, Atari unveiled the STacy, its first real crack at a portable computer. (The company never produced the portable 8-bit 65XEP it introduced at CES in 1985.) The company billed the 16-bit STacy as a "low-cost portable laptop computer, fully compatible with Atari's line of Mega and ST computers." Atari launched the STacy in the UK later that year, but not until June 1990 in the US. You could buy it either with a built-in 3.5-inch floppy drive for $1,495, or spend $1,995 for a model with an additional 20MB hard drive on board.

Ira Velinsky, the designer of the original ST, was also responsible for the STacy's attractive, edgy design. The STacy featured a full-travel, 95-key keyboard. To the right, a built-in trackball sat with two mouse buttons positioned just above it; above that was a full numeric keypad. Welcome back to 1989: The STacy weighed a whopping 15.2 pounds with 12 C batteries installed and measured 13.3 by 15 by 2 inches (HWD). Thank goodness there was a handle built into the bottom edge of the case. No one today would ever consider the STacy a laptop as such, but it was portable in a way an ST desktop system with a monitor wasn't.

The STacy's Epson-sourced backlit supertwist monochrome display featured the same 640-by-400-pixel resolution as the SM124 desktop monitor. The machine also worked in the lower two graphics modes. The combination meant the STacy was compatible with all ST software, and an external monitor port let you use it as a desktop computer as well. The STacy came in 1MB, 2MB, and 4MB RAM configurations. It included an 8MHz 68000 processor and 192KB ROM similar to the 520ST and 1040ST. The STacy even had the blitter chip from the Mega 2 and Mega 4 machines. As with all ST computers, the machine featured MIDI In and Out ports, two joystick ports, an RS-232C modem port, a Centronics parallel port, a cartridge slot, and a DMA port for hooking up an external hard drive.

To go with the STacy, Atari was rumored to be working on a portable laptop laser printer. *STart* covered it in the April 1989 issue, saying it was "displayed for the first time at a private soiree in the home of a high-ranking Atari official." It would print at 300 dots per inch, work with any ST with at least 1MB of memory, and consume a "modest" 650 watts of power—not a lot for a laser printer, but a lot for just about anything else. The printer was supposed to land that June and retail for $2,400, and that included the massive power pack necessary to run the thing away from an outlet. The printer never made it to retail shelves, though the magazine did run a photo of someone holding a prototype laser printer in their lap. Honestly it looked just as big as any other laser printer—and that was without the power pack pictured.

Unreleased printer aside, many musicians liked the STacy for its relatively easily portability and built-in MIDI interface. And for a time, according to one of the ST FAQs floating around Usenet, even Mac users cross-shopped the STacy because it beat Apple's own clumsy, expensive Macintosh Portable.[1] For a short time, Atari had a desirable portable in the STacy. As long as you weren't expecting color, which had its own lower-resolution issue on the platform, the STacy was a zero-compromise, transportable ST.

The STacy also contained the long-awaited TOS 1.04, commonly known as Rainbow TOS. It shipped in April 1989 and included support for the STacy hardware, a new file selector, and worked better with external hard drives. TOS 1.04 was considerably faster in day-today use, and included the ability to format a DOS-compatible disk in addition to reading it. The new OS also brought additional bug fixes.

Atari 1040STE (1989)

Atari unveiled its long-awaited 1040STE in Europe in August 1989.[2] The 1040STE ($699 at launch) looked the same as the 1040ST, but it boasted a number of key improvements. The biggest boost was to the color palette, courtesy of updates to Shifter—now 4,096, up from 512—as well as built-in hardware horizontal, vertical, and split-screen scrolling, and the ability to write into the video counters.[3] That finally put the ST on an even keel with the Amiga lineup for the first time. The STE also included the blitter chip first seen on the Mega 2 and Mega 4 ST, which made quick work of formerly challenging memory moves for graphics. With this launch, the low-end ST finally got the graphics coprocessor it was missing all along, and it was a more significant addition here for home entertainment and gaming than in the more expensive, business-focused Mega, where it came into play primarily for CAD and animation. A new stereo (two-channel) audio chip could play 8-bit sampled PCM digital sound at 44kHz, and the YM2149 remained for three channels of synthesized sound. The machine's RAM was contained in industry-standard SIMMs, making it much easier to upgrade. A new set of enhanced analog joystick ports were backward-compatible with the original. Both of the 9-pin ports were moved to the side of the case again (this time on the left), which was much more convenient.

The 68881 FPU math coprocessor expanded the ST's native computational abilities. Math coprocessors became highly sought after, especially on the PC side; as long as you had software that was written to take advantage of one, the benefits could be tremendous. The STE also included Genlock support for synchronizing video output, making the STE an excellent choice for video production. On the software side, STE machines first came with TOS 1.06, a new version dated 6/19/89, just four months after 1.04; its only real change was internal rewrites to support the STE's architectural changes. Fewer than six months later, Atari released TOS 1.62, which included bug fixes for TOS 1.06. Hardware and TOS changes in the new STE resulted in a significant portion of existing software being rendered incompatible with the STE at first. Some developers quickly patched their software so it worked properly on the STE.

Figure 8.2: The STE brought stereo sampled sound, hardware scrolling, a blitter chip, and a much larger color palette to the low end of Atari's ST lineup, better positioning it to compete with the Amiga 500.

Atari continued to play up the ST's advantages in its advertising. Compared with the Amiga, the ST booted up much more quickly thanks to its built-in OS on ROM chips, and the ST also had built-in MIDI ports and cost less. The ST came with a standard GUI, unlike DOS machines. And next to the Macintosh, the ST had a larger software library (at the time), and professional applications for desktop publishing and music recording cost less on the ST.

Although the STE was undeniably superior to the original ST models, it remained a bit behind the times. Critically, the STE was still limited to a maximum of 16 colors on screen at once in low-resolution (320-by-200-pixel) mode, and four colors in medium resolution (640 by 200). This was despite Atari's earlier claims that it would be able to display up to 256 at once at low resolution, and 16 colors at high (640-by-400) resolution. The 1040STE still ran at 8MHz, which was quick for 1985 but no longer considered fast. There was still no internal hard drive. Atari didn't upgrade the enclosure at all, so you still had to lift it to unplug and attach joysticks and mice, and the keyboard remained as mushy as before.[4] Worse, an early batch of machines shipped with a faulty DMA chip, which led to frequent data loss with hard drive connections.[5]

The ST community was optimistic about the STE, but also wary about the challenges it presented. Software would have to be written to support the STE hardware upgrades. While Atari planned a 520STE and a 1040STE for Europe along with appropriate marketing, more concerning was Atari's approach to the US market—or lack thereof. "[The] STE's success…depends more on advertising and dealer and product availability than on the product specifications themselves," a preview story in *STart* said.[6] And true to form, Atari didn't launch the 1040STE in the US until March 1990, and the machine didn't hit retail stores until June along with the STacy.[7] The 1040STE had an attractive launch price of $699, but despite the numerous upgrades, the STE still gave Atari a model that only matched the Amiga 500 and didn't beat it in any significant way aside from the obvious ST-specific differences that were there since the beginning. For the market then, that wasn't enough, and few developers took ultimately advantage of the STE's increased capabilities. In the fall of 1990, *STart* magazine said although the 1040STE "may not be an Amiga killer," the "STE's increased colors, stereo sound and relatively low price [made] it a good buy." *STart* hardware editor David Plotkin wrote he would have liked to see enclosure and keyboard improvements, an overscan mode for proper multimedia display, an expansion bus, and at least the ability to display 32 colors on screen instead of 16.

New Peripherals

Atari unveiled several new monitors as the 1980s came to a close. The SM125 was the successor to the SM124; it still had a 12-inch tube, but it now had a separate stand (finally!) that could move in four directions. Otherwise it was similar to the SM124, with a built-in speaker, 640-by-400-pixel resolution, and a 70Hz refresh rate. The stand made it look a lot like a regular PC monitor of the time. The SC1425 was a 14-inch iteration of the SC1225. This one still didn't come with a stand, but it had additional picture controls behind a hinged door on the front underneath the tube. It also contained a headphone jack. The SC1435, a rebranded Magnavox 1CM135, included stereo speakers for the first time that worked nicely with the 1040 STE's upgraded sound chip. A stand was optional for that model.

Removable hard drive cartridges were a kind of holy grail of storage for a while. The idea was to give you essentially unlimited capacities and fast speeds, but in a flexible medium that also delivered the portability and archival features that floppy disks offered. Atari's Megafile 44 was designed in this idiom. This drive was shaped like the Megafile 20 and 30, and was also meant to fit neatly into a stacked Mega system. It employed a SyQuest removable storage cartridge. Each one held 44MB, and the enclosure could be daisy-chained with other drives in the system via DMA ports. To change disks, you pushed the button on the front panel, waited until the drive spun down, flipped the eject lever, and pulled out the cartridge. Then you put the new one in, flipped the lever back, and waited until it spun up.

The Megafile cartridges themselves were well designed, considering you couldn't just seal them up and sandwich the platters between metal the way you could with regular hard drives. SyQuest built in a small mechanism inside the drive to blast the area with high-pressure air that cleaned any dust off the platter.[8] Plus, the cartridges each came with sleeves to protect them when being stored, much like floppy disks. A March 1990 review of the Megafile 44 in *STart* said the disks cost about $100 each, which was reasonable enough that you could purchase a few and get your money's worth out of the unit. The review compared the drive with the Carter Graphics SQ-44 and the Toad Computers Toadfile 44; all three behaved similarly in testing. All delivered access speeds of roughly 25ms, putting SyQuest drives right on par with fixed internal and external hard drives of the time.

Today, most of these drives and cartridges survive, and seem to have held up just as well as regular hard drives. The same can't be said for mid-1990s Iomega Zip and Jaz drives on PCs and Macs. That has to count for something, right?

Spectre GCR (Gadgets by Small, 1989)

Despite the ST's aggressive pricing, the Macintosh began to pull away in sales in the late 1980s and started to get software that wouldn't become available on Atari computers. Consequently, there was demand on the ST for some kind of emulation, which a company called Gadgets by Small began to serve with Spectre GCR. This hardware device plugged into the ST's cartridge port, though it wasn't complete on its own. You also had to purchase your own Macintosh 128KB ROMs and System 6 in order to get it up and running, thanks to the ever-present fear of lawsuits from Cupertino.

On the plus side, once you had it all, you could not only run Macintosh software but even read Macintosh floppy disks right from the ST hardware, as your system now contained actual Macintosh chips. Performance was excellent for an emulator as a result, although you had to stick with programs like HyperCard and PageMaker (as opposed to running games). Gadgets by Small recommended 2MB of RAM, which meant either an upgraded ST or STE or a Mega machine was ideal for the program. Another good option was a STacy plus Spectre GCR, which together still cost just half as much as the least expensive portable Mac. This would no longer be true once Apple introduced its revolutionary PowerBook 100, 140, and 170, the dark gray machines with the large hand rests and center-mounted trackballs that came out in 1991. A comparable product called PC-Ditto allowed for MS-DOS program emulation on the ST, although it was in software and therefore much slower than even an XT.

Atari Transputer Workstation (1989)

The ATW800 Transputer Workstation was a T800-20–powered machine based on the INMOS transputer, but with the 68000-based front end of a Mega ST. This high-end workstation was capable of 10 million instructions per second. It was designed to tackle CAD projects at a then-whopping 1,024-by-768-pixel resolution and 256 colors. It was also designed for 3D modeling, animation, desktop publishing at up to 1,280-by-960-pixel resolution and 16 shades of gray, and with a tremendous amount of foresight, Lisp- and Prolog-based artificial intelligence programming. (I will never think of Lisp without thinking of my college computer science classes, and how a professor once described Lisp as an acronym for "Lots of Irritating Stupid Parentheses," which is exactly what it is.) In addition to AI, Atari also targeted robotics, speech recognition and synthesis, and ray tracing as potential uses for the machine.

To harness all this power, the ATW800 Transputer Workstation ran Helios, a distributed UNIX-based OS designed for parallel processing, with X-Windows on top. That made it incompatible with the existing ST, meaning that it required custom software to work. On the plus side, you could network several Transputer Workstation machines together, if one wasn't enough. The system supported up to 16 additional T800 processors with so-called transputer farm cards internally, and "an unlimited number" externally. Don't ever say Atari wasn't ambitious, even with Jack Tramiel at the helm. To its credit, Atari did build and sell the Transputer Workstation, but ultimately it didn't succeed. Throughout the late 1980s, the company repeatedly showed off the unit at COMDEX and other expos and scored a fair amount of press coverage in magazines. Atari began selling the machine in May 1989, but in the end only managed to move 350 of these beasts before giving up on the idea.[9]

Software Packs

In the UK, Atari began to sell existing 520STfm models with impressive bundles of software. The upside of this was it brought lots of new buyers into the fold later in the platform's life cycle by giving them killer value. Each pack came in a special box (sometimes more than one) and featured a tremendous variety of top-notch games and other software, little of which was filler. The bundles did much to launch the low-cost ST into the public consciousness in Europe, even several years after the first ST launched.

Let's take a quick look at some of the most popular packs. The Summer Pack was released first in April 1988, and included the following software: 3-D Galax, Arkanoid, Chopper X, Defender of the Crown, Enduro Racer, International Karate, Into the Eagle's Nest, Leviathan, Marble Madness, Mouse Trap, Plutos, Q-Ball, Rampage, Rana Rama, Road Wars, Slap Fight, Strike Force Harrier, Super Sprint, Tetris, Trailblazer, Warlock, and Winter Olympiad '88.

The Super Pack, released in October 1988, replaced the Summer Pack and included Arkanoid: Revenge of Doh, Beyond the Ice Palace, Black Lamp, Buggy Boy, Chopper X, Eddie Edwards Super Ski, Ikari Warriors, Marble Madness, Organiser, Quadralien, Rana Rama, Return to Genesis, Road Wars, Seconds Out, Starquake, Summer Olympiad, Test Drive, Thrust, Thundercats, Wizball, Xenon, and Zynaps.

The Power Pack, which supplanted the Super Pack, was released in June 1989 and included After Burner, Black Lamp, Bomb Jack, Bombuzal, Double Dragon, Eliminator, FirST BASIC, Music Maker, Nebulus, Organiser, Out Run, Overlander, Pac-Mania, Predator, R-Type, Space Harrier, Star Goose!, Starglider, StarRay, Super Hang-on,

Super Huey, and Xenon. This one was also popular thanks to all the Sega arcade conversions, which were hugely desirable, as was evidenced by 16-bit Sega Genesis/Mega Drive cartridge sales.

More packs soon followed. A Discovery Pack replaced the Power Pack in March 1990. Atari also released two Family Curriculum packs; a Discovery Xtra pack; a Professional Pack; a Discovery Pack Plus; an STE-specific Turbo Pack with multiple boxes each containing two games such as Blood Money and Anarchy, and Out Run and Super Cycle; and even a MIDI Music bundle for the STE in 1991 that frankly should have come sooner.

There was a huge downside of these packs for Atari hardware and software sales. Many consumers, fully satisfied with lots of applications to run and games to play, often never went beyond what came with the system. This phenomenon meant poor sales for software developers and publishers, and it ultimately hurt the overall ST market.[10] It was a tricky balance, and it's significant Atari never offered anything comparable in the US. As time wore on, the Packs also pulled precious consumer marketing attention and sales away from newer STE machines, because they were such good values, and because the STE didn't really have enough software support to justify the increased expense.

New Games for 1989

Developers continued to build out the ST's software library. Some of these new titles arrived before the STE and STacy announcements, as Atari unveiled those systems later in the year, but altogether the year brought much to celebrate. The key difference here is that for the first time, some of the following games played just as well on the PC, but only if those titles supported EGA or VGA graphics cards and Adlib or Sound Blaster sound cards. Nonetheless, as long as you had an ST and a color monitor, you enjoyed a full experience regardless.

Battle Chess (Interplay, 1989)

At this point, there were many good chess games on the market, complete with impressive AIs, tournament-style play, and three-dimensional board views. How do you shake that up and introduce something new? Interplay had the answer with Battle Chess, a game that finally showed what you always imagined chess pieces did: fight each other to the death.

Figure 8.3: If you're going to play chess, might as well make it fun, right? Battle Chess gloriously showed us the combat we imagined happens when one piece captures another.

Unlike strategy-action hybrids such as Archon on 8-bit computers, this game was still purely chess, with all of the same rules. When one piece captured another, it always won the ensuing "battle." The battles were humorous, too. For example, when a pawn captured another pawn, it stomped on the other's foot with its staff; as the captured pawn hopped in pain, the attacking pawn would then knock it over. Each piece had its own special animations. Queens cast spells that vaporized their enemies. The rooks were always my favorite; they animated into stone golems and clomped their way to their new positions. There was no in-game soundtrack—probably for the best, given the cerebral nature of this game—but digitally sampled sound effects captured all of the footsteps, clanks of weapons, and howls of agony.

The game had 10 levels of play and a 30,000-move opening library. Several magazines criticized the AI engine, but no one buying this particular chess product was in it solely for the strategy. Although Battle Chess played a good game of chess, it was the graphics, animation, and sound effects that made this title. The game was well received and a big seller. Battle Chess spawned two sequels, one focused on Chinese Chess, and the other, Battle Chess 4000, set in space. Neither of those made it onto the ST.

B.A.T. (Ubisoft, 1989)

This expansive, ambitious point-and-click adventure game, developed for the Atari ST, featured more than 1,000 scenes to explore. As an agent from the Bureau of Astral Troubleshooters (B.A.T.), your mission was to stop a scientist-and-crook team from detonating bombs in Terapolis, the largest city on Selenia, in 10 days. Along the way, you needed to use the programmable computer implanted in your arm, called the Bidirectional Organic Bioputer, or BOB. To find clues, you talked to inhabitants across the seedy city, flying from place to place in your Drag (which the manual describes as a difficult-to-pilot "flying chariot") using what amounted to an entire flight simulator embedded in the game.

You navigated the game's interface with the mouse. The cursor changed depending on the object you hovered over. The graphics were done in a distinctive, cartoonlike style. Although there were some RPG-like elements, such as character stats, they weren't the focus of the game. A December 1990 review in *ST Format* praised B.A.T., awarding it a 92 percent score. *Computer Gaming World* was a little more hesitant in its June 1991 review, but still recommended the game and also included a hint section that could help you give it a whirl today.

One innovative feature was the included sound hardware. A 16-channel card, dubbed the MV16, plugged into the ST's cartridge port and had a built-in headphone jack. That meant to hear the game's enhanced sound, you had to listen via headphones or plug in a set of speakers. Ubisoft planned to use this card with more games, but as the STE came out later that same year with integrated digital sound, and because Amiga already had digital sound in hardware, the MV16 didn't serve much purpose long-term.

Blood Money (Psygnosis, 1989)

This side-scrolling shooter recalled Thunder Force, Gradius, and R-Type, with its futuristic, colorful backdrops, neat "alien sweepstakes safari" concept, and fast action. The game took place across four hostile planets, each with different bounties to reward hunters. The manual was written as a sweepstakes brochure, complete with "small print" that said the company accepted no responsibility for any loss of limbs, eyes, internal organs, or any other parts the body. Always good to cover your bases.

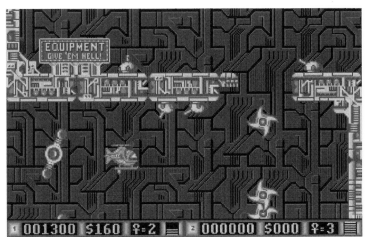

Figure 1: The late 1980s saw a slew of addictive scrolling space shooters like Blood Money, a game that seemed as if it belonged in an arcade or on a Sega Genesis.

On each planet, you flew a different craft. Planet 1 cost 100 credits and gave you a helicopter gunship. Planet 2 was 200 credits and put you in control of a submarine in an undersea world. Planet 3 cost 300 credits and you received a personal jetpack. Planet 4, at 400 credits, put you in the cockpit of a fighter jet. Blood Money featured improved graphics and animation over Menace, another good shooter that came out a year earlier; both were programmed by David Jones. This port of the Amiga game was done by Wayne Smithson, the same person who developed Baal. Smithson said in a September 1989 *ST Format* interview the main issue was writing new sprite animation and horizontal scrolling routines for the ST to compensate for the lack of them, because the Amiga had those in hardware.

"If the ST had a blitter chip as standard, then it would be faster than the Amiga," Smithson said. Case in point: If you compared the game running on an ST with the same game on an STE (or in an emulator in STE mode), with its standard blitter chip, you'd see gameplay change from sluggish and choppy to fluid and SNES-quality. It was a significant jump and turned the game from something that looked impressive in 1989 but didn't stand out, and didn't necessarily warrant coverage in this book, to something you would have wanted to play again and again.

Lucasfilm Games/LucasArts

Lucasfilm Games broke ground on the Atari 8-bit with the breakout titles Rescue on Fractalus!, Ballblazer, Koronis Rift, and The Eidolon—all landmark genre-pushing games that were some of the best ever seen on that platform. But it wasn't until the company began releasing sophisticated point-and-click graphic adventures that the division hit its stride. All of these titles were simultaneously released on PCs and sold more copies there. But there was plenty of crossover right around this crucial 1989-to-1990 time period, as many ST fans remember playing these games on Atari before moving over to a PC or Mac. (In 1990, this division of Lucasfilm was renamed LucasArts, so depending on the time of release, most of the ST versions were labeled LucasArts.)

I'll detail just one of these phenomenal games as a sample. Based on the biggest movie of 1989, Indiana Jones and the Last Crusade: The Graphic Adventure brought the escapade to your computer screen in an accessible point-and-click format. Designed by Ron Gilbert, Noah Falstein, and David Fox, The Last Crusade was set in 1938. Indiana Jones, an archaeology professor at Barnett College, went on a grand adventure to rescue his kidnapped dad and stop Hitler and the Nazis from finding the Holy Grail, which gave eternal life to anyone who drank from it.

The game's interface was devoid of typing; it was point-and-click through and through. You had to point and click on words on the screen, such as "Walk to" or "Open," to enact the appropriate actions. Many of the puzzles had multiple solutions, which was uncommon for the era. You started out the game in your office, which looked like a tornado had stopped by for lunch earlier. You had to pick up a few items at the university and at your father's house first. Then you could get started on the main adventure, which tracked closely with the movie's story but allowed you to spend a lot more time touring Venice and its underground catacombs, a castle in Germany, and a Zeppelin in flight before you reached the Grail Temple.

Many LucasArts adventure games ranked among the best the Atari ST had to offer. In most cases, they were straight ports that differed little between the ST, the Amiga, and the PC. Other favorites of the time included Loom, Maniac Mansion, Zak McCracken and the Alien Mindbenders, and The Secret of Monkey Island. It wasn't just adventure games, either; Their Finest Hour: The Battle of Britain was a solid combat sim. But the adventures will always hold a special place in my heart. Part of me wishes I could go back to 1989 or 1990 and do them all over again. I'm still going to at some point, because I'm sure I've forgotten big portions of each by now. (That's the good thing about getting old and senile; you can enjoy things over and over again, because you can't remember them.)

Midwinter (Maelstrom Games/Rainbird, 1989)

One of the most significant releases of its time, Midwinter was a post-apocalyptic strategy game and survival sim with plenty of stealth and action elements, as well as tremendous depth and attention to detail. The game was set in the year 2099. The world was plunged into a new ice age, and the snowy, barren island of Midwinter became the last semi-inhabitable place on Earth. You had to defend this priceless piece of land, which spanned 160,000 square miles, from other forces that wanted it for themselves.

In Midwinter, programmed by the late Mike Singleton, you started the game as a police officer on skis. Most of the game took place in first-person mode as you explored the island and met its inhabitants. Ultimately, you had to persuade and then manage a staggering 32 recruits, each with 14 personal attributes and a unique history. In addition to the board and strategy elements, the game included skiing, hang gliding, cable car, and snow buggy sequences, each of which was rendered with the game's light-sourced, fractal-based 3D graphics engine. Somehow, the title morphed from turn-based strategy to first-person shooter, years before anyone called a game by the latter term.

Midwinter was released for the ST in 1989 and the Amiga a year later. ST Format awarded the game a 96 percent score in its April 1990 review, saying, "What keeps Midwinter addictive is the strategies you can employ to win. Depending on your position on the map, all sorts of possibilities present themselves—do you rescue another team member, do you go for the buggy instead, or do you blow up the factory? The choice is yours and any option may lead to success."[11]

Eurogamer contributor and Midwinter fan Dan Whitehead started an effort to develop a remake in 2014 (apparently since abandoned at the time of this writing), and even released a comic book telling the story of the game in 2016. Midwinter was a game that had to be seen to be believed, even if it was ultimately a bit too complex.

Pirates! (MicroProse, 1989)

The famous Pirates!, designed by Sid Meier, put you in "an era of new kings and empires, of new tests of strength and power," as the manual said. As a budding captain of a majestic sailing ship, you had to seek out fame and fortune across the Spanish Main by trading with other countries, engaging in maritime battles in the Caribbean, rescuing members of your family, switching allegiances along the way whenever necessary, and even searching for buried treasure. You could play as either the English, Dutch, French, or Spanish. The game was set by default in 1660, although you could choose any historical time period from 1560 to 1680, which would affect the level of non-Spanish influence and activity in the region.

Figure 8.4: Pirates!, Sid Meier's strategy game of 17th-century seafaring and trade, arrived on the ST with improved graphics and a MIDI-enhanced soundtrack.

This open-world game had plenty of action sequences that functioned as minigames, including fencing in a zoomed-in view from the side with your opponent, dueling ships, navigating the seas in an overhead macroscopic view, and invading land. There were also considerable strategic elements, such as discussing politics with governors, smuggling goods for local merchants, and even finding a romantic partner. The game contained more than 50 islands to explore. In addition to starting a new career, you could also try out famous expeditions. These were short adventures featuring historical characters such as Henry Morgan and Baron de Pointis, and were meant for more experienced players. In the main Career mode, there was set point when the game ended, though you usually wanted to retire before your health declined and fighting became more difficult.

The 78-page manual offered plenty of atmosphere and details that fleshed out the game as well. Each time you played, enough aspects of the game were randomized, such as relations between the four nations and individual events, that it never felt repetitive. Sid Meier would go on to even greater things, most notably the Civilization series (which we'll get to later) and Railroad Tycoon. But Pirates! was his earliest and perhaps most notable achievement. It was also a marked departure for MicroProse, which had become known primarily for its wartime simulations. Pirates! took an extra year and change to arrive on the ST, but when it did it brought noticeably improved visuals over the original on the Commodore 64. The game's soundtrack also played through the ST's MIDI port.

Populous (Electronic Arts, 1989)

The isometric title that kickstarted the "god game" genre, Peter Molyneux's Populous made you a deity. You had to direct and manipulate your followers and use your divine powers to eliminate the opposing player's followers. You could play against the computer or another human. The game was played on a virtual tabletop, with a zoomed-out view presented in a book paradigm and a zoomed-in view beneath it. A strip of icons ran along the top-right side of the main view. You normally started a game by raising and lowering land such that it gave your followers a place to build and expand. With your orders, they would farm the land, fight, or if they got out of hand and started setting fire to things, cause you to unleash fury upon the land. The more followers you accumulated, the more mana you received, which in turn gave you additional divine powers such as generating earthquakes, plagues, and floods for your opponent.

Populous's interface was transparent in its icon-based simplicity, which helped the newcomer get off the ground in what was then a new kind of game. In 1990, *STart* magazine called the ST port of the title "a fascinating, fun and challenging game. Populous went on to win countless awards in the gaming press. It also spawned some sequels such as Powermonger, a battle-focused game that added weather, carrier pigeons, and more to the formula; and Populous II: Trials of the Olympian Gods. Both sequels made it to the ST, and all three are still impeccably balanced, addictive, and worth playing today.

Stunt Car Racer (MicroProse, 1989)

This UK-developed game put you in the driver's seat of a custom stunt car with a giant, turbocharged V8 engine and a well-damped, long-travel suspension system. At the start of each race, a giant crane lifted your car onto each elevated track, which was complete with banked turns. Your goal was to score the most points by executing stunts, such as jumps, barrel rolls, and more. As you can imagine, it was easy to accidentally go off either side of the track and crash to the ground below. Even just performing the stunts put strain on your car and could cause it to come apart.

You raced against computer-controlled opponents; your score was based on lap times as well as whether you won each race. The game contained eight courses, with two in each division made up of three drivers for a total of six races in a season. The graphics consisted of filled polygons, and you raced with a first-person view from the cockpit. The frame rate on an STE was solid, and you felt a sense of speed with this one—that was assuming you could keep your lunch down on some of the bumpier tracks. A Super League doubled the speed of the cars, if you wanted to push it even further.

The only disappointment was the sound, which was sparse throughout. In addition, there's the truism that any 3D game on the ST may have been advanced in the late 1980s, but can't help looking dated now, and in a way that 2D sprite-based titles don't. My heart probably still lies with Brøderbund's Stunts on the PC, which was released the year after this game and gave you a much wider variety of cars and courses to drive. But there are those who think Stunt Car Racer was one of the best games on the ST; give it a whirl and see where you stand.

Ultima V: Warriors of Destiny (Origin, 1989)

Depending on your viewpoint, the fifth installment of the Ultima series was either the second-best (after Ultima IV) or the best for its more

204 | Faster Than Light: The Atari ST and the 16-Bit Revolution

sophisticated text parser, polish, and overall sense of a living and breathing game world. Designer Richard Garriott in fact shares the latter view, even though Ultima IV is probably always going to be considered the most significant and influential game in the series. Ultima V introduced some incredibly sophisticated dynamics for the time, including night-and-day cycles, NPCs with daily routines, an astronomy model, and lots more.

The game's dark story played *The Empire Strikes Back* to Ultima IV's *A New Hope*. Basically, Lord British went missing on an expedition, and in his place stood Lord Blackthorn, a totalitarian ruler who twisted and bent the eight virtues into strict distortions of their original meanings. Meanwhile, mysterious Shadowlords travelled the land of Britannia and basically scared everyone to death. You had to learn how to dispatch the Shadowlords, remove Blackthorn, and rescue Lord British so he could resume his rightful place at the throne.

I originally played Ultima V on a PC, because I could never find it for the ST. I was somewhat embarrassed to find out much later Ultima V had in fact come out for the ST platform, and it was just that my local computer stores in Brooklyn didn't carry it in 1989.

In replaying the game for this book, I've come to find the ST port a little strange. Granted, it would have been better to play this port than the PC one, thanks to the ST's inclusion of the full soundtrack from the original Apple II version (which itself required a memory upgrade and an added sound card). But the ST port also put the music in different places relative to the Apple II, and inexplicably, it showed a somewhat squashed "Ultima V" logo on screen at all times beneath the play window, shrinking the available viewing area. I don't know about you, but I don't usually forget the name of the game I'm playing and need a constant reminder, especially if I'm playing the thing for 40 or 50 hours. Finally, Ultima V had a couple of infrequent crash bugs that have reportedly never been patched, but that aren't deal breakers as long as you save the game periodically.

Regardless of which machine you play it on, Ultima V must be seen and enjoyed to be believed. Open-world CRPGs 30 years later are still drawing influence from innovations first seen in Garriott's masterpiece.

Atari had begun to sharpen its efforts on gaming, especially after the XE Game System's mediocre showing at retail. (What did Atari expect with eight-year-old hardware?) Specifically, the company took an interest in the sleek Epyx Handy, a portable color game console developed by two former Amiga designers. Atari entered into an agreement with Epyx to build and sell the Handy, but Epyx soon went bankrupt, so Atari had to go it alone. With a few minor hardware changes, Atari released the Handy as the Lynx in September 1989, beating all comers to market with a full-color, backlit, active-matrix TFT handheld gaming system.

The chunky portable packed some serious hardware, including hardware sprites, zoom, and distortion, separate chips for graphics and math processing including a blitter, all of which stacked up favorably not just against the NES but the upcoming, Mode 7–equipped Super NES. The Lynx's launch lineup, with just five titles, was solid—I had all of the games, including the futuristic ElectroCop, the addictive California Games, and the space shooter Gates of Zendocon. But the platform picked up some real steam after a couple of years and held up well positioned next to the monochrome (and non-backlit) Nintendo Game Boy and, for a short time, even the color Sega Game Gear introduced in 1991.

As a certifiable Atari nut, I owned two Lynx systems—one in the original, larger form factor (not the most portable in the world), and one of the sleeker Lynx II models I picked up on a heavy discount in the late 1990s from B&C ComputerVisions. The Lynx II was a better deal in 1991 at just $99 with a smaller size, rubber handgrips, and improved battery life. The newer tabbed and ridged cartridges were easier to use than the original flat ones. All told, 72 cartridges were released for the Lynx through 1993. Atari ran into several problems with the Lynx, from an early shortage of parts that gave the Game Boy a huge head start, to generally poor battery life, and an inexplicable delay of more than a year before more cartridges began to appear in stores. The company also put zero effort into tying the Lynx to the STE, or marketing the two next to each other. You wouldn't have known the company was selling its brand-new STE computer system at the same time it was launching a 16-bit handheld console.

It may not have mattered. The word on the street, or at least in Atari enthusiast circles, was Atari had already begun to abandon its efforts in the computer market, even with the STE just being released in October and the TT on deck for next year. Some were bullish; in response to a question from *Computer Chronicles* cohost Stewart Cheifet asking whether Atari could turn around its fortunes in the US computer market versus Europe, *STart* editor Andrew Reese said he thought so. "Part of the problem has been that Atari was short of DRAMs and directed what output they had to Europe," Reese said, adding that "1989 is Atari's year according to them, and they are going to make a major push into this market."

Atari fans were loyal, but they were never blind. Issue after issue of *ST-Log* and *STart* had columnists and readers alike (in letters to the editor) expressing their frustrations with Atari and what was happening, or not happening, with the ST in America. In an ominous sign, Larry Flint Publishing, which purchased *ST-Log* and *ANALOG Computing* in early 1988, decided to fold the two magazines back into a single publication— a strategy that lasted for precisely one issue: December 1989, still called *ANALOG Computing*. Then LFP shut it down altogether.

9 | Thirty-Two

The personal computer market was evolving, and not in Atari's favor. Microsoft had the biggest impact when it released its breakthrough version of Windows in 1990. Although Windows 3.0 still ran on top of DOS, it brought the PC desktop much closer to the way other GUIs worked, a huge improvement over its confusing earlier Windows/286 and Windows/386 incarnations. Clone PC vendors were sprouting up by the dozen, chasing market leaders like Dell, Compaq, and Gateway 2000 by taking out eight-page ads in *Computer Shopper* magazine and undercutting the larger PC manufacturers on price. In Cupertino, Apple was busy cementing its growth in both the education and creative markets, and was building out a full lineup of color machines; the IIcx and the new $6,000 IIci had been introduced at the tail end of the prior year, and the much less expensive LC and IIsi would be out soon. The industry was beginning to show the first signs of the Windows-and-Mac duopoly that has come to define the computer industry we know today.

Clearly, Atari had its work cut out for it. It also had a killer machine in the works.

Atari TT030 (1990)

Atari reached for the stars with the TT030 and targeted the high-end graphics workstation market. At first, Atari had intended it to run UNIX. Inklings that Atari would produce a machine like this appeared as early as the 1040ST's launch in 1986, when the company began to tease a new high-end computer system referred to as the EST. The

EST was conceived as a 32-bit system with a Motorola 68020 CPU and a 68881 math coprocessor. It appeared along with an accompanying mockup image of a possible prototype in the May 1986 issue of the German *Data Welt* magazine, as Curt Vendel of Atarimuseum.com documented. The EST would have 4MB memory, second-generation blitter and Shifter chips, and come with either TOS or UNIX System V.[1] Not much was heard about this model in the ensuing years, though a passage in the Summer 1988 issue of *STart* magazine covered the EST's supposed progress:

> The EST is another product ST users have been anxiously awaiting, and provides yet another opportunity for Atari to revolutionize the world of personal computing. At about the Mega price point, it will offer three additional screen resolutions, including a 1,280-by-960 full-page, monochrome mode.
>
> The attendant ease-of-use in word processing and desktop publishing applications has the opportunity to tear the competition to shreds. Comparable performance from an IBM or Macintosh currently costs the user thousands of dollars more in additional hardware and software. Although a prototype of the machine has been up and running in Atari's R&D lab for a while, a few of its custom parts initially gave Atari's suppliers some trouble. Development, however, is now in its final stages.[2]

The EST was never released as such, but many believe its design became the TT030, including former Atari TOS developer Landon Dyer.[3] The name TT stood for Thirty-Two/Thirty-Two, for its 32-bit data bus and 32-bit processor, in comparison with the ST's Sixteen/Thirty-Two roots. Atari ended up going with TOS for the TT030, in fact, because the company was taking way too long (upwards of two years) to complete its port of UNIX System V Release 4.0. The final TT030 contained a much faster 68030 processor running at 32MHz with a cache, a 68882 math coprocessor, and two new VGA graphics modes: 640 by 480 with 16 colors, and 320 by 480 with 256 colors (both out of 4,096 as on the STE). Notably, the TT lacked a blitter chip, because Atari never developed one that would go faster than 8MHz, but that mattered much less given the TT030's intended mission: It also supported a monochrome mode with a whopping 1,280-by-960 resolution, which Atari specifically marketed as ideal for

DynaCADD, Calamus, PageStream, and other pro-level graphics and desktop publishing applications. The TT030 had 2MB RAM standard and was expandable to a whopping 26MB, which was way beyond comparable MS-DOS machines.

Figure 9.1: The 68030-class TT030 would have been a giant killer for both high-end workstations and desktop publishing, but it arrived too late and without the UNIX operating system it needed to truly compete.

The TT030 retained the ST's full lineup of ports, including for MIDI and the cartridge slot. It also had the upgraded sound chip from the STE. The machine contained an AppleTalk-compatible LAN port, which Atari unfortunately never developed a driver for. There was also a VME bus card slot for expansion, giving the TT030 the means to connect to Ethernet networks, along with the existing ASCI DMA channel for Atari laser printers and hard drives. The TT supported both internal and external SCSI drives. A running change swapped the 720KB floppy drive for a 1.44MB model, which brought a high-density format to Atari computers for the first time and matched what was increasingly found on PC-compatibles. Crucially, the cartridge port remained, making this also an ideal machine to run Macintosh applications using Spectre GCR. On the software side, Atari released TOS 3, which was most notable for its newfound 68030 and TT RAM support in the kernel. TOS 3 was also required to use the TT's higher screen resolutions. Versions labeled 3.01, 3.05, and 3.06 were released, the last two with additional bug fixes.

Atari unveiled the TT030 at CeBIT in Hanover, Germany, and began shipping the machine there in 1990, with release in America by the start of the following year. In the US, the TT030 retailed for $2,995 in a configuration with 2MB RAM and a 50MB internal hard drive. Atari also launched several new products alongside the TT030. The SM195 was a 19-inch monochrome monitor intended for desktop publishing and CAD, and was designed to complement the TT030. It supported resolutions up to 1,280 by 960 at a 70Hz refresh rate. The company also announced the SM147, a successor to the SM124 that included a 14-inch screen instead of 12 inches, as well as grayscale support. Finally, Atari made available a Megafile 60 for its Mega line, which featured (you guessed it) a 60MB drive.

Dave Small wrote in the February 1991 issue of *STart* that the "TT can be perceived as many different machines rolled into one," including a faster model with more capabilities, a UNIX workstation, a networkable server, and a VME-bus expandable computer, and that while that's good from a multifunction perspective, "it's bad, in that all the extra hardware [for these capabilities] is costly…the machine is pricey to an ST audience wanting only a more powerful ST."[4] Small also noted the TT's more expensive competition also offered more power and raw performance, like the $4,999 NeXT workstation and its object-oriented NeXTSTEP development system (an OS that eventually became the code underneath Mac OS X). And then there was the matter of Atari's port of UNIX System V, which didn't arrive until the middle of 1992.

Still, in many ways, the TT030 was the most powerful computer Atari ever released. As with the 1040STE before it, several key factors hobbled the TT030 at launch, in this case the missing UNIX System V port that thwarted Atari's attempt to break into the workstation market; some architectural incompatibilities with major software packages like C-Lab's Notator, and Steinberg's Cubase and its sound processing program Avalon, only some of which ultimately received patches; and a price that put it out of the reach of just about anyone considering the TT as an upgraded ST. After Atari discontinued the TT030 in 1993, open-source enthusiasts would port the then-new Linux OS to the TT, one of the first non-Intel computers to get it, as well as the Falcon and Amiga.[5] Some developers for Atari's ill-fated Jaguar console used TT machines as workstations.

Hotz MIDI Translator (Atari, 1990)

The Atari Hotz MIDI Translator, commonly referred to as the Hotz Box, was a wild piece of music gear designed by Jimmy Hotz and code-veloped with Atari. It was essentially a giant MIDI controller of the kind you see today with light-up buttons (as with the Ableton Push) or even giant touch screens. But this is 1990 we're talking about, when musicians with excess hairspray were experimenting with all these new-fangled Atari ST–controlled recording studios and looking for new ways to spark their creativity.

The HMT138H Translator, dubbed the Master Unit, was this mas-sive 22-by-37-by-6-inch (HWD) black instrument with 10 parallel CPUs inside. On the front were 124 touch-sensitive pads arranged in six large groups and eight smaller groups, all in different shades of blue. This was the playing surface; musicians could program the pads in scales such that the third and fifth of a chord were always at the ready in each group of pads regardless of a song's key signature. That meant you could solo over a chord progression and not "make a mis-take" even if you hit the wrong pad. Around back were six quarter-inch inputs, some proprietary connectors to attach additional units, and a full MIDI interface with Thru and Aux ports. A 48-pad expansion unit called the Translator Wing added even more possibilities.

The Hotz box package started at $5,000 and went up from there. There are must-see photos and YouTube videos around the web of Fleetwood Mac, Jon Anderson of Yes, and other musicians wailing away on this thing. One popular ad showed Fleetwood Mac standing next to a pair of Hotz boxes and an Atari STacy open to a MIDI se-quencer, and surrounded by touring road cases. No word on whether any musicians set a Hotz box on fire on stage after finishing a solo.

NeoDesk (Gribnif Software, 1990)

Desktop shells were all the rage in the late 1980s, as software vendors such as Norton and Xtree looked to capitalize on the PC's difficult MS-DOS-based interface by creating much simpler and more flexible de-signs. Windows itself was a desktop shell of sorts, considering it ran on top of MS-DOS for years. For the ST, the best-known shell was NeoDesk, which billed itself as a "complete replacement of the bor-ing, built-in desktop that comes with the Atari ST," and it was onto something. NeoDesk let you put frequently used program icons on the desktop, similar to aliases on a Mac or shortcuts in Windows. It also let you customize icons for files and folders, and beginning with version 3, it let you put folders full of files and even write notes on the desktop. In addition, you could create your own icons, file templates, hot keys, and macros. These are all things we take for granted today, and some of which you could already do on a Mac. On the ST, it was a godsend.

NeoDesk read 5.25-inch floppy disks and could format them so that they worked on PCs. A recoverable trash can let you undelete files, and a special developer's kit let other programmers write utilities that worked with NeoDesk or otherwise extended its abilities even further. NeoDesk reportedly only took 35KB of memory, and Gribnif Software took special care in reducing the amount of disk swapping so that the program felt snappy in day-to-day use. In the end there was only so much you could cram onto even a 640-by-400-pixel monochrome screen, although Falcon and TT users would have received their money's worth.

Deluxe Paint ST (Electronic Arts, 1990)

Although the ST had NEOchrome, Degas, and Degas Elite to tide over visual artists for years, Deluxe Paint had become something of a standard on other platforms such as the Amiga and MS-DOS. In fact, Deluxe Paint was developed and unveiled in time for the Amiga's 1985 debut, and quickly became the platform's best paint program. You may have seen the gold-and-blue image of the King Tut death mask in print advertisements.

When Deluxe Paint finally arrived on the ST, it was worth the wait, as the program included support for the STE's 4,096-color palette. The new icon-based graphical interface made it easy to get started. It included some high-power features such as a Bezier curve tool, an airbrush with different levels of intensity, custom brush shapes, and the ability to create various kinds of dithered and gradient patterns and other special effects. A stencil tool let you lock part of the image you were working on so you couldn't lose it even if you started to draw over it.

Deluxe Paint also included a bunch of animation tools, which put it closer to Cyber Paint than Degas or NEOchrome. It supported the creation of animation sequences, and let you flip, rotate, distort, and otherwise modify your images so they looked as if they were truly moving. There were also robust text-entry facilities, including the ability to design your own fonts, and you could print images at up to poster size.

Deluxe Paint wasn't a must-have for every ST user, but it was ideal for anyone who owned an STE or later machine and took visual art seriously. At the time of its release, critics said it was better than any of the existing Amiga and MS-DOS versions.

Gaming Powers Up

The bad news was the ST was beginning to be left behind in 1990. The good news was for the next several years, ports of some of the best titles in computer gaming history would nonetheless make it to the ST platform anyway. Not only that, but the ST did continue to get some exclusives, or at least, some games that only appeared on the ST and the Amiga and not the PC. Let's take a look at a few of those first.

Lotus Turbo Esprit Challenge (1990)

One of the most popular supercars of the 1980s was the Lotus Turbo Esprit, a faster iteration of the Esprit coupe that was released in 1977 and made its big-picture debut as James Bond's vehicle of choice in *The Spy Who Loved Me*. The turbo model was known for its wound-to-the-nines 2.2-liter four-cylinder, and every kid who doubled as a car enthusiast had a picture of this thing on their wall. Naturally, someone had to make a game about it, and thus was born the Lotus series, a three-title trilogy with the Esprit Turbo at its center.

The first and best-known of the three games was Lotus Turbo Esprit Challenge. It put you behind the wheel—er, joystick—of a red Esprit Turbo in the guise of a seriously addictive action game that built on Sega's Out Run concept. The game contained 32 road courses of all kinds and three levels of difficulty, and you raced up to 20 competing cars. You could play this one in a split-screen two-player mode as well as a single-player racer. Periodically you needed to pitstop for fuel, and that affected whether you could still win the race.

The ST also saw both sequels, Lotus Turbo Challenge 2 and Lotus III: The Ultimate Challenge. The second game included a serial-port-style local networking mode for hooking up a second ST and, therefore, players three and four. The third installment included a Racing

Environment Construction Set for building your own courses. All three games were worth playing and solidified the ST's bona fides in arcade-style racing, especially at a time when gamers were turning their attention more and more to 16-bit consoles like the Sega Genesis.

Speedball II: Brutal Deluxe (The Bitmap Brothers, 1990)

This futuristic sports game combined soccer and ice hockey, with graphics that were equal parts Tron and gothic. Although the first Speedball game established the concept and was fun in its own right, Brutal Deluxe took it to another level, adding eight-direction playfield scrolling, more players on each team (now nine), more weapons and strategic elements, a league system, and individual player management with different skillsets and even substitutions.

The arena shot at the beginning set the mood, portraying a single player entering a tremendous arena filled to the brim with spectators. Late-1980s, tracker-style techno played in the background. In the gym before a game, you could upgrade your individual warriors by purchasing training packages. That's with fake in-game currency, none of this in-game purchase baloney from today using real money. And it mattered, as you would see the changes on the field—"just try buying one of the Star Players and see what happens!" said *The One* in its November 1990 review of Brutal Deluxe, awarding the game 94 percent overall.

The field in Brutal Deluxe was two screens wide and five screens long. The pace was fast; you passed from player to player, or chased players on the opposing team when they possessed or intercepted the ball. You had to pick up tokens on the playfield while you played— that's how you got the in-game currency. "Where other sports simulations fail because they look weedy and indistinct, Speedball 2 succeeds because it looks hard and clear," wrote *ST Format* in its January 1991 review. "[T]he players are all clearly visible, to the extent that you can actually see fists landing on heads."

Although 1990 was already getting late for the ST's influence, games such as this—with only the barest of improvements on the Amiga, ticking the on-screen colors up to 32—showed how much power the platform continued to wield. This game could have done well in the US, but its release was restricted to the UK and other European countries. As we've seen by now, enthusiasts in different countries experienced the ST in different ways, meaning I myself didn't get to play this game the first time around and am thrilled to have discovered it more recently.

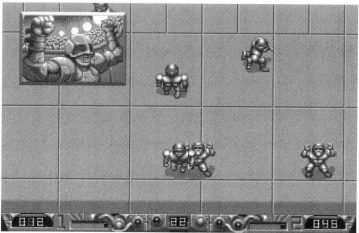

Figure 9.2: The futuristic sports game even non-sports fans can get behind, I dare you to play this and not become instantly hooked.

Wings of Death (Eclipse Software/Thalion Software, 1990)

This colorful, imaginative, vertical-scrolling shooter was developed by former demo coders as an ST exclusive before being ported to the Amiga. The digital stereo soundtrack on the STE was a cut above anything the YM2149 could produce. There's nothing immediately groundbreaking about the game itself: You had to destroy waves of ground targets and enemies in formation, collecting power-ups and new weapons as you went. Nothing was friendly—you had to shoot everything that moved.

But it's the way Wings of Death played, with bullets flying in all directions and gigantic enemy sprites that showcased the ST's graphics prowess, that kept you coming back. And the fantasy theme did it a lot of favors. In Wings of Death, the evil witch queen Xandrilia turned you, the magician Sagyr, into a winged creature. You had to fly and battle through seven levels of nasties, starting in your own castle and ultimately arriving in the witch's lair to find and destroy Xandrilia, at which point she would turn you back into a human. Some of the aforementioned power-ups (really spells) along the way turned you into other forms, such as a griffon, eagle, and dragon, along with their respective weapon upgrades.

If you were picky, you would notice the lack of hardware sprites, the same as with so many shooters on the ST. Not everyone figured out the slick routines found in Goldrunner, and one review of the Amiga port complained the game relied a bit too much on luck. That was a fair criticism—sometimes I had no idea where a bullet came from and couldn't get out of the way in time, but that only made me want to play it more. All told, this game did a convincing impersonation of a 16-bit arcade game, thanks to its accurate sampled sound, fast action, and challenging gameplay, and easily stood up to anything on the Sega Genesis.

Prince of Persia (Brøderbund, 1990)

Jordan Mechner's second masterpiece, after Karateka for 8-bit computers, was Prince of Persia, a beautiful action-adventure game with rotoscoped animation. And thanks to its appearance on 16-bit computers with sharp resolution, it was a huge upgrade in graphics, animation, and sound prowess. Your goal was to penetrate 12 palace dungeon levels in ancient Persia to confront the Grand Vizier Jaffar and save the Sultan's daughter. You had 60 minutes to pull this off.

Along the way, you confronted many obstacles, such as spiked traps, pits, guillotines, falling floors, and an array of enemy swordsmen you had to fight using the joystick. Hidden plates on the floors sometimes activated traps, or just opened and closed iron gates that made satisfying clanking sounds. You had three units of health, and there were healing potions here and there, though if you sprung a trap and fell into it you died instantly. Each time that happened, you restarted at the beginning of the level, but the timer kept going. A brilliant twist at the end posed a well-executed challenge.

The ST's 16-color graphics looked sharp, although PCs with VGA cards were able to display 256 colors on the screen at once, a mode Prince of Persia supported and that gave it an organic, less cartoony look. One of my favorite things about this game was the way it used leitmotifs; each character had his or her own little musical phrase, and these resurfaced in different ways as the story advanced. You also needed an add-in card on PCs to hear decent sound, although that was fast becoming the norm. Exactly zero of the game's awesomeness was lost on the ST.

Prince of Persia has been called the first truly cinematic plat-former. It's hard to debate that notion.

SimCity (Maxis, 1990)

The city-building title that launched one of the most storied fran-chises in gaming, SimCity is where it all started. Programmer Will Wright developed it after working with a tool for the 8-bit game Raid on Bungeling Bay that let him create his own maps during develop-ment. It turns out Wright "had a lot more fun building the islands than I did flying around in the helicopter," which led him to this pro-ject.[6] That, plus a burgeoning interest in urban planning, laid the groundwork for SimCity.

In this game, you were the mayor of a city. You had to grow it by building residential, commercial, and industrial zones, as well as roads, power plants, parks, and more. Major aspects of city planning were included, such as tax rates, budgets, and the locations of police and fire stations. The actual inhabitants of the city, referred to as "sims," went about their business on their own, such as building houses, apartment buildings, stores, and hospitals.

These decisions were affected by pollution levels, proximity to other buildings, crime levels, and available transportation and levels of traffic congestion. All of this was thanks to a sophisticated urban ar-chitecture-based AI engine that reportedly was presented to actual city planners at a conference in late 1989.[7] Sometimes you had to rebuild after natural or man-made disasters such as earthquakes, tornadoes, and plane crashes. There was no specific endgame.

Wright developed SimCity, initially called Micropolis, on a Com-modore 64 in 1985, but couldn't find a publisher for it. He cofounded Maxis along with Jeff Braun to publish the game. SimCity landed on the Mac and Amiga first, thanks to a distribution deal with Brøder-bund, and then quickly made it to the ST and a host of other platforms. Brøderbund brass thought SimCity wouldn't sell unless it was more of a "game," so the final versions also included some timed scenarios with specific goals.[8] The ST port contained a sluggish GEM-based interface wrapper. It ran in low-resolution (320-by-200) mode and admittedly wasn't the best way to play this game. But for a generation, SimCity was the prototype "software toy" and as addictive as they come. Even a less-than-optimal interface on this port couldn't get in the way.

Mega STE (1991)

Although the market for PCs and Macs with GUIs continued to pick up, there was still room for more development on Atari's part despite its shrinking resources. The Mega STE, introduced in November 1990 and released in January 1991, was a wholesale upgrade from Atari's business-focused Mega ST lineup to bring it more in line with the 1040STE's changes. The new form factor was similar to the expandable, high-end TT, but now in gray instead of off-white, and it did get the nicer TT keyboard this time around. The $1,699 Mega STE came with 2MB RAM and an internal 50MB SCSI hard drive; a 4MB model cost $1,849. A running change during production swapped the 720KB floppy drive for a 1.44MB mechanism, the same as with the TT030.

Figure 9.3: The Mega STE was highly desirable for its faster speed and other enhanced STE-like features.

The biggest upgrade in the Mega STE over the 1040STE was its processor, which now ran at 16MHz instead of 8MHz, along with a static RAM cache. You could switch the processor's speed of operation back to 8MHz whenever you wanted, in case a piece of software wasn't compatible with the faster speed. Having the extra speed boost on hand, configurable via a single button press in TOS, gave the machine plenty of extra flexibility.

The Mega STE also came with the blitter chip, support for 4,096 colors, stereo DMA sound, and external GenLock support, all similar to the lower-end STE, and the Mega STE was also expandable to 4MB RAM. It had two serial ports, plus an AppleTalk-compatible LAN port. A removable panel on the back of the computer hid a VME bus card slot, and you could add an optional MC68881 or MC68882 math co-processor, both unlike the lower-end 1040STE. Atari marketed the machine alongside its new 15-inch SC1435 color monitor. Technically, the STE was Atari's last ST machine, although few separate the 16-bit ST line out from the 32-bit TT and the 32/16-bit Falcon at this point.

The Mega STE came with either TOS 2.05 or TOS 2.06 in RAM, depending on when the machine was manufactured. The new versions of TOS let you add custom icons to the desktop, and they contained a new Control Panel desk accessory for color and sound setup as well as a mouse accelerator. You could tell the difference between the two TOS versions by whether the machine booted up with an Atari logo and RAM test; if so, the machine was running 2.06.

Atari marketed the Mega STE as a do-it-all mainstream personal computer, for graphic design, audio production, publishing, and even for school assignments and record keeping, despite its still-high price. Atari ran a series of ads in various European countries that focused on its music prowess, although there was nothing the Mega STE could do that earlier ST's couldn't in this regard aside from the improved hardware specs. The faster processor, internal hard drive, VME slot, network port, and optional coprocessor support were all nice upgrades. But for most consumers, they weren't $1,100-extra nice, considering the Mega STE was still limited to 16 colors on screen at once, and a maximum 640-by-400 resolution with a monochrome monitor, both just like the first 520ST in 1985. A regular 1040STE went for $599 in early 1991[9] and left plenty of room in the budget for an external hard drive and a memory upgrade.

STBook (1991)

The STBook, designed by Tracey Hall, was Atari's underrated attempt at bringing the STacy into the 1990s. The machine looked much more like a contemporary laptop. The STBook measured 8.5 by 11.4 by 1.4 inches (HWD) and weighed just 4.2 pounds. Inside was a 40MB, 80MB, or 120MB hard drive with 19ms access time (fast for its day) and either 1MB or 4MB RAM. Instead of a trackball as found on the STacy, the mouse was a pressure-sensitive "VectorPad" in the top-right corner of the bottom half of the machine. You moved the cursor around with small pushes in the direction you wanted the cursor to go. The harder you pushed, the faster the mouse moved.[10] The keyboard's keys had good travel, and typing on the machine wasn't much of a compromise.

Figure 9.4: The svelte STBook was a stunningly lightweight and usable ST computer, but its high price and lack of a display backlight and floppy drive made it a nonstarter.

The central feature of the STBook was its monochrome, non-backlit, 10.4-inch passive matrix display, or to be precise, a 640-by-400-pixel reflective Super-Twist Nematic (STN) panel. The Epson Custom Module display looked somewhat similar to today's E Ink–based ebook readers at first glance, albeit with more graphics and less text thanks to the GEM desktop. As Atarimuseum.com notes, the STBook was quite fragile, and susceptible to cracks in the plastic enclosure and display.

There was also no internal floppy drive, and no ability to drive an external display. The machine ran TOS 2.06 only and did have the blitter chip, but was otherwise identical to an original ST (68000, 8MHz). MIDI ports were still standard; the ST was a MIDI-compatible platform from beginning to end. Atari offered an optional fax modem with the machine, a very 1991 thing to do.

The STBook was never sold in the US, although Atari reportedly sent some to musicians as a preview. In Europe a limited number were sold, albeit without rechargeable batteries; you had to install seven AA batteries, and battery life with them was poor.[11] Atari promised up to 10 hours of battery life with either the rechargeable packs or the 7 AAs. If you get a hold of one of these today, I wouldn't bet on the rechargeable NiCad packs holding any charge. You probably don't need me to tell you that.

Atari STPad "STylus" (Prototype)

Many entrepreneurs and companies alike took a crack at pen-based computing, and Atari wasn't about to be left out of the fray. The company developed a thick tablet prototype with a non-backlit 640-by-400-pixel Epson Custom Module screen, the same one from the STBook. The system came with an electronic pen attached with a wire that was stored in a special compartment on the back when not in use.

Thanks to Curt Vendel at Atarimuseum.com, a prototype STPad was on display at VCF East 2019, which I got to check out. You could hold and use the STPad in your lap or on a table. It ran a modified TOS with a few pen-based modifications grafted on. Underneath the hood was 1040ST-class hardware (8MHz 68000, 1MB RAM). For storage, the machine had no floppy or hard drive. Instead, it contained two slots for special high-density RAM cards of unknown specification (and who knows what they would have cost at retail). The machine featured an array of ports on the left, including serial, parallel, RJ-11 (presumably for some kind of modem), and an external bus connector.[12]

The STPad never made it into production, not even to a select few the way the STBook did. Apple would release the Newton two years later, and we all know how that turned out (and we all still argue to this day over how influential it was, despite its failure as a retail product). The STPad could have been successful, but Atari was already in the process of winding down its computer business, so the company would have probably either screwed it up, run out of money, or both, just as with everything else it did around this time.

Music Trackers

The ST may have single-handedly lead the MIDI revolution in music studios the world over, and its sound chip, while far from revolutionary, generated plenty of memorable soundtracks that helped spur the chip tunes movement of today. But one kind of audio in some ways dominated the late 1980s and especially the early 1990s computer and demo scenes over everything else. So-called tracker music is a kind of hybrid of sampling and storing music as data. They sound great, take up little space, and are fun to listen to and collect.

To understand a tracker file, let's first look again at MIDI. MIDI files are records of data that control the notes, velocity, duration, and other aspects of 16-channel multitrack music. They leave the actual sound generation and output to external sources such as synthesizers and rack-mount sound modules. Sampling is the direct recording and digitization of audio waves such that they can be played back through a single mono or stereo (one- or two-track) channel, which allows for the most realistic recreation of voices and live instruments, at least at high-enough sample rates. Digital audio requires orders of magnitude more storage space.

Trackers split the difference. They combined the data-based approach of recording music events, except also employed tiny sample-based instruments and vocal snippets for more realistic playback, and without the need for external sound sources. Trackers supported four channels of audio, and recorded discrete music events across a vertical-scrolling timeline. It was a kind of step-sequencing of small samples using numbers. The result was a MOD file (a module containing both the data and the samples) not much bigger than a MIDI file—say 80KB instead of 25KB, with plenty of room for variation, and still fairly easy to download—but one that sounded much closer to sampled music, and that could be created with a computer keyboard and mouse.

The Amiga made tracker music popular, thanks to its four-channel DSP audio from the get-go. But plenty of it made its way over to the ST, especially after the advent of the STE and its built-in digital stereo sound. Some of the most popular trackers on the ST included TCB Tracker, Noisetracker, and ProTracker, though there were others.

Trackers also made it over to the PC and Mac, and added support for more channels. Anyone looking for a way to hear high-quality music on their computer without having to buy extra hardware around this time period probably dabbled in tracker music.

As the mid 1990s approached and more and more people bought computers with optical drives built in, trackers and MIDI soundtracks began to give way to the immense storage and audio streaming capabilities of CD-ROM games. Although game developers increasingly targeted CD-ROM drives as a hardware requirement, the tracker movement persisted and dovetailed with the demoscene. Enthusiasts looking to show off their programming prowess and visual artistry tended to want better-sounding audio that could also be packaged with the demo in such a way that didn't add appreciably to its storage requirements or download time. And tracker music lent itself to techno, house, and other subgenres of electronic music, which was often produced with more expensive and elaborate hardware that nonetheless mimicked the same exact digital data/waveform hybrid trackers espoused.

Another World (Delphine Software, 1991)

One of the most original and atmospheric adventure games to hit the ST was Delphine Software's Another World. Nothing had the game's mixture of sci-fi-infused style and sound design, and you could argue nothing has since, either. This game was also known as Out of This World in other North American releases, but not on the ST.

In this game, you played a young scientist named Lester who, after an experiment in particle physics went horribly awry, was teleported to another dimension on an alien planet full of dangerous beings. The game featured polygon-based rotoscoped animation, a beautiful soundtrack, and cinematic camera shots such as close-ups, zooms, and panoramas. You controlled Lester with the joystick, not the mouse, similar to Prince of Persia. You pushed left or right to move in each scene, and pushing up or down jumped or ducked. Tapping the button kicked or fired a weapon (though you started the game unarmed), while holding it down made Lester run. Although it was an adventure game at heart, there were challenging action elements to it as well.

Eric Chahi developed Another World on the ST and Amiga by himself, with the exception of the soundtrack by Jean-François Freitas. Chahi wrote Another World in a mixture of 68000 assembly and GFA

Basic. This game won accolade after accolade, and became part of a 14-game 2012 exhibit at the Museum of Modern Art. Both 15th and 20th Anniversary Editions were released for a wide variety of platforms. Neither of the updates impressed critics, many of whom were coming in as new gamers who didn't understand what all the fuss was about with the original game—mainly because of its slow pace relative to today's games and high difficulty level, similar to so many titles of the ST's era.

Gods (The Bitmap Brothers, 1991)

In The Bitmap Brothers' Gods, a smarter-than-it-looked platformer that looked a lot like a Psygnosis game, you played Hercules. The gods gave you a quest: You had to explore the ancient City of Legends and the dungeons below in order to find the gift of immortality and godhood for yourself.

Gods was presented in a side-view perspective. The game included a wide variety of beasts to fight, plus 15 different weapons and 20 different power-ups and potions. Unlike many platformers of the time, there were plenty of adventure game elements, including secret rooms, keys, and puzzles, plus some interaction with other characters and a save game function.[13] More than 30 artifacts could be found, and shops appeared twice per level so you could upgrade your equipment. There were four main sections of the game, with each divided into worlds and then levels.[14]

If you played Gods on an STE, you would find its speed and animation quality were tremendous leaps over Psygnosis titles such as Barbarian and Baal, even if still shots of the graphics looked somewhat similar. Gods was a fluid game that stood up to anything you would find on a console. There was still no in-game music the way there was in Wings of Death, but the opening track was good and there were multiple channels of sound effects playing throughout the game, which lent it more of an arcade feel.

Gods came out for the ST and the Amiga first, before seeing ports to other platforms such as MS-DOS, the Acorn Archimedes in Europe, and even the Sega Genesis and Super NES. In 1992, *Computer Gaming World* called it one of the year's top four action games, saying the combination of its "fast and furious arcade-style action" and exploration and puzzle-solving elements raised it "above the typical action crowd."[15]

Lemmings (Psygnosis, 1991)

Psygnosis's brand recognition launched into the stratosphere with the release of Lemmings. This unforgettable game, programmed by David Jones and Mike Dailly and ported to the ST by Brian Watson, would soon have you screaming "No!" as lemming after lemming plunged to its death because of something you screwed up. It's an ideal example of a puzzle-based platformer that successfully used the mouse, rather than a joystick or gamepad, as the primary input device.

In this humorous and madly addictive game, you had to guide a group of blue-and-green lemmings from the entrance of each level (a trap door on top) to its exit, and past certain obstacles along the way. To do so, you could make each lemming perform one of eight tasks: walk, climb, float with an umbrella, block each other, build bridges, blow up blockers, and dig tunnels. You had to figure out a combination of these skills to assign different lemmings that would, in turn, affect the way the others moved so they could safely exit the level. If you saved a high enough percentage of the lemmings within the allotted time frame, you'd beat the level and move onto the next one. The game included levels divided into four groups: Fun, Tricky, Taxing, and Mayhem. Each screen was more difficult than the last. Not only that, but you couldn't cheat and queue up skills in advance if you paused the game. You had to do it all in real time, even as the lemmings approached dangerous situations.

Psygnosis introduced expansions and sequels, such as Oh No! More Lemmings, and Christmas/Holiday Lemmings, plus new games such as Lemmings 2: The Tribes and 3D Lemmings. The original remains my favorite, though, and is reported to have sold more than 20 million copies across all platforms just by itself. This book has included numerous Psygnosis titles, but it's worth nothing many people learned about the company because of this specific game and its offshoots.

Lethal Xcess (Eclipse Software, 1991)

Lethal Xcess, also known as Wings of Death 2, was probably the peak of the ST platform's graphics, sound, and animation capabilities. The game, created by Claus Frein, was originally designed to stand alone. But it became the sequel to Wings of Death and a continuation of that game's story, albeit now in a futuristic, science-fiction setting rather than high fantasy.

The mage Sagyr triumphed over the evil witch Xandrilia and once again became human—but the witch still managed to transport Sagyr thousands of years into the future. In this new world, the witch's descendants, known as the Xandrilians (I'm not making this up), attempted to take over using an array of machines and monstrous creatures. Sagyr had to find the Xandrilians' home planet and destroy it. This time around, your player stayed in one form (a spaceship), but there were now eight different weapons (not counting upgrades) and even more sprites on the screen at once than in Wings of Death. There was also a fun two-player mode.

Lethal Xcess was a game that many players loved, but it reportedly didn't do well at retail. That was to be expected this late in the ST's existence; even if the platform had survived for years after, there weren't enough dedicated owners to buy lots of new software. Nonetheless, it was another game UK players enjoyed then and all ST fans can enjoy now. On the STE, the game featured interrupts (to get more color on screen), hardware scrolling and blitter support, and stereo sound.[16] If you enjoy space shoot-'em-ups at all, Lethal Xcess is a must-play on an STE or in an emulator in STE mode.

Llamatron (Llamasoft, 1991)

Llamatron was based on Robotron: 2084. You played as, well, a llama, and you had to stop an alien invasion while rescuing "Beasties" (instead of the last human family on Earth). These included camels, sheep, goats, and more llamas. Because there was support for only one joystick, you would shoot in the same direction you were moving. The game was stocked with bizarre enemies such as Coke cans, space invaders, and televisions. A Herd Wave took the place of the Brain Wave, requiring you to get as many of the beasties as possible.

Jeff Minter, who developed Llamatron on the ST before ports were released for the Amiga and MS-DOS, marketed Llamatron as shareware, a movement that was starting to gain steam. Shareware let you distribute the game for free and play a significant portion of it (or even the whole thing) up front. A donation was requested to either unlock the rest or just in an effort to trust that users would pay for good software.

With the exception of the beasts and some nutty sound effects, the game played and sounded similar to Robotron, which was especially funny given a proper conversion of the original was also available for the ST. The difference was Minter was only asking for £5 at first, making it a nice value for the amount of gaming you'd get. People who paid to register the game would also receive another game from Llamasoft, a newsletter, and a fold-out poster. (Later the price went up to £25.)

After Llamatron, Jeff Minter went on to do what was widely considered his most famous project, the Tempest 2000 remake for the Atari Jaguar game console. One final note: The game's official name was Llamatron, but it was displayed on the title screen as Llamatron: 2112. Unbelievably, the title of this game contained not just a call-out to Robotron: 2084, but another reference to the same Rush album that Ultima II did. Nerds, the whole lot of us.

Turrican II: The Final Fight (Rainbow Arts, 1991)

This one was originally developed for the C64 and came out for the Amiga first, but I'm including it because it lost little in the ST translation and ended up being one of the best late-stage ST games to hit the platform. Turrican II was a shoot-'em-up on foot that vaguely resembled Metroid on the NES. It was more of a pure arcade game, though, with five worlds and a half-man, half-robot end boss called The Machine, and played similar to the side-scrolling levels of Contra (albeit set in space).

The game's introduction told the backstory in an anime-style storyboard. Essentially, the Avalon 1 ship was about to leave the Milky Way to explore new galaxies, before it was suddenly attacked by an enemy battle cruiser and boarded by mutants who killed off every crew member save one (you). The Machine itself even temporarily boarded the ship and surveyed the damage without realizing you had survived. You had to fight the invaders and save the galaxy all by yourself. You did so by donning one of the latest athletic and armored Turrican fighting suits and then plunging into battle. As you played, you collected power-ups that amped up your weapons arsenal. Later stages of the game put you in a spaceship, changing up the gameplay and keeping things interesting.

The game's graphics looked good, with fluid scrolling and impressively shaded objects (considering the limited on-screen color palette).

The music was memorable, thanks to a stunning and now classic electronic score by Chris Huelsbeck. The whole presentation, especially the first level, reminded me more than a bit of Sonic the Hedgehog on the Genesis, a comparison I'm sure is going to garner me some hate mail. Turrican II did see distribution in the US as well as overseas.

Although some of the ST's best games wouldn't come out until after 1990, I'd still peg the golden age of ST gaming as the late 1980s. The reason for this is simple: ST games had better graphics and sound than PC and Mac games of the time. This included popular titles such as Populous, Arkanoid II, and just about anything that worked in CGA. Even some EGA games didn't match the ST; EGA was functionally equivalent to the ST's low-resolution mode, but games often still lacked sound support. That meant titles such as Indiana Jones and the Last Crusade: The Graphic Adventure, and Ultima IV and Ultima V all played better in their ST incarnations than on a PC.

It's at this point, with ports of significant games such as Prince of Persia and Loom, that the limitations of the ST started to become more apparent. Any "best ST games" roundup should absolutely include titles such as these, and if you're looking for what to play next (or again) on your ST, these are worthy of mention. But with the advent of VGA cards that could display 256 colors on screen at once, Sound Blaster and MT-32 support for multichannel digital sound effects and beautiful orchestral and electronic music, and faster 386 systems on PCs, the titles arriving on the PC in the 1990–1991 time frame began to leave the ST behind.

It soon became clear Atari was done with computers, at least in the US. If you read the last four issues of *STart* from late 1990 through 1991, for example, you'll notice that there are virtually no ads in it from Atari, aside from one showing the PC-compatible Portfolio, in what amounted to the single most important place where Atari should be advertising its ST computers and peripherals. Even the February/March 1991 issue, which had the TT030 on the cover and a huge feature story inside dedicated to the new computer, had no ads for the TT or any other ST machine from Atari Corporation. If Atari wouldn't even take out advertising in the last ST-only magazine left in America, it was a good a signal as any that the company had abandoned the US and would only focus its dwindling ST-related efforts on Europe from then on.

The ST's story remained a lot stronger on in music production, and on both sides of the Atlantic. We'll go into that further in the next chapter. But although Atari management had already lost interest in the platform, the engineers hadn't. A significant portion of the existing several million users and thousands of software developers hadn't, either.

10 | Falcon

By late 1991, no one would argue Atari had the wind at its back anymore. IBM-compatible PCs and Macs were beginning to coalesce into the final personal computer platform war that mattered. Both the ST and the Amiga were sliding in the US. They still held strong in Europe, although the writing was on the wall there, too. Despite its total lack of a clear strategy for the ST, Atari still had one absolutely stellar computer up its sleeve. It still excites me to think of it now, even if Atari botched the launch. And even if, ultimately, it wasn't enough to save Atari.

Atari Falcon030 (1992)

The Falcon030 was in most ways the ultimate Atari machine that ran TOS. It was also instantly recognizable to any Atari ST fan worth his or her salt. Although the Falcon sported the same-shape enclosure as the 1040STE, it featured dark gray keys instead of white and had a rainbow-color Falcon030 logo to the top right of the numeric keypad. Detractors complained Atari didn't unveil a new enclosure for the Falcon, the same way they complained when the company stuck with the same design for the 1040STE, saying that it signaled a half-assed approach to such an important new model introduction. But the Falcon's enclosure and new colors were so sleek, I wish the machine had been more popular than it was, for this and many other reasons.

The Falcon's specs were quite impressive, though not as good as what Atari and Jack Tramiel had initially envisioned. Atari wanted the Falcon to have a Motorola 68040 processor, meaning it would leapfrog existing Intel 386 PCs common in the market at the time and would also include the TT's faster RAM and expansion bus. An Atari team lead by John Horton began to develop this machine in Atari's Dallas R&D office,[1] while a separate small team in Israel designed a prototype card code-named Sparrow, which could turn a 1040STE into a dual-processor machine with Motorola 16MHz 68030 and 32MHz 56001 DSP chips along with a 68882 math coprocessor and a TOS 2.07[2] Atari soon canned the faster Falcon design in light of the tremendous R&D investment it would have required, and decided to turn the lower-cost Sparrow into the basis for the retail Falcon model.[3] Meanwhile, Atari fans and computer buyers spent most of 1992 not hearing anything new, until details finally became available closer to the end of the year in both the UK and the US. There was also (big surprise) internal strife at Atari as to what the new machine should do. Atari Germany wanted the Falcon to be a serious computer to rival the PC, similar to what Jack and Sam Tramiel envisioned; Atari UK continued to push the importance of the gaming market and competition with the Amiga.[4]

Figure 10.1: Atari's last hurrah on the desktop was the Falcon030, a beautiful personal computer with a fast processor, upgraded graphics and DSP, and support for higher screen resolutions.

In August 1992, Atari unveiled the Falcon in Germany and launched it at retail shortly thereafter in several countries. The Falcon's CPU was a 32-bit Motorola 68030 running at 16MHz, and the system finally contained a new blitter chip that also ran at 16MHz. More impressive still was the on-board Motorola 56000 DSP chip, which ran at 32MHz and handled a variety of tasks such as compressing images, adding effects to audio, or even working as a modem thanks to a modular port on the back of the machine. Eight 16-bit digital audio channels could record and play back at up to a 50KHz sampling rate, and the machine had stereo 16-bit input and output ports.

The Falcon's new VIDEL video chip enabled resolutions higher than 800 by 600 with 256 colors from a palette of 262,144, along with 40- and 80-column text modes from 320 by 200 to 640 by 400. One mode even displayed 16-bit color (65,356 colors on the screen simultaneously), although at reduced CPU performance. The Falcon also had an overlay video mode for video titling and special effects. The machine supported a maximum of 14MB of memory, and came with a high-density 1.44MB floppy drive and, optionally, a 2.5-inch, 84MB internal hard drive with a faster SCSI interface instead of ASCI.

Atari's last major upgrade of its GEM-based, proprietary OS, TOS 4 was necessary for Falcon machines. It added support for the system's DSP chip, 16MHz blitter, and video overlay. It also included the OS's last single-tasking AES 3.40, which added pop-up menus, 3D windows and dialog boxes, 256-color animated icons, soft-loaded fonts, drag-and-drop between applications, background window manipulation, extensible file systems, and a new international localization module. Along with the Falcon, Atari also unveiled MultiTOS, a ground-up rewrite of TOS based in large part on the free operating system MiNT. MultiTOS featured memory protection and preemptive multitasking that let you run several programs simultaneously. Although Atari advertised MultiTOS along with the Falcon, it didn't begin to ship the software until the middle of 1993. Even then, MultiTOS came on disk; you had to load it on top of TOS. In ROM, TOS 4.00, 4.01, 4.02, and 4.04 exist, with the last being the final one Atari released publicly. Unfinished beta copies of 4.92 still float around that include MultiTOS built in. (It probably would have been called TOS 5.)

The Falcon debuted at $799 with 1MB RAM and a floppy drive, $1,299 for 4MB RAM and the 84MB internal hard drive, and $1,899 for an additional bump to 14MB RAM.[5] Atari marketed the machine under the awkward term PIMS, for Personal Integrated Media System; I don't think a single person outside of Atari headquarters ever used this term for anything. (Around the same time, PIM became an acronym for personal information manager, for handhelds like the Sharp

Wizard and its competitors that were known as PIMs, but those had nothing to do with the Falcon.) If you got past that mouthful, Atari touted the machine's various new capabilities, such as acting as a "better-than-CD quality digital recorder," and "an electronic canvas with more than a quarter-million possible colors," along with the animation studio, musical instrument, and other production possibilities STs had always had. It also introduced some surprising niche uses, such as "adding surround sound to your VCR" (how exactly?) and "running a home security system," which is only finally happening more than 25 years later with the Nests and SimpliSafes we have today. If you know of anyone that used a Falcon as an alarm system, please write me. Atari also promised "optional, soon-to-be-released 386 PC emulation" and touted the Falcon's carryover ability to read MS-DOS disks.

Unfortunately, the Falcon landed gently in late 1992, a year after it was announced and at a time when fully 32-bit systems had become the norm. And although the Falcon sported a 32-bit 68030 processor and a 32-bit video bus, the rest of the machine still only had a 16-bit data bus and a 24-bit address bus, both of which hobbled real-world performance enough to show up in reviews and comparison tests. That probably didn't affect the machine all that much in the marketplace, though, and the Falcon played games with rendered 3D animation much more quickly than the ST ever could. But in the UK, the Amiga 1200 cost £100 less and was still a better game machine.[6] The fact of the matter was the Falcon should have come out in 1990, when Apple was already releasing 68030 machines and IBM-compatibles were already three years into the 80386. In 1992, it was already time for the 486 and the 68040. The Falcon didn't get the 68040 and wasn't competitive enough.

Despite Atari's struggles at the hardware and OS levels, the Falcon was in many ways the best computer Atari ever made. It offered everything the ST did, with more speed, higher graphics resolutions, more simultaneous colors on screen, digital sound, DSP, a blitter chip, and multitasking, and it was backward-compatible with most of the ST's software library. But by the time the Falcon was released, there were no more Atari-computer-specific magazines left in the US, and Atari itself was in a precarious financial position. The Falcon didn't have a chance long-term. In 1993, Atari even announced an official attempt at a second-generation Falcon 040 model, which helped tank already middling sales of the current model for several months, only to never release it.[7]

AtariWorks (HiSoft, 1992)

AtariWorks was an example of the kind of software the ST needed all along. It was a packaged office suite, similar to ClarisWorks for the Mac and Microsoft Office circa the early 1990s. The suite combined word processor, spreadsheet, and database programs, and you could put together basic presentations from within the spreadsheet. It came packaged with the Falcon030 in the UK and was also available separately at retail.

The word processor contained plenty of contemporary features, such as a full WYSIWYG page editor, support for inline images, a spell checker and thesaurus, and even text and audio notes. The spreadsheet supported up to 10,000 rows and 256 columns, with hundreds of formulas; numerous text, chart, and graph options; and the ability to set automatic or run manual calculations. The database featured flexible, resizable fields on templates, and the ability to view records as forms, lists, and sorted searches. All three modules shared a similar GEM interface and supported SpeedoGDOS fonts, and you could cut and paste data between modules. The whole package was easy to use and had just enough power for most home and business users.

In addition to two floppy drives or a hard drive, the program required 2MB of memory and performed best with 4MB. That put it out of the reach of STs and even STEs without memory upgrades, although Megas, TTs, and Falcons were fair game. Nonetheless, many ST users who stuck around long enough to see the Falcon release used this, or even received it bundled with their Falcon in the first place. Browsing old Atari SIG newsletters from 1993 and 1994, you'll find tons of people using AtariWorks and looking for tips and the latest updates.

I still wonder how much better the ST would have done with this type of cohesive suite just a couple years earlier. Ashton-Tate Framework and Lotus Symphony both launched in 1984, and by the time AtariWorks arrived, the office suite ship had already sailed on both the PC and Mac. AtariWorks was great for existing owners and Falcon buyers, but I'm pretty sure it didn't convert a single PC or Mac user to Atari by that point.

Demoscene

As time wore on, the Atari ST became the platform of choice for a sizable portion of the burgeoning demoscene, a subculture of talented programmers and enthusiasts who performed increasingly impressive and efficient feats of coding, visuals, and music. Largely European, demoscene coders often went on to either work at or form their own video game companies. Some tie the demoscene's roots—dating as far back as the late 1970s—to those who first began "cracking" software so you could illegally copy retail disks and trade them with others for free. Usually the crackers would add their own little title screens and introductions, like a software example of graffiti. These screens became increasingly elaborate and colorful through the 1980s until creating the graphics demos branched off and became a subculture all its own.[8]

Hundreds of demos were coded on Atari STs. Some of the most popular and well remembered were made by groups such as The Lost Boys, The Exceptions (TEX), ULM, and The Carebears (TCB). The colorful demos were often dedicated to demonstrating specific programming and graphics techniques, such as fast parallax scrolling, raster graphics, and vector graphics, all while complex electronic music played in the background. Often, demos were programmed in assembly, with a focus on accomplishing the most visual tricks with the least amount of code and using the smallest possible amount of memory. Later, demoscene coders moved to C and C++ once it became more practical to get the most out of the hardware in this manner.

The scene started with the ST and STE, and eventually, the best demos were made on the Falcon 030, as was to be expected thanks to its improved graphics, DSP chip, and sheer speed; STE and Falcon 030 demos tended to incorporate tracker music. There was a fair bit of testosterone-infused peacocking in the on-screen writing that accompanied some of them, in a combination of programming braggadocio and in put-downs of both other demo programmers and especially fans of other platforms like the Amiga.

Eventually, the demoscene migrated to MS-DOS PCs. Many of the most famous PC demos from the early 1990s, such as Future Crew's Unreal, Panic, and Second Reality, came at what was the tail end of the ST's retail presence. The PC was just coming into its own by this point not just for regular gaming but specifically for graphics-demo-level prowess. For more about the vibrant ST demoscene in Europe, check out Microzeit's Borders series, a trio of beautiful visual histories by Marco A. Breddin that focused specifically on the creative efforts and the people involved.

Music Production in the 1990s

We've covered in deep detail the significance of the Atari ST in gaming. But another key legacy of the ST was in computer music. By this point, the machine was well established in studios the world over. A few systems such as the Mac and even C64 predated the ST with optional MIDI interfaces. But the ST was the perfect confluence of built-in ports, a mouse-driven GUI, and sheer processing power, all at a budget-friendly price. This gave it an enormous advantage, much like the way the iPod wasn't the first MP3 player but quickly went on to dominate the industry.

"I got my Atari 520ST in 1986 along with an AKAI S900 sampler," said Norwegian producer Per Martinsen, AKA Mental Overdrive, who spent much of 1989 operating the Atari ST used at the R&R Records studio in Ghent, Belgium.[9] "I'd been fiddling with synthesizers and drum machines for a few years before that, and it was all about hardware sequencers that were hard to program. When I first saw the ST coupled with C-Lab software, I was thinking, 'This is so good.' I could make tracks from scratch and finish them."[10]

"The Atari STs in combination with the AKAI S900 and S950s definitely played a large part in the development of the UK house, techno, hip hop and drum 'n' bass scenes," said Cliff Charles of Spiral Music. "It was now possible to make creative records on a really low budget."[11]

Atari had built up a truly impressive clientele of top-name musicians with ST computers. In its advertising during the late 1980s and early 1990s, the company regularly dropped names like Madonna, Mick Fleetwood, Tangerine Dream, Peter Gabriel, and The Moody Blues. Numerous ST machines were visible driving synthesizers on stage during Jean Michel Jarre's "Paris La Defense" free concert on July 14, 1990; you can easily see them if you watch the concert video of the show. About 2.5 million people attended the performance, which set a Guinness World Record. But most musicians, when you asked them why they stuck with the ST, talked about not just getting what they wanted out of the software, but specifically how "locked in" the ST kept different pieces of equipment and the sound of the groove. This was at a time when other systems sometimes introduced a slight millisecond-level MIDI delay or variance in controlling synths (exacerbated by long cabling distances) that could detract from the quality of the song.

"Something not enough people talk about is the Atari ST's fast MIDI attack," says Alec Empire, whose Atari Teenage Riot band was named in honor of the machine. "Some of the music we made was only possible because of the amount of MIDI information the Atari can process. The Atari just delivers a certain punch."[12]

Long after the ST went out of production, music studios continued to use the ST for its accurate MIDI timing and sheer ease of use that came with its top software packages from Steinberg, C-Lab, and Passport. Depeche Mode was still using Notator for its 1997 album *Ultra*. William Orbit created most of the tracks for Madonna's 1998 record *Ray of Light* on an ST running Cubase 2.0. Fatboy Slim's 1998 electronic big beat album *You've Come a Long Way, Baby* became known among Atari fans for being created on an ST with Notator, and the machine is pictured in the foldout album inlay next to a rack of samplers and a large eight-bus mixing board. As late as 2017, Fatboy Slim still had the same ST at the center of his project studio, along with five spares, "because people have been giving them away to me...people will just give them to me going, 'you're the only person I know who might still use this...'"[13] By the new millennium, few thought the Mac or PC couldn't control MIDI as well as an ST anymore, and they were beginning to acquire additional features like recording digital audio tracks and running the first wave of software-based synthesizers.

Even as Atari wound down production of its computers, the ST's established position in the music industry meant it would live on long after the last Falcon030 rolled off the assembly line. The ST could remain as a self-contained component of a studio, and not used for anything else other than recording and playing back music tracks. And this is how recording musicians continued to use the platform. This is only fitting for what *Red Bull Music Academy Daily* called "the personal computer that was the first major step in the democratization of electronic music production."[14]

Best of the Last Games

As the ST platform rolled to its natural (unnatural?) conclusion, some of the most compelling games were released for it. I'll touch on four here that came out in 1992 and 1993. But anyone reading from the UK, or who at least was in the UK in the mid 1990s, may recall some other excellent titles on the ST as well. Rest assured I'm not going into all of them because of space constraints, and because many of them were also playable on PCs and therefore not especially significant in a historical sense on the ST side. These four, however, had too much impact to ignore.

Civilization (MicroProse, 1992)

For me to summarize the greatness of this turn-based strategy game would still pale in comparison with the vast amounts of praise it has garnered in the 25 years since its release. The original Civilization only ran on the ST with what is now considered low-resolution, EGA-equivalent graphics, including just 16 colors on screen at any one time. Yet, all of the goodness of this strategy game came through.

If you've been living under a rock for the past several decades, let me explain what could well be the best god-style title ever created. Each game started at 4,000 B.C., and time moved forward—at first quickly, and then more slowly until it became year by year in modern times. You played one of many competing civilizations, from three to seven in any one game. The goal was to win the game either by vanquishing other civilizations or by being the first to win the space race by 2100 A.D.

The game was played over a map of the current world. As you played, you would encounter roving bands of barbarians and representatives from other civilizations, at which point you had to begin some level of diplomatic relations with them. You had to research new technologies (reading, the wheel, bronze working, mapmaking, the alphabet, physics, and so on), build and develop your own cities, and manage the creation and deployment of military units, civil society improvements, and more. You could also build special Wonders of the World that boosted your nation's prestige and afforded it unique benefits.

Later Civilization games arrived for other platforms approximately every five years, along with numerous expansion packs and a couple of offshoots. Some of those were well done either out of the gate at launch or after a couple of those expansion packs refined the rules. Many fans have their preference for a certain iteration. On the ST, you could only play the one that started it all. It's still an incredibly deep, expansive, and addictive title today. Civilization was a game to get lost in, to play again and again and pass the hours with.

Formula One Grand Prix (1992)

Maybe the best racing simulation of the early 1990s, Formula One Grand Prix (F1GP) put you right in the cockpit of a Formula One car. It was considered the first true Formula One simulation, as opposed to earlier games that were arcade racers, such as Pole Position (the first popular such title) or Accolade's 1988 release Grand Prix for the PC (which looked closer to F1GP but lacked oversteer).

Figure 10.2: The racing series that became a legend, this game delivered the feel of being in Grand Prix races with real (simulated) Formula One cars instead of the usual arcade-style treatment.

In F1GP, you were one of 26 drivers competing on the grid. All 16 international Grand Prix tracks were included. There were five levels of difficulty and six included driving aids to help you get into the game. The cars were designed to handle, accelerate, shift gears, and brake just like the real thing. You could even modify the cars by adjusting the wing angles, brakes, and gear ratios.

This was one of the best games ever to come out for the ST, though there's a caveat now. Playing this again today is fun for nostalgia or research purposes, and it's a well-balanced drive. If you weren't a fan then, though, it may be difficult to get into this one, simply because so many games do this much better compared with the early 1990s.

Even then, the PC version could display textured pavement, thanks to the PC's VGA graphics and ability to show multiple shades of gray simultaneously without detracting from the rest of the on-screen colors. And today, Codemasters is busy releasing F1 game after F1 game, modeled after each season of the real thing and adding more and more realism as it goes.

But F1GP is where it all started. Other racing games on the ST were also solid, with Vroom as a worthy call-out, and of course Stunt Car Racer has its fans for what it is. The rest are much more on the arcade or arcade-like side, such as Super Monaco GP, Super Cars, Out Run, the top-down Super Sprint, the Lotus series, and the Crazy Cars series. For a pure racing sim, though, F1GP was the pinnacle of what was achieved on the platform and the start of a long-running and incredibly successful franchise.

Cannon Fodder (Sensible Software/Virgin, 1993)

In this action war game, you played as one or more soldiers behind enemy lines. You moved around each level and searched out recruits you had to kill, depending on the outlines of your current mission. Each level contained a variety of terrains, including jungle, arctic, desert, and more. You fought grunts, snipers, artillery, engineers piloting vehicles, and even an enemy air force.

You controlled the game with the mouse. The left button sent your troop leader to whatever spot on the screen you clicked. The right button turned the cursor into a target and then aimed where you were shooting. Your additional troops could be set to shoot various weapons, throw grenades, pilot five types of vehicles, or just run around all on their own, in addition to following whatever the troop leader did. An interface box on the left provided buttons for additional weapon types and whether you wanted the troops to split up.

The game contained 24 missions, each with different goals and terrain. Some missions were split up into multiple phases (with a maximum of six in one mission). Thankfully, you couldn't shoot your own troops by accident with regular bullets, because if you could the game would be over quickly. Other weapons could well harm them, though. As you progressed through the game, and if you survived long enough, your troops would increase in rank up to 16 times, all the way from private to general.

The game delivered mixed messages about war, from war "has never been so much fun" on the box, to "war, as Cannon Fodder demonstrates in its own quirky little way, is a senseless waste of human resources and lives," in the manual. "We hope that you never have to find out the hard way." Those were wise words, and also interesting given the run-and-gun games that preceded this one, and the hyperrealism of today's first-person shooters. For now, at least, it's safe to say there will always be video games about war.

No Second Prize (Thalion Software, 1993)

No Second Prize was a motorcycle racing simulator that pointed the way forward for future racing sims. The game, developed by Chris Jungen, set the mood with an ultrasmooth cinematic intro made with solid-filled polygons. The best part was the gameplay itself was just as slick, even with other bikers on the track at the same time.

You could select from six different riders, each with a number of different stats and skills. You raced in first-person view, with a picture of the bike's dashboard that showed what gear you were in and an oversize digital speedometer. The game contained a career mode and 20 different tracks, so there was plenty to see and do. You controlled the bike with the mouse, which somehow quickly became natural—you could choose from five levels of sensitivity, and you accelerated and braked using the mouse buttons. You could also choose a manual or automatic gearbox.

The biggest shock here in first-person view versus playing, say, a third-person arcade game such as Super Hang-On (where you see the motorcycle you're controlling on screen), or even a car racing sim from the cockpit, is that the view tilts hard to the right or left as you lean on the motorcycle in the corresponding direction. It feels as if you're banking a plane in a flight simulator, but more quickly. Of course, this is what happens in real life, but unlike on a real motorcycle, you can't move your eyes so that the horizon line stays fixed! The whole thing just lurches to the right or left. Amazingly, it's easy enough to get used to, and the game's graphics aren't realistic enough to make you sick the way some newer simulations can.

The game somehow managed to feel good even though you were limited to mouse control, but it was the frame rate that sold the game on the ST in the early 1990s. Even now it's impressive, especially when compared with other, less-slick first-person games.

Clones and Accelerator Cards

As Atari itself faded from the computer scene to focus on the Jaguar, several clone manufacturers stepped in—to not only support the large existing ST base but also produce new machines and accelerator cards that were faster and more powerful than anything Atari had released. For a time, these computers, while expensive and rare, extended the life of the ST platform into the rest of the 1990s and even the 2000s.

The most famous of these were from C-Lab, the music software company responsible for Creator, Notator, and Logic. C-Lab purchased the rights to the Falcon hardware design from Atari and began production of its own machines. The first model, the MkI, was essentially the Falcon030 back on the market again with TOS 4.04 chips. Then C-Lab introduced the Falcon MkII, a machine the company billed as optimized for music and digital audio production with hard drive recording. Inside the machine was 14MB RAM and a 514MB SCSI drive. C-Lab also added a line level input that negated the need for a mixer, similar to what you find on USB audio interfaces today.

The company claimed with a Falcon MkII and Logic Audio or Steinberg Cubase Audio, you could record up to 16 tracks of digital audio along with dozens of MIDI tracks. C-Lab also boosted the regular Falcon's A/D and D/A converters for its eight channels of digital audio. A late-1994 ad for the machine showed a stamped logo that read, "DONE DEAL: Atari Falcon License to C-Lab 15/11/1994 for dedicated products in music and pro audio worldwide." C-Lab said the machine was also ideal for running Apex Media, an animation studio program, or Vidi-ST, a video digitizer package. Lastly, C-Lab introduced the Falcon Mk X, a machine in a 1U rack-mount case (the standard 19 inches wide) with extra space for internal SCSI hard drives and an external keyboard.

The C-Lab machines were the only clones that had a finished look and feel, similar to the Falcon030. The rest of the models we'll discuss below were usually either sold as motherboards you would then install in a PC case, or in some cases, a rack-mount unit, as opposed to any model-specific enclosure, drives, and power supply.

In 1995 and 1996, Medusa Computer Systems released two models: the T40, a TOS-compatible computer with a 68040 processor, and then the Hades, an upgraded model with a 68040 or 68060 processor, a PCI bus with four slots, and up to a then-astounding 1GB of RAM—all specs that brought the ST into the new millennium and made it comparable to Pentium-class PCs of the time. One source on Atari-Forum says about 100 T40s and 200 to 300 Hades machines were produced.[15]

A couple of years later, Milan Computer, which was based in Germany and located on the web at milan-computer.de, sold new TOS-based systems. These were essentially a motherboard you could then install in a PC case along with floppy drives, hard drives, and a CD-ROM drive. The motherboards came with either 040 or 060 processors and modified versions of TOS 4.04. According to Gaiyan on Atari-Forum, who spoke with one of the Milan developers, about 580 Milan boards made it out the door, most of which stayed in Germany.[16]

GeSoft's Eagle computer was a clone of the TT030 with a 32MHz 68030 processor and a 68882 FPU. GeSoft unveiled the machine at ProTOS in Germany in late November 1994.[17] A December 1994 test of a prototype in *ST Computer* said it was ready for release, and early tests running Calamus and several unnamed word processors put it at about 70 to 100 percent faster than the TT030 it was based on.[18] The machine was also designed to support faster 68040 processors and included what GeSoft called Eagle Channel, a proprietary bus with room for eight slots for things such as memory upgrades all the way to 256MB of TT RAM and 14MB ST RAM. GeSoft also planned to ship its own graphics card with the system. An Atari-Forum member named AtarimuseumDE showed a photograph of an Eagle in his collection (it looks like a beige desktop PC from the early 1990s) and said about 50 were made before GeSoft filed for bankruptcy.[19]

A company called PowerPhenix produced two accelerator card products for the ST. The CT60 was designed for Falcon030 machines. It contained a socketed 68060 processor running at 66MHz with an included FPU, and support for up to 512MB of RAM. You did need to upgrade the Falcon's power supply, or more likely, fit the combination board into a PC case with a proper ATX power supply. The CT60 also came with a connector to enable the front panel features of ATX cases, such as the power and reset switches, and the two LEDs for power and hard drive access. A slightly faster model called the CT63, clocking at 80MHz base and possessing a couple of other minor hardware changes, was also produced.

Other accelerator boards for the Falcon included the Nemesis Falcon System Accelerator, Centek's CenTurbo II, and the Afterburner 040. There are other cards too numerous to include here, but many of them were produced in very small quantities in the 1990s or not at all. Some enterprising modders are still working on 32MHz and 40MHz speed boosters for earlier machines like the STE lineup to this day.

Sunset and Coda

In the end, inexplicably, it wasn't enough. Atari's precarious corporate position hobbled the Falcon launch, and management soon decided it wanted to focus on its new Jaguar game console. By the end of 1993, Atari discontinued Falcon production just one year after the machine hit the market. Atari also canned the "Panther" game console it had started developing years earlier, in an aborted effort to compete with the Sega Genesis and the Super Nintendo. Atari's final console push— well, at least before we get to today and the re-imagined VCS, about which the jury is still out—was seriously impressive. The Jaguar promised to deliver not 16- or 32- but 64-bit gaming. The Jaguar used the same enhanced joystick ports first found on the 1040 STE. Instead of joysticks, though, the Jaguar came with…gargantuan gamepad-style controllers, complete with full numeric keypads.

The system launched at $250 with the mediocre Cybermorph as a pack-in. Third-party developers had little lead time and few support tools and documentation to work with, leaving them to give up and program the 68000 they already knew with game logic instead of the Jaguar's powerful custom "Tom and Jerry" processors. Some of the Jaguar's additional games were excellent—Jeff Minter's Tempest 2000 was a groundbreaking action title with an awesome soundtrack. Alien vs. Predator was also good, and the Jaguar ports of Doom and Wolfenstein 3D put up solid frame rates. Later, Atari released a CD-ROM add-on console called the Jaguar CD, a revamped controller with even more buttons, a primitive VR headset that never saw mass production, and a few other accessories. But once the Sega Saturn and Sony PlayStation arrived in 1994 and 1995, it quickly ended any hope the Jaguar would become one of the dominant game consoles.

In an ignominious postscript, extra stock of the Jaguar's sleek black plastic housing ended up as part of dental equipment. A company called Imagin Systems purchased the molding plates for the casing and used them for its dental imaging cameras, while the cartridge housings made for useful memory expansion cards.[20] I wish I was making this up, but the Atari fan community has known about it for many years.

In short, Jaguar and the Lynx, while both good, weren't enough to pull Atari out of its second fatal nosedive. We can all blame the company's poor management—and we do! But it would also be impossible to tell the story of Atari computers, whichever ones, without mentioning software piracy. Periodically in *STart* and other magazines, the subject of piracy specific to the ST platform came up. It was something that dogged Atari ever since the 400 and 800 launched in November 1979. The problem continued throughout the ST's life span. Atari computers never quite shook their reputation for rampant software piracy.

The reality is US sales of the ST dropped off dramatically even by 1990.[21] A series of articles by Al Fasoldt called "Who killed the Atari ST? A drama in three parts" appeared in the *Syracuse Post-Standard* in 1989. "Atari, the American company that makes the ST, has chosen to leave the U.S. market in the cold. Instead, for the last two or three years it has pushed the ST in Europe," wrote Fasoldt, who made it clear he was a fan of the computer. "As much as 90 percent of all STs have been sold there. In most American cities, even large ones, it is impossible to find an ST dealer. Many stores that used to carry the ST have dropped it because the manufacturer did not support its own products in the same way that Apple or other companies do."[22] Fasoldt closed with some faint hope for a resurgence in 1990 thanks to what would become the STacy, the 1040STE, and the TT030.

So why *did* the ST fall off so quickly in the US, if it did well for many years in Europe? "The reason is very simple—distribution channels," said Shivji recently. "Atari did not have any distribution channels to speak of in the US. In Europe, we had a great cadre of ex-Commodore people and dealers we could use."[23] And what about the later machines such as the STE, TT, and Falcon? "The problem is that Motorola lost the processor battle," Shivji said. "The TT was based on the 68030, a successor to the 68000. This processor was clearly inferior to the 386 and 486 from Intel." That's true, but it doesn't explain how Apple was not only able to sell the IIci, a machine powered by a 68030 running at 25MHz, at the same time as the STE and TT, but it was able to do so to the point where it was one of Apple's top-selling computers.

For its part, the Amiga also faded from the scene. It was tempting as a total ST fan to have celebrated this, but the reality was it was just as sad as the ST not making it. Both platforms dissolved around the same time. As with the ST, the Amiga held on longer in the UK, with Commodore filing for bankruptcy in 1994 and then disappearing in 1996, the same year JTS bought what remained of Atari's assets.

To this day, I find it frustrating that Atari just let the platform languish until the public slowly gave up on it. The ST could have been so much more, and could have endured for far longer than it did. It deserved much more than that. Fortunately, great computer platforms don't really die, as we've learned. They just fade away...and then, for the most dedicated enthusiasts, they return stronger than ever, not only by passing into the emulator afterlife but in an expanding enthusiast community for the original hardware and software that's bursting with activity today.

11 | Emulation

One of the best things about the ST is the continuing interest in the platform today. If anything, it's only grown. Now, there are so many ways to plug into the community of fans, enthusiasts, and experts who can help you get the most out of your system—and often, much more out of it than you could back in the ST's heyday.

What I want to do in the next four chapters is present a 10,000-foot view of the landscape for ST enthusiasts today. I'll cover emulation, collecting, ST mods, new software, forums, fan sites, and more—everything you need to know to get back into this wonderful hobby, including its robust modding community, the increasing value of some ST models, and how to get started with one now if you missed it the first time.

The absolute simplest and least expensive way to fire up ST software today is, of course, emulation, so let's tackle that first.

ST Emulators

Emulation has become a go-to technique for anyone looking to enjoy older computers and game consoles on today's machines. This would extend to our beloved ST line, including the top-end TT and Falcon machines, the youngest of which is still upwards of 25 years old. But despite the ease of leaving behind aging, sometimes temperamental hardware and just using the much newer computer already in front of you, it turns out it's considerably trickier to emulate the ST than it is, say, the Atari 8-bit line. This is despite the fact that software emulators for the ST have been around since the 1990s.

There are many reasons for this difficulty, and none have anything to do with the old culprit of whether the emulating PC in question was powerful enough. They're all powerful enough now. But unlike the Atari 8-bit or Commodore 64, the ST's underlying hardware and OS changed several times in significant ways over the course of the platform's life span. Newer ST models, such as the Mega, the 1040STE, the TT, and the Falcon, each brought hardware upgrades and a new set of TOS versions. Some of the hardware, such as the Mega's blitter chip and the Falcon's on-board DSP, delivered additional capabilities that only certain programs took advantage of, and that may have interfered with programs written before it existed (and often did, especially with regard to the TT and Falcon). There's the split between floppy disks, both single- and double-sided, and hard drives that connected with ACSI or SCSI interfaces. Hard drives were more convenient, but not all ST software supported them. In addition, copy protection often came in the form of hardware dongles (such as with Cubase and Notator), and software copy protection needed to be broken if you wanted to install and run some programs from a hard drive without also needing the floppy inserted. Finally, not only do you need legal access to ROM files, but you also need access to a genuine TOS image—and as mentioned above, you often need to choose the right one or your program won't load.

This is not to say emulation doesn't work; your own favorite ST programs may fire up on the first try. But put it all together, and it's not always as simple as installing an emulator and copying a bunch of ROMs to a folder. ST emulators need a well-tuned balance of preferences, OS, and disk images in order to run different software correctly. Let's look at some of the most common emulation setups and cut through the noise—in this case, outdated information that turns up all the time in Google searches but that you no longer need with today's PCs.

Hatari

ST fans looking to run their favorite software in an emulator on a Windows, Mac, or Linux machine should begin with Hatari, one of the few continually updated Atari ST emulators available today. Hatari, developed initially by Thomas Huth and now with several regular contributors, is extremely powerful and accurate. But because of its complex interface, combined with what I wrote earlier about the various iterations of the ST, TT, and Falcon, and the different TOS versions and CPU speeds available, you'll need to do a tiny bit of tweaking for each program you want to load in Hatari. You also need patience; Hatari loads ROMs more slowly than other emulators. Once you get the hang of the way Hatari works, though, it's easy.

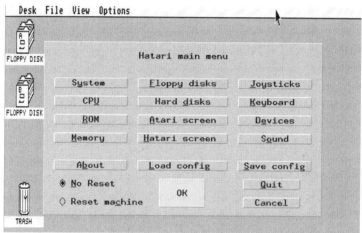

Figure 11.1: The best all-around ST emulator, Hatari also covers the STE, Mega, TT, and Falcon, and runs on PCs, Macs, and Linux machines.

To get started with Hatari, head to hatari.tuxfamily.org/download.html and grab the latest release for your computer platform. It will include a copy of the free EmuTOS to get around copyright restrictions. For most software, though, you'll need a copy of a genuine Atari TOS ROM. TOS 1.04 or later is required for hard drive support, and at least TOS 1.62 is required for stable STE emulation. Some initial tips: When you fire up Hatari, the first thing you'll want to do is capture the mouse cursor so it doesn't constantly jump out of the Hatari window and onto your regular desktop (especially if it doesn't reach the end of the ST desktop first). You do this by pressing ALT+M on a PC or Command+M on a Mac. Hatari lets you resize the window or even run in Full Screen mode, but you may run into issues retaining the aspect ratio. To do so, resize the window while holding down the Shift key; this will retain the original aspect ratio as you go larger or smaller. If you ever mess it up so it looks out of proportion and you can't get it back to the way it was, enter Full Screen mode and then exit; that will restore Hatari to the originally sized window mode.

To load a program, "insert" the appropriate floppy disk image into Hatari's "A" virtual floppy drive and then click Emulator > Cold Reset. You can also set up a folder on your computer for Hatari to use as a virtual hard drive. The easiest way is to select a GEMDOS folder and then put some ROM files for apps or games inside that folder. These programs must be set up for hard drive use; you can't use regular images of floppy disks, which means you'll need to secure converted programs in order to fire them up from the virtual hard drive. The upside of this is many of the patched games have STE support and even cheats added to them, if you're so inclined, for things such as unlimited health in Gauntlet and unlimited air in Airball.

In Hatari, I usually use a mix of hard drive installs (mostly for games) and regular floppy-based images (regular apps, and some games), depending on what's available. That lets me use most Atari ST software. As for the choice of machine, I'll cue up an original 8MHz ST with 1MB RAM and TOS 1.0 for maximum compatibility with older (1985–1988) software, and an 8MHz STE with TOS 2.06, 4MB RAM, and the built-in blitter for any 1989+ games, or any title I know works better with an STE and doesn't run too fast. The latter configuration is also good for all the patched, hard-drive-compatible games. For applications and demos, I tend to go with a Mega STE, TT, or Falcon, depending on the program.

Another important tip is to create config files you can save and load for frequently used setups. I have one for TOS 1.00 (an original ST), one for TOS 2.06 with a virtual hard drive, and several extra configs for STE machines, the TT, the Falcon, and so on, but you can do this any way you want. Whatever you want to be the default Hatari configuration on startup should be saved in the default config directory as hatari.cfg (there may not be one already present). Then you can load and save other CFG files whenever you want, but Hatari won't always start up with EmuTOS and possibly other settings you don't want or never use. You could even set up dozens of CFG files that have the hardware tweaks you want and the appropriate software loaded into the floppy drives, and then call up each CFG file as desired.

Other Emulators

Numerous other emulators also deliver accurate ST emulation on different platforms. I tend to stick with Hatari, because I'm often switching between a PC and a Mac and just want to use the same emulator in both places, and Hatari covers the most bases for the most people. But you may find one of these other emulators does the job better, or is at least simpler to use.

The biggest alternative often used today is Steem SSE, which is commonly cited as a friendlier and easier-to-set-up emulator than Hatari. The original Steem hasn't been updated in several years, but Steem SSE is a newer, PC-only version maintained by Anthony and Russell Hayward. Many Steem fans prefer its interface to Hatari's. Although Hatari is still the most cycle-accurate ST emulator maintained today, Steem SSE has become quite good. When you load Steem SSE for the first time, it walks you through setting up the default folders for your floppy disk images and virtual hard drive. Loading images is much faster than with Hatari, and you can capture the cursor and pop in and out of the emulation in a single step with the F12 key. Steem SSE also plays a fun sound effect that imitates the audible whirr of SF314 and SF354 floppy drives, except that the originals were never this quick. If you have a Windows PC, give this one a shot and see what you think.

ARAnyM bills itself as a virtual machine for running 32-bit ST/TT/Falcon OSes such as TOS, MagiC, FreeMiNT, and Linux-m68k as well as regular TOS/GEM applications. The program attempts to provide a holistic, singular approach to emulation that picks the best possible compatible hardware even if it wasn't modeled after a specific machine—in this case, a 68040 with MMU, a 68882 FPU, accelerated OpenGL-compatible graphics, up to 4GB RAM, and an array of simulated peripherals. The group behind ARAnyM says the product is similar to a software iteration of a (much more expensive) hardware clone of the ST, such as the Milan or Medusa Hades, and that it's more powerful because it's only limited by the performance of the host computer. If this sounds like your cup of tea, head over to aranym.github.io for the latest ARAnyM release.

You're not going to read any Android-versus-iOS stuff in this book; the last thing I want to do here is cause yet another flame war. With that said, and as gingerly as possible, one advantage to Android phones is you can run emulators on them for old computers and game consoles. The ST is no exception, thanks to a free app called Hataroid. It's a port of Hatari that works on Android phones and tablets, and includes an on-screen representation of the ST keyboard. Part of why I love playing with ST hardware and desktop emulators is so I *don't* have to use my

254 | Faster Than Light: The Atari ST and the 16-Bit Revolution

phone and its cramped touch-screen keyboard, but if you want ST software on the go, there's nothing more portable than Hataroid.

Digging a bit further down into the rabbit hole, you may come across SainT, an older, software-only, cycle-accurate emulator that originally ran on Windows 9x, NT, 2000, and XP machines. In its day, it was good at running games and demos. The emulator is sparsely updated now—there have been just nine updates in the last 12 years, though the last one was in December 2015. But it's still worth a look thanks to its rich ST and STE graphics and sound support, complete with emulation of the blitter and DAC. There's no TT or Falcon emulation, though.

Finally, and at least historically the most important, The Gemulator was the original Atari ST hardware emulator. The Gemulator dates all the way back to the early 1990s, when the ST platform was still (at least technically) alive. Back then, the commercial package, made and distributed by Branch Always Software, required a 386 or 486 PC and sold for $229. The product contained the Gemulator expansion board, custom emulation software, and TOS 2.06 ROMs.[1] It didn't claim to run any games or music software, but it did support a hard drive partition and was able to run professional applications such as PageStream. It also supported on-the-fly monochrome and color "monitor" switching with a single keypress and could address 8MB of "virtual" ST RAM, more than any real ST machine. With Gemulator 2.1, according to a 1993 FAQ, the program needed at least a 486-33 to match or exceed the speed of a standard 8MHz ST.[2]

There's a kind of nesting-doll aspect to using old hardware to emulate even older hardware. I've seen quite a bit of Spectre GCR-related experiments lately, even though a real Mac that's a good 10 or 15 years newer than an ST and much faster costs 100 bucks on craigslist. But that's the fun in this sort of thing.

12 | Mods

If you have original ST software and want to enjoy the machine again the way it was in the late 1980s and early 1990s, by all means, leave the hardware stock. But modding an ST means you get to do all sorts of things with it you couldn't back then.

Before we get started with mods, I recommend having a Windows PC of some kind handy to help with things like prepping SD cards and loading firmware. Procedures do exist for doing some of these steps from a Mac or a Linux box, but it makes it considerably more difficult to track things down. Plenty of ST fans in recent years have programmed and zipped up little utilities to help out with these endeavors, and I tend to find that almost all of them run in Windows. For this sort of project, if your main computer is a Mac, picking up any spare PC running Windows 7, 8, or 10 will do. It could be a $400 laptop on Amazon, a slow-as-molasses netbook, the old Compaq tower you have in the closet—anything with an SD card slot or a couple of free USB ports for plugging in a card reader and/or USB thumb drives. Having a PC also means you can try out Steem SSE instead of just Hatari for emulation, and you can run the now-defunct (but still amazing) Best Game Pack for quick access to more than 600 Atari 8-bit games as well.

At any rate, regardless of which model ST you have, you'll want to run lots of software on it. There are many ways to jump into modding an ST, but the single most important thing you can do today is to add some type of flash storage to serve as a "hard drive," albeit one bigger than anything available during the ST's heyday. Whether you want to risk running a 30-year-old spinning drive inside a Megafile 30 or a

Falcon some more is up to you, but I would personally choose a modern flash-based setup. Flash memory lets you run the most software as easily and quickly as possible, and it makes it much easier to transfer files between a modern computer and the ST.

Figure 12.1: The SD-card-based UltraSatan is like having an ST with a virtually unlimited, reliable, fast hard drive.

UltraSatan

My favorite storage upgrade for STs is UltraSatan, a product expressly designed for this purpose by Miroslav Nohaj (aka Jookie), a software developer by day and a hobbyist hardware designer by night. The original SatanDisk model came out in 2007, and many people still use these today. UltraSatan, introduced in 2009, features two slots, letting you copy information from one SD card to another or hot-swap either card. The upshot is with as little as an 8GB card, you can store every program ever created for the ST, access them much more quickly, and back them all up easily. It's especially desirable for running applications and games that require multiple disks. SD cards have no moving parts to fail, though I'd still make good and frequent backups over relying on the ST's OS and file system over a long period of time; I've already had one just suddenly stop working with my 1040STE, taking all of the data with it (and it's one of the later STEs with the right DMA chip, so it wasn't that).

In the process of "research" for this book, I purchased a unit from Lotharek's Lair, along with an ASCI cable, a power supply, and a formatted SD card preloaded with numerous partitions full of games and demos. The UltraSatan unit itself is just a circuit board, although you can buy it with an enclosure (the way I did). The one Lotharek sells includes room for the two card slots, plus a small power switch on the back and a power LED on the front. You can power the UltraSatan with any micro USB adapter that would charge a Kindle or power a Raspberry Pi. The whole thing is ever so slightly larger than the stock Atari ST mouse—meaning it's much smaller than an external hard drive or even a 3.5-inch floppy drive.

There are several ways to format an SD card for use with the ST. The two methods Jookie recommends are ICD PRO, which is free but doesn't let you transfer files to a modern PC, and HDDRIVER, which is a paid solution that does. HDDRIVER (via www.hddriver.net) costs €45. It comes with a manual in English and several tools for formatting media, configuring your devices, and running self-tests. It works with a wide variety of ST models (including some accelerated and clones) and SD cards, SSDs, and hard drives. It also supports MiNT and MagiC, along with larger FAT32 partitions and long filenames.

A third, less expensive method, and the one I used with my Ultra-Satan, is Peter Putnik's custom PP driver (atari.8bitchip.info). For just $10, Putnik will send you the software you need for your setup, and it takes up less memory and in some cases is more compatible with some patched games thanks to its lack of timer dependence. The one thing I'll mention here is I couldn't figure out how to set it up from a Mac, so I used the PC in my home office "lab" instead. Once set up properly, the drive will function like an ACSI hard drive would have back in the 1980s, with the obvious changes being it's much smaller and quieter, and the partitions are much larger and faster. There are also ways to add an UltraSatan as a replacement for the internal hard drive in the Mega ST and Mega STE, either with a SCSI adapter or conversion to IDE.[1] All told, I love using the UltraSatan. Between this for the ST and my SIO2SD setup on my Atari 8-bit, I can't imagine ever going back to floppy disks for anything.

Gotek

Unlike the UltraSatan, which emulates a hard drive, a Gotek drive emulates a floppy disk drive. It's a two-part solution that consists of the drive itself and a separate piece of code from the IIxC Floppy Emulator project. The combination works with all manner of computers, not just the ST, and it even works with old music synthesizers that have internal or externally connected floppy drives.

In the case of the ST, swapping in a Gotek and plugging in a USB drive means you can run native floppy disk images from it, and not have to find patched, hard drive conversions of popular software (although those are pretty easy to find for most of the programs discussed in this book, if not all). A Gotek drive has either a three-segment LED or an LCD display, a USB input, two buttons that cycle up and down between the available disk image files, and a status LED that works similar to a regular floppy drive's "busy" or "drive is being accessed" light. The back of the unit contains a floppy cable ribbon connector, a power connector, and some headers for jumpers. Because the Gotek is connected through the floppy disk bus, you'll be limited to sluggish floppy disk speeds, and you'll have to manually "swap" disks by cycling through multiple images.

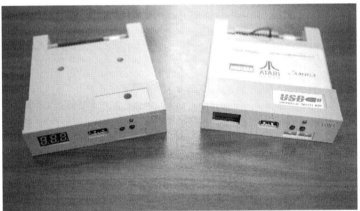

Figure 12.2: This inexpensive virtual floppy disk simulator is a nice, sort-of-drop-in replacement for the actual floppy drive in the 1040ST.

Nonetheless, a Gotek solution is much less expensive than an UltraSatan drive, and with some work is a drop-in replacement for the internal floppy drive inside a 1040ST or STE. You'll also need HxC firmware or a competing version like Flash Floppy (which some have found more stable); you can get the HxC firmware from hxc2001.free.fr. With a Gotek, you need some electronics knowledge; for example, you may want to solder in a header for the smaller set of nine holes, and you have to make a number of connections of pins to other pins. There's also the aspect of fitting it into the ST case;

numerous people have designed rails and made the files available, for example, so you can make them on a 3D printer yourself.

A basic Gotek drive has a three-digit LED readout; I picked up one of these new for just $27 from Amazon, and they're readily available. However, a three-digit LED means you have to number the floppy images and then remember which numbers correspond with which images. HxC firmware now supports Gotek models with two-line LCDs that show folder and filenames; this started out as a hack, and you can easily add a nicer display to an existing unit, but now you can buy a drive like this from the get-go. I found one with the display upgrade, an 8GB USB drive, and the appropriate optional cable extender from eBay user kevinmount for a total of $81, including overseas shipping to the US, but there are plenty of available options.

If you're not comfortable doing hardware mods on this level, I highly recommend going with an UltraSatan setup instead. A few people have even figured out how to add a Gotek in an external enclosure for use with smaller 520ST models. Hardware modder Piotr Bugaj designed a Micro Gotek that fits more easily inside the ST enclosure.[2] Bugaj also made a version that lets you toggle between the original floppy drive and the Gotek in an external enclosure, if you want the Gotek but don't want to mess with the case or lose the existing floppy drive.

Other Storage Options

The HxC floppy emulator (hxc2001.free.fr), designed by Jean-François Del Nero, emulates different kinds of floppy drives—for our purposes, obviously the Atari ST—similar to how a Gotek drive works. In fact, some with Gotek drives who have run into compatibility issues have purchased the HxC firmware separately just to flash the Gotek. Lotharek sells a variety of HxC floppy emulator versions, both with and without cases, that add features such as multiple drives at the same time (great for multidisk programs), fancier displays, and truly quality external housings. (Tip: If you want to nerd out on vintage flight simulators, oscilloscopes, glass cutters, and other odd use cases for floppy disk emulators, check out all the pictures located at the above link.) An HxC floppy emulator lets you use an SD card like the UltraSatan, but without having to search out patched versions of games for virtual hard drive installation, and you can still set up a boot menu on the card.

Another option specifically for the TT030 and Mega STE is the Lightning VME, a USB interface with two USB 1.1 ports, a 600Kbps transfer rate (in a TT030), and a compact design that fits inside those two systems' enclosures. It requires that the system is running either TOS 2.06 or greater, MagiC, or MiNT. The Lightning VME supports USB hard drives, keyboards, and mice. It takes power from the Atari's internal supply and you can use both USB ports at once. Visit wiki.newtosworld.de for more information on this project.

For those with a few more bucks available for mods, Jookie's latest project, the CosmosEX, is also worth a close look. You can find out about this one at Atari.sk/comsosex-3-0/. The Raspberry Pi–powered CosmosEX requires hardware modding like a Gotek, and also works as an SD-card-based hard drive on the ST. But its higher price compared with an UltraSatan nets you several additional benefits, including Wi-Fi and a shared network folder, three hot-swappable floppy images via a hardware button, and the ability to plug in a USB controller, mouse, or keyboard. It opens ZIP files, and you can download images from the internet. You can even use it to control an ST from a remote computer through a browser window. You do lose the UltraSatan's second SD card slot, though. The newest CosmosEX model 3.0 has pre-fitted RPI, ACSI, and SCSI support.[3]

Memory

Upgrading an ST's memory became much easier with the advent of the STE and its support for standard-size SIMMs. A good target for most of the lineup remains 4MB, though TT and Falcon users may want to shoot for 12MB to 16MB. At the time of this writing, Jay's Retro Computer Sales is still selling a handful of original 4160 STE nameplates (sourced from an unreleased Atari SKU) for the top panel of your upgraded STE model. The store has extras from some 2MB and 4MB models sold in Europe way back when. There's room to run here; I've seen TT030s with 64MB of RAM, which for TOS is absolutely cavernous.

The MonSTer board (www.fairlite.co.uk) combines a dual-IDE interface, an alternate RAM bank (up to 6MB), and a flashable TOS image. There are several versions available that work with Mega ST and STE models.

If you have a 520ST and you want to boost it in some fashion, plenty of upgrades were released in the late 1980s to enable doubling the onboard memory to 1MB. An older Magnum 16MB RAM expansion was designed for the original STs and is harder to find; other upgrades abounded, like Frontier Software's Xtra-RAM, and newer ones you can buy now like Exxos's 4MB "LaST Upgrade," available at www.exxoshost.co.uk/atari/last/4MBMMU/index.htm.

It's reported that most 260STs in the UK had 512KB anyway, as memory prices dropped soon after and Atari decided to build all of them the same way, including using all the labels it had already printed for the 260ST.[4] So if you really have a 256KB model, it's best to leave it alone thanks to its relative rarity; upgrading the memory would negate its single most distinguishing feature.

Operating Systems

Unless you're looking for maximum compatibility with the earliest ST software out there, it's worth considering an upgrade at least from TOS 1.00, if not a newer version. Many enthusiasts feel TOS 2.06 strikes the best balance of new features, speed, hard drive (read: SD card) support, and backward compatibility. But 2.06 is also a blanket, "safe" choice in the case of hardware upgrades; I have these chips installed in my 1040STE. If you're upgrading an older 520ST or 1040ST, 1.04 is another good starting and stopping point, as it better supports hard drives and adds a few other nice features that improve the system's day-to-day usability. Peter Putnik has also patched 1.04 and 1.62 with additional bug fixes, support for larger FAT partitions, and virtual floppy drives.[5]

If you can't decide which TOS version you want to commit to, why not install several? The way you do this is with a TOS switcher. Many people load up, say, 1.62 and 2.06, and then switch between them whenever a piece of software requires it. The Exxos Store sells Dual TOS kits for 1.62/2.06 and 1.04/2.06, plus all manner of TOS ROM upgrades.

Toward the end of the ST's time on the market and for some time after, alternative operating systems began to appear. We've already discussed MiNT, which formed the basis of MultiTOS, but it could also be run as a standalone OS on the ST. The current FreeMiNT is actively supported, complete with a mailing list, and offers XaAES multitasking and TeraDesk, an open-source desktop environment. In 1992, Mag!X appeared with its own version of preemptive multitasking and

MagiCDesk, an update of the GEM desktop with support for background file operations, long filenames, and aliases. In 1995 the name changed to MagiC.

It's also a great time to run an updated desktop shell like Gribnif Software's NeoDesk or the multitasking Geneva, especially if you've got at least a 4MB machine. Jinnee 2 (pronounced "Genie") runs on top of MagiC and adds drag-and-drop, file and folder desktop icons, faster file operations, and a recoverable trash can.

Processor

There's all sorts of stuff you can do to speed up an ST. For starters, you can reference the previous chapter's section on clones and accelerator cards and focus on the latter. But in addition to finding a card made in the 1990s that will speed up your current machine (the Falcon has the most options available), you can also try one of Exxos's latest speed boosters for the STE. At the time of this writing, the store carried a 32MHz STE booster, two STfm boosters for a 16MHz upgrade, and a 16MHz upgrade for the Mega ST. These boosters all require some electronics knowledge as well as ROM chip updates.

Display and Graphics

There are numerous ways to improve the display output. CENTscreen is a software utility that adds new resolutions and color modes to a Falcon running either TOS or MiNT. You can get resolutions like 768 by 512 with 65,536 colors, or an interlaced 1,024 by 768 with either 16 or 256 colors. European ST owners can hook up any flat-screen TV with a SCART port by buying a cable adapter that's readily available on the internet.

Many LCD monitors out there support Atari NTSC and PAL refresh rates, as long as you hook up the proper RGB-to-VGA cable; a full list is located at 15khz.wikidot.com. More interestingly, you can connect an ST via HDMI. There are HD converters that offer SCART-to-HDMI and VGA-to-HDMI; Analog Thinker has an excellent video showing these options at www.youtube.com/watch?v=c25dlHFW584. Exxos forum user Smonson has been working on an HDMI/DVI output for the STfm, which you can follow at www.exxoshost.co.uk/forum/viewtopic.php?f=29&t=330. Numerous forum threads cover which LCD monitors work with the TT030's 1,280-by-960-pixel High resolution. NVDI is a useful piece of software that updates the code underneath GEM to offer faster screen draws, more printer support, new fonts, and other nice updates.

An Atari system with a VME slot means you can install an upgraded graphics card. The Tseng Labs ET4000 offered SVGA-level graphics on PCs of the early 1990s; a Nova version was available for the TT030 and the Mega STE. ATI Mach32 cards also worked in these two machines with a Nova VME adapter.

Internal Sound

As far as internal audio goes, all machines from the STE on have stereo sound, and the Falcon even has support for eight channels of digital audio. But if you have an older ST, STf, or STfm and want to do something with the YM2149 chip, there is hope. The Tweety Board was another Practical Solutions product, like the Mouse Master and Monitor Master, that enhanced your ST; in this case, it added stereo and three-channel sound capability to any pre-STE machine that lacked it, simply by splitting the YM2149's three internal voices into different outputs. Those boards are very hard to find now, but the schematics are out there to build your own version. Most ST enthusiasts believe it makes more sense to simply upgrade to an STE or later machine so that you can get genuine software support for stereo sound, instead of a hack like this without much support.

Let's say you love the YM2149's chiptune-like output. It turns out you can easily add a virtual instrument to any modern digital audio workstation with ymVST, a free VST plug-in by Gareth Morris that does a reasonable job of emulating the YM2149 so that you can write music for it without needing an actual ST—although if you're reading this, chances are that you've got a real one! Nonetheless, it's cool that someone developed this. You can grab a copy via the project's home page (www.preromanbritain.com/ymvst). Fun aside: Steinberg, creator of Pro-24 and Cubase for the ST, later developed the VST standard for software instruments that so many people use today in music studios around the world. Sadly, there's no way to run VST plug-ins on an ST, as even if the code existed, it would require way too much horsepower for an ST. Even a 68060 would struggle with this sort of thing.

Mouse

I love the Atari ST and all, but…it's a little hard to sing the praises of the ST's stock mouse. Fortunately, you can buy an Atari-to-USB adapter that lets you use a much newer optical model, so you don't have to put up with its ultra-angular ergonomics and stiff buttons, or even better, clean the original's ball and rollers all the time. Or if you prefer to keep the look all original, you can pull up schematics for a board that updates the STM1 mouse with a laser kit: www.dropbox.com/s/49nhklf374ef5kv/Atari%20Laser%20Mouseboard.pdf.
You can even buy a premade one yourself from this (augh!) Amiga store: amigastore.eu/638-laser-upgrade-kit-for-atari-stm1-mouse.html.

Networking and USB

Fortunately, you don't need a modem, a copper wire line, and dial-up software to get your ST online anymore. First up are Ethernet options. The Netusbee adapter plugs into the ST's cartridge port and adds an Ethernet port and two USB ports to any ST, STE, Falcon, or TT computer. You can order one (or several) from Lotharek's Lair. A Netusbee Lite option drops the USB ports, so it's for Ethernet only. The older EtherNEC board is still available in a few places, although it's an ISA-based solution that requires a case to house the card. Don't forget the CosmosEX storage upgrade I mentioned earlier, which also adds wireless network support, at least locally. There's no way to use the CosmosEX to access the internet from your ST, at least not at the time of this writing.

Once all networked up, what you can do with your ST? First, you can set up a home network, where you can transfer files via FTP between computers (using software such as Litchi and aftp). You could also get on the internet. There, you can run free programs like the Crystal Atari Browser (CAB), an ST web browser, or Newsie, a combination email-news-FTP client. These programs are not going to replace the latest version of Chrome or Firefox on a modern computer, and will give you a distinctly early 1990s look at the web (assuming the pages even load in the first place). But it can be done, and like a dog walking on two legs, it's awesome that it can happen at all.

FireBee

To heck with 68040 and 68060 upgrades—what if you could build a completely modern PC running TOS, with built-in networking, fast drives, high-resolution desktops, and SD card support? Fortunately, some dedicated ST enthusiasts came together to answer this question. The FireBee is an actual new "Atari" computer. Known as the Coldfire Project throughout its development in the 2000s, the first FireBee machine appeared in May 2012. The group is still selling computers today and providing full support, including driver and firmware updates and new documentation. I have not sampled one of these machines, but a survey of current owners around the web indicates customers are happy with their purchases. I put this in the Mods chapter because you may want to approach the FireBee as a giant mod more than anything else. It may be super-fun to work with, but it's going to take some tweaking to run your favorite software one way or another.

Diagnostic Software

This isn't so much a mod, but if you are doing them, it helps to have some diagnostic tools. GEMBENCH is a useful program that tests the performance of an ST. This is useful for testing accelerator cards, additional memory, and the various clones that have been developed, or just pitting several STs against each other to see how they perform. GEMBENCH 4.03 was the last official version, but the community has since developed 5 and 6. SYSINFO does what it says on the tin; it will tell you your machine's processor and FPU (if installed), whether you have a blitter chip, how your system's memory is set up, and lots of other details. You can also buy any number of official Atari Field Service Diagnostic cartridges; Best Electronics stocks individual models for each hardware platform along with accompanying manuals, although scans of the manuals are also available at the Internet Archive.

13 | Collecting

There's never been a better time to get into the ST. Unfortunately, lots of people have begun to discover this, and the market has tightened up a bit. Depending on your viewpoint, hunting for vintage computer gear is either fun or annoying. For me it's both; the fun part is obvious, but the annoying part comes when you know you had Atari ST gear back in the day and can remember how inexpensive it all became in the late 1990s and 2000s, only to go back up in value again now. I wouldn't go so far as to call the ST expensive to collect for, but it gets costly quick if you're looking for complete-in-box games, or if you fancy a TT or Falcon. Even the 1040STE is pushing $300 to $400, at least in America, and working STs rarely go for less than $150 anymore.

To cite one example: While I was researching this book, within 24 hours of the listing appearing, someone on eBay clicked on Buy It Now for a $450 "complete system in boxes" that included the 520ST, an SM124, and an SF354, with $50 shipping. Never mind this collection would have gone for $150 20 years ago, because this is how supply and demand works. Nonetheless, I nearly pulled the trigger myself, but didn't see any photos of the machines themselves and hesitated—and then it was too late. Hopefully this worked out for the buyer, because if the pieces were in like-new condition as implied by the description, that would have been a solid buy these days.

Note that I'm quoting prices for eBay auctions. Some people are charging way more in fixed "Buy It Now" listings, of course, and you can safely ignore those listings. If you look at actual transaction prices ("Sold" transactions on eBay), you'll find more that are like what I was quoting above. But if you have the patience and prefer shopping in "real life," you could find much better deals haunting local garage and estate sales or local craigslist ads, especially when buying complete "lots" of equipment and software. Overseas options are also worth a look, as STs were more common in Europe and therefore often sell for considerably less even once you factor in the increased shipping cost to America. You'll also do much better if you're flexible with regard to what you end up with. For example, you may not want a copy of Dungeon Master that's missing the box, but if you have the chance to pick it up cheap, it's probably worth going for anyway.

What I've Bought Recently

As I've mentioned earlier, my 1980s system was a super-early 520ST, though we exchanged it relatively soon after for one with the ROM chips installed. I had an SF354 drive, an SF314 drive, and an SC1224 color monitor. I used the Epson FX-85 printer and a Hayes Smartmodem 1200 I already had from my Atari 800 and just moved them both over to the ST once I shut the 8-bit BBS down. Much later on, in the late 1990s, I picked up a 1040ST and a Mega 4 with a 20MB hard drive for cheap. I also had dozens of boxed games with manuals, although I had also sold some in Usenet newsgroups, including some adventure games I had solved but now wish I had held onto. I sold it all as I moved around a lot and lived in various cramped New York City apartments, and I'm sure I needed the money then for something or other.

This time around, in anticipation of writing this book, I knew I wanted to get at least one STE machine as well as an ST. I spent several months browsing eBay and looking at local ads before bidding on and winning a 1040ST and SC1224 "in the box" but "not tested," and a 1040STE upgraded with 4MB RAM and TOS 2.06. I purchased these systems from individual sellers. I also picked up a brand-new Atari ST mouse, a sealed copy of Starglider, and a 1040ST manual in the shrink-wrap from Best Electronics. I didn't even open the copy of Starglider; I just wanted it because it was the first game I remember owning on the ST complete-in-box. Finally, I knew I wanted some kind of flash storage, so after some initial research I decided on an UltraSatan from Lotharek's Lair.

The 1040ST ended up dead on arrival; it booted to a black screen. Nonetheless, because the machine looks fantastic, with zero yellowing and no visible wear, it became the cover model for this book. The 1040STE, meanwhile, has proven an able performer with the UltraSatan and a joy to use. I also bought an SM124 monitor to get the full "monochrome" experience with High resolution. Next up, after this book, will be Falcon and TT purchases as soon as I can afford them. I've got an old (well, 2006-era) 1,280-by-1,024-pixel NEC LCD1990SXi MultiSync flat-panel monitor ready to go for the higher resolution modes of those computers.

Retrobright

As I hinted at above, one of the biggest problems with owning or collecting vintage computer gear today is what happens to the cases over time. Thanks to sunlight exposure over a period of years, the plastic on some computer and peripheral cases can take on a distinct yellow tinge. The ST is subject to this phenomenon. Plenty of machines with little to no yellowing sometimes pop up on eBay or show up as "unicorn" finds at garage sales or in thrift shops. But for the most part, you'll be dealing with some yellowing with whatever vintage computer or game console gear you pick up. Often, there will be different degrees of yellowing between various peripherals, and sometimes the white keyboard keys yellow in a different fashion than the case does.

There *is* a way to deal with the problem, but it's a bit of a pain. Commonly called Retrobright (or, more properly, Retr0bright), it's a chemical formulation and step-by-step process you can apply to old hardware to remove the yellow effect and bring out the plastic's natural coloring. This process works on both ST enclosures and on keyboards and trim (which, you'll note, can sometimes differ a bit and offer a distinct "two-tone" yellow look for added fun). Some computer enthusiasts first developed the mixture in the late 2000s as a kind of open-source effort. Now there are numerous ways to approach the process, all of which are collectively called "Retrobright." Regardless of the details, it works on most vintage beige hardware, as well as the light gray you'll find on Atari ST and XE-era machines.

The basic idea is simple: Mix some hydrogen peroxide and the ingredient TAED (for Tetraacetylethylenediamine, with a common example being the heavily advertised Oxy active laundry booster) into a creamy paste. You apply an even coat of the paste to the yellowed plastic, and then find some source of ultraviolet light rays, usually from either direct sunlight or a UV lamp. Place the treated plastic under the light and let it sit for a day or so. Many enthusiasts whip up their own batch, though you can also get most of the way there with a hydrogen-peroxide-based hair bleach cream. Some claim the process weakens the plastic, and a few believe the procedure is just temporary and that the cases will yellow again. But most people who have had success with retrobrighting say they love the result, and some have reported their restored hardware still looks good even years later. And lately, some folks have reported seeing improvements from just putting their machines out the sun with no mixture applied.

Do you *need* to retrobright your machine if it has some yellowing? Absolutely not—this is purely an aesthetic decision, and as they say, beauty is in the eye of the beholder. There are also alternatives. For example, simply taking the machine apart and spray-painting the case to a nice, light gray could make it look brand new again even if there's a tiny difference in the shade used. (If you pick the color correctly, even a slightly different shade of light gray will still be much closer to original than a heavily yellowed model.) Painting an ST case black also works nicely; I've seen several now that I found stunning, and one enterprising modder even makes his own replacement laser-engraved ST badges, including versions with inverted lettering for black cases. Of course, the keys are somewhat trickier, because you can't just take the keyboard apart and spray the keycaps with white paint without losing the labels.

Repairs

As for repairs, these systems are quite old now and could, in fact, require some. Opening up a 520ST or a 1040ST is fairly straightforward, although it does take a lot of steps thanks to the different pieces of shielding inside. It's even easier to get inside one of the larger models like the Mega ST, Mega STE, or TT. The 1040STE is a little tricky, I've learned, because you have to take it out of the bottom half of the plastic enclosure before you can take off the rest of the shielding, which is not true for the 1040ST. Once you know that, it's also pretty easy. If you search the web you will find numerous threads for all of the possible ST models and how to get at the insides.

If your ST is still running with all of the original hardware intact, you may want to do a little preventative maintenance. The easiest thing to do is to open up the machine and reseat all of the socketed chips, such as for TOS, or possibly a blitter if your machine has it. Be sure to check each PLCC socket for oxidation, and if your machine has memory sticks, reseat those as well. Battery-backed clocks in the later STs are also huge source of trouble; you'll want to either replace the battery, or just remove it before it leaks and makes your life much more difficult.

Capacitors can also leak, and the beautiful power supply in an ST can eventually fail. Fortunately, replacement parts are available around the web. In fact, even if a given machine is running fine, sometimes enthusiasts recommend replacing the caps and the power supply before you run into problems in order to keep the ST running well into the future. While you're in there, if you have an STE model, you may want to check which DMA chip you have. The faulty chip reads C025913-38; if you have this, you'll want to swap it out, because it can lead to data loss with an UltraSatan or another method of SD flash storage (although there is some controversy over whether the DMA chip is implicated, the way it was with the initial batch of STE shipments in late 1989). If the chip is labeled C398739-001A, then it should be fine regardless.[1]

Keyboards and mice can also be sticking points—quite literally, and if you're having trouble with a certain key or button either registering presses or bouncing back from them, pressing them repeatedly a few dozen times in quick succession can loosen them up. Beyond that, it's possible to open up the various STs to get at the keyboard (either inside the 520ST or 1040ST-style enclosure, or in one of the removable versions like the Mega ST or the TT). The Mega ST keyboards lack tactile feedback, because they use very early Cherry MX Black switches and are designed that way.[2] The original ST has key-and-plunger-mechanism pairings, and replacements are available on eBay.

Which System Is Right for You?

If you're looking to pick up a new system now, it's tough to go wrong with any of the different ST models. Most of them will let you do most of what you want. Around the edges of use cases, there are some differences. Rest assured, even a less expensive 520ST with an external drive, or a 1040ST, would be a smart purchase. These machines will let you run the vast majority of software ever created for the platform.

Further up the pricing spectrum is the 1040STE, which remains highly desirable today for its additional abilities. Enthusiasts have finally upgraded some existing ST software to take advantage of the STE. Even so, most software still doesn't utilize the additional hardware. Some prefer Mega STs in general for their separate form factor and detachable keyboards; these, too, are more expensive than regular STs, but not absurdly so.

The rarer Mega STE is where the pricing hysteria begins to take hold, although three-digit pricing is still within reach at the time of this writing. Mega STEs are desirable today for their internal hard drives and switchable 8/16MHz processor and cache speeds. Then there are the TTs and Falcons, both of which regularly go for four-digit sums on eBay and are quite difficult to find. With their faster processors, higher-resolution graphics modes, and differing sets of capabilities, these two machines are the most desirable of all. (Don't be put off too much by potential incompatibilities with some models and some software; just about everything has been patched these days and is readily available.)

There's also the matter of software. Personally, I can't ignore the conveniences of modern SD-card-based storage. Hard-core complete-in-box collectors may disagree, but I can no longer afford to get back into that racket now; it's more for genuine collectors. Every time I search eBay, today me only gets even more upset with past me for letting go of all of my original Atari computers and software so cheaply 20 years ago. I suppose that describes a lot of us. Suffice to say that if you've held onto your original equipment and all the software, you've done the right thing!

One other note: The ST had several software calculators and related desk accessories available. But as many Atari fans know, the company also sold actual calculators in the mid 1980s, many of which matched the ST's styling and color scheme. They came in all varieties, including pocket-sized, handheld, solar, desk, and even desktop printing. This was only fitting, since calculators were a big part of Tramiel's business at Commodore before the era of desktop computers.

The Daily Driver Question

Invariably, ST fans may want to try using the computer for tasks you normally do on a PC or Mac. After all, it's much less of a stretch than, say, using an Atari 800 or Commodore 64 would be, given the ST platform's native 80-column display, mouse-based desktop interface, and support for hard drives and laser printers. This is especially true if you're using a modern SD card for storage and not vintage floppy disks, which are even slower than you remember, or a 30-year-old hard drive, which could well continue to work another 30 years, but we all know how subject to chance that is. And early drives were more prone to failure even when new. Flash storage, when combined with patched software that lacks copy protection and loads much faster than it did on a floppy, makes using an ST today downright pleasurable. At the top of the market, a TT or Falcon would make the best daily driver, since both work at screen resolutions beyond 640 by 400 in monochrome or 640 by 200 in color. The Falcon also excels at playing back digitally sampled music, and you can mod one with a much-faster 68060-class CPU and more memory.

So what could an Atari 16- or 32-bit computer do today? Basic word processing, number-crunching, document prep, and terminal emulation should all work the same way they did in the 1980s and early 1990s. Playing games is a given, and you could program new software and demos for the ST in any number of languages. For more contemporary tasks, such as digital music playback, viewing images, and browsing the web, you'll want to take a look at some newer software written after Atari ended ST production, like CAB, Newsie, and both MP3 and MOD music players. Texel is a newer spreadsheet that reads early Excel and Lotus 1-2-3 files and can import CSV files.

Music Recording and Demos

Finally, let's talk quickly about two major scenes for the Atari that are still going on. The first is music recording. As you can probably surmise, nothing is stopping anyone from using an ST as a studio computer today, as they're still as effective working with MIDI now as they were more than 30 years ago. If you want to run Cubase or Notator, you'll need the appropriate dongles, which are pretty hard to find these days. But if you don't have those, you can give sequencers like Master Tracks Pro, Breakthru, and Cubase Lite a whirl. Some of the algorithmic composition tools we discussed in chapter 8, like Presto, are still available today as well, often without modern analogs on the PC or Mac.

Certain things about the music recording process have changed considerably. For example, a small project studio 30 years ago would have contained an analog mixer for your synthesizers and various sound modules, which meant more cabling both for the audio outputs and also for the MIDI connections to the computer (or each other). On the ST, it would be nice to have the aforementioned editor-librarian software for the patches in addition to the sequencer. And on the mixing board, you likely had one or more outboard reverb units and at least one compressor you could patch in on an insert. You may still want some of this gear to go with your ST.

On the plus side, you could take advantage of later innovations, such as powered monitor speakers where you no longer need a separate amplifier. For digital audio recording you don't need ADAT or DA-88 machines—to say nothing of their expensive tapes—and you probably don't need a mixdown deck like DAT. In fact, some kind of hybrid is probably best, where you can compose or record music on the ST and then mix it more thoroughly in Pro Tools, Logic, or another modern digital audio workstation using as many software compressors, reverbs, equalizers, and limiters as you want. You can also add vocals, sampled loops, and other live instruments this way, instead of dealing with the extremely limited (by today's standards) memory in old Akai samplers. Finally, remember that an SD-based storage solution like an UltraSatan is completely silent, unlike hard drives from the 1980s and 1990s—perfect for a room that you need to keep as quiet as possible for whenever the Record button is pressed.

ST demoscene fans will be thrilled to know—or already know—that scene continues to live on as well. The ST remains a fun platform to program for, the same as it always was. To get an idea of the kinds of incredible coding feats ST programmers are still pulling off, along with fresh-sounding electronic tracks no one imagined in the early 1990s, check out new demos like "Big Apple" by fenarinarsa, done on an 8MHz 1040STE, and "Zero Three Zero" by Excellence in Art and The Pixel Twins, done on a Falcon 030. For more, AtariCrypt has a good section highlighting some of the best recent demos from Demozoo.

We do things with our computers today that are beyond anything possible in the early-to-mid 1990s. No matter what you do, you're not going to end up with a machine that supports cloud storage and the latest HTML5-based web services. Nor will you be able to store digital photos from your phone, spit out Microsoft Word DOCX and PDF files, or edit and produce high-definition videos. But if you're interested in connecting to text-based BBSes and Usenet, creating documents and spreadsheets, listening to music, controlling a MIDI-based recording studio, and doing some simple (if rather strained) web browsing, you'll be pleasantly surprised at what's possible with an ST today. People are still programming these machines and making music with them now. Not bad for a computer first introduced in the Reagan administration.

14 | Community

Perhaps the best thing about the Atari ST scene as it exists today is the genuine sense of community. There has always been one, though it used to be confined to Usenet groups, special interest groups (SIGs), and email lists. Today it spans web forums, Facebook groups, YouTube channels, podcasts—it's almost impossible to keep track of it all, which if you're an ST fan is an excellent problem to have. The ST has benefited from being one of the last products to go before Atari Corp. was liquidated in 1996. As a result, even some (very) early websites dedicated to the machine were built, some of which are still running in 2019 on who knows what servers—you'll pick these out right away for their cramped layouts, early tiled backgrounds, and the little animated GIF that proudly claims the site is best viewed in Netscape Navigator 2.0.

In short, there's a ton of info online from the later portion of the ST's heyday. Many newer websites also now exist that serve the ST community as destinations of knowledge, sometimes with regular new blog posts and plenty of embedded videos if you're so inclined. If you're looking for more information on any number of ST-related topics, far beyond what I could ever detail in a single book, check out the following sources.

Note: I'm going to keep this list Atari ST focused, if not in whole then at least in part. If I were to expand it to the greater vintage computing and retro gaming communities, where there may be occasional ST mentions but largely cross-platform focused, this chapter could end up being its own book! Nonetheless, it's worth noting many of them have sections and/or tags that filter all of the content, and that by clicking Atari or Atari ST, you can drill down and see the latest coverage that matters to you most.

Forums

Two forums stand out. Atari-Forum is the big one, with lots of subforums broken down by interest area. You'll find dedicated forums for Hatari, Steem, the Falcon, Menu Disks—the list goes on. It's mostly UK focused, though there's plenty here for ST fans stateside as well. AtariAge is the one most famous for its extensive and active 2600 and 8-bit computer forums, but it also has a good ST forum section that runs back many years and has been picking up significantly in popularity lately. This one is more US focused, but as with Atari-Forum.org, there's plenty of cross-pollination.

For the curious or the simply nostalgic, there's a tremendous Usenet archive, mostly centered around comp.sys.atari.st, which you can easily access these days via Google Groups. It's not active anymore, as is the case with most Usenet newsgroups that peaked in the 1990s and then fell by the wayside in favor of fragmented but much easier to access website-based forums that included support for inline images, hyperlinks, user profiles, direct messages, and more. Nonetheless, the old comp.sys.atari.st archive is a solid source of information and is worth digging through for tips and tricks you may not have thought of. Or, if you're like me, that you knew 25 years ago but eventually forgot about. It was where current ST owners talked all the time, back when the ST was still a current platform.

Websites

The venerable archive site Atarimania has a full catalog of ST software in its database, including snippets from magazines, some box and manual scans, and more. I used Atarimania often in helping me gather research for this book. I could spend hours just lost in it (and have, in fact, done this). There are mini-conversations happening on many of the individual product pages, done in a kind of Kilroy-was-here manner as people and even original developers have left comments for others to see years down the line. ST fan Marko Latvanen works hard behind the scenes to bring us the most updated information.

Atarimagazines.org is Kevin Savetz's venerable trove of scanned and OCR-ed Atari magazines that includes *STart and ST-Log,* plus all the earlier *Antic* and *ANALOG Computing issues* from early 1985 onward that carried ST-specific information. Without this site, I would have had to re-buy all my old *Antic* and *STart* issues, both of which I had subscribed to right until the end, and then buy the entire *ANALOG Computing* and *ST-Log* run just to see what I missed the first time around. Savetz's other side project, AtariArchives.org, hosts lots of research info from the old Cleveland Free-Net Atari SIG's 16/32-Bit Computers Support Area that Bruce Nelson maintained in the early 1990s. If you want to get a sharp picture of what it was like to read about the latest on the ST online back then, make this your first stop.

The Internet Archive team has done miraculous work in preserving computing history, among other things, and ST documentation, magazines, books, and brochures are no exception. At the time of this printing, there was no way to run ST programs in a browser on the Internet Archive, as there is for old Macs, the Atari 8-bit lineup, the Commodore 64, and more (and given what we talked about in the Emulation chapter, is it any wonder why?). But it's still packed with ST-specific resources.

Peter Putnik's Atari.8bitchip.info site is packed with modding information for the ST, including tweaks of his own design that I've already covered earlier, and he also has a full catalog of Atari ST hard drive games he has patched. The patches include the ability to install on a hard drive, plus broken copy protection, 4MB support, cheat codes, STE-specific enhancements, and other fun stuff. Bill Lange has a new site (theahlcollection.blogspot.com) dedicated to former *Creative Computing* founder David H. Ahl's extensive trove of files, many of which cover the ST and the Atari Corporation era in general.

One of many things AtariCrypt has, aside from an excellent blog about the ST, is a page dedicated specifically to Peter Putnik's patched STE-enhanced games that now take advantage of the blitter chip and improved digital sound located at ataricrypt.blogspot.com/2018/03/enhanced-games.html. Updated titles include Dungeon Master, Oids, Menace, Xenon II, and (thank heavens) Gauntlet, and range from improved frame rates and scrolling to digital sampled sound upgrades. Sometimes the updates are simple; a new Rogue patch for the STE lets you add your own background music.

Atari Legend (atarilegend.com) is another tremendous resource of ST content. It has ST news, sections on screenshots and key figures related to the ST, game reviews, interviews, and more. Hosted by Maarten Martens, it's also linked up with www.atarigamer.co.uk, where you can find copies of two issues of the indie *ST Gamer* magazine produced by Darren Doyle. Mark Grogan's The Code Show is a traveling museum dedicated to the preservation of 16-bit computers like the ST, the Amiga, and the Acorn Archimedes in the UK. Enthusiast James Mackenzie (jamesfmackenzie.com) has written several how-tos on creating a bootable Atari ST game disk and setting up an UltraSatan.

YouTube and Podcasts

You won't be surprised to learn, if you don't know it already, there's a tremendous community of enthusiasts out there creating videos and podcasts about the ST. Some worth checking out include those from Wasabim and the series *The Nostalgia Nerd* by Peter Leigh. While you're surfing YouTube, don't miss the old episodes of *The Computer Chronicles*, several of which featured the Atari ST in the 1985 through 1989 period. For podcasts, ST fans will want to check out *Into the Vertical Blank* and InverseATASCII's *16/32*.

Stores

Plenty of mods are available for the ST, as we saw earlier, and it turns out there are numerous go-to destinations for parts on the web. While eBay and craigslist remain the best places to find used and vintage ST hardware, software, and related products, sometimes you'll need a newer mod or one-off design that's difficult or impossible to find in the used market. That's where these stores come in; while I mentioned some of these earlier as places to buy specific products, I wanted to round them up in one place for easier shopping. Note: Some of them sell portions of their catalog on eBay either in tandem with the web store or just route all of the purchases through eBay. But combined with a PayPal account, you'll be able to buy just about anything from these stores, whether it's direct with a credit card or on eBay.

The two most venerable stores selling Atari ST products have been around for decades: Best Electronics (www.best-electronics-ca.com) and B&C ComputerVisions (www.myatari.com). Both have finally depleted most of their original Atari sealed stock, but they still have lots of OEM parts and shrink-wrapped software, not to mention mods like upgraded Atari joystick kits and improved Mylar layers for 8-bit keyboards.

Lotharek's Lair (lotharek.pl), run by the esteemed Przemyslaw Krawczyk, has all kinds of wonderful mods available for the ST, Atari 8-bit, and some other vintage platforms, as you may have already seen by the numerous times I've called out Lotharek in this book alone. I can personally vouch for the UltraSatan he sells, and he stands by his products as well. Jay's Retro Computer Sales (www.ataristsales.co.uk) is based in the UK and sells power supplies, keyboard parts, TOS upgrades, and other useful bits for the Atari ST, including packages of screws that I need to make a note of and go order when I'm done writing this paragraph. Wait, where was I?

The Exxos Store (www.exxoshost.co.uk/atari/last/storenew/) sells not just parts, but mods that you won't find anywhere else, including accelerators and speed boosters for various ST machines. The site also has a forum for tips and support. Retronic Design (www.retronicdesign.com) sells numerous adapters as well as a Gotek-style drive with an 8GB USB stick preconfigured with the software needed for the ST (among other platforms). Atarian Computing (www.atariancomputing.com) is based in Finland these days (formerly Canada). It has been buying, restoring, and selling 16- and 32-bit Atari computers for more than 20 years, and also has plenty of online resources, programming tips, and modding tips for the ST. Finally, Rhayader Computers (www.rhayadercomputers.co.uk) in Wales sells some nice mugs and mouse mats for the ST. Come on, you know you want at least one of each.

Even with everything covered in this chapter, I've only touched on what's available for the ST today. As you read this, enthusiasts are programming new games and new demos, crafting new hardware mods, rediscovering old computers and peripherals in closets, and digging up complete-in-box games for sale or trade on eBay. Just this past week while I was going over this chapter, I found several people who were working on new adventure games using STOS Adventure Creator. My friend Peter Fletcher was tweeting examples of generating output from DynaCADD running on a TT and then opening those ST files natively on a Mac using Lemke Software's GraphicConverter. (They looked amazing, and that Mac program also opens NEOchrome and Degas files.) I've seen recent threads where UK-based ST fans shared their memories over getting into the computer because of the Power Pack deals. At the time of this writing, IRATA.ONLINE operator Thomas Cherryhomes was developing an ST port of PLATOTerm to complement his 8-bit Atari version. Even Flappy Bird made it over to the ST.

There is so much out there, just as there is with the Atari 8-bit line, the Apple II, and just about every other well-loved computer from the 1970s, 1980s, and 1990s. If you pull off a cool ST mod, or just want to show off your setup, feel free to drop me a line: jamie@lendino.com.

15 | Forever

Right until the end, Atari had a tense and at times tortured relationship with gaming. Throughout the 1970s and 1980s, in both of Atari's incarnations, some executives there were thrilled at how the word Atari became synonymous with video games in the arcades and at home. Others at the company aspired to "more," and wanted to beat Apple, Commodore, and IBM in the personal and business computer markets (in both the 8- and 16-bit eras). This tension was never fully resolved. Ask a group of people today what they think of when they think of Atari *computers* and you'll get widely divergent answers. Most will still mention video games in some capacity, regardless of what Atari's various computer division incarnations wanted. A 1994 iteration of an Atari ST FAQ, clearly still wrestling with the question itself, stated:

> [T]he ST is known in many European countries as not only a great professional computer but also a great entertainment computer. When we hear the name 'Atari' in the United States, we think of games and even though that's not the entire story behind what the ST can do, like it or not, that sure is part of it…[Ask] around and you'll find out that there is most likely a game that you'll love playing on the ST.

For some, the ST was a music machine, plain and simple. The ST's influence on the music industry, especially in Europe but also in the United States, was enormous. A thriving demoscene, still active today in spots, paints the Atari as an early leader in graphics and programming tricks and marrying that to chip and tracker music. Gamers who had the ST loved its lineup, even if it was a little soft in spots in comparison with its 8-bit predecessor and to its 16-bit Amiga competition. And the ST saw discrete pockets of success in desktop publishing, in CAD, and in other vertical markets in Europe, thanks to its powerful processor and low cost of entry.

To its detriment, the platform had a split personality, thanks to the different experiences you got when sitting in front of a monochrome monitor and a color monitor. The medium-resolution color mode looked so strange and out of proportion. In desktop publishing, music production, and CAD, and for general business productivity, the monochrome monitors ruled. Games and demos were color only, full stop. Nearly all ST users were stuck with one monitor and didn't get the most out of the machine. With the TT and Falcon, you could get sharp, proportionate text *and* color graphics with a single monitor, but the ST platform was already in decline by then.

In the end, the ST remains an early and key platform in the history of the personal computer. It holds this status regardless of its limitations or the shortsightedness of various key executives, both before and after the Tramiel takeover of Atari. It was sad to see the ST go, but I'm happier than ever at the support it's seeing today in what is turning out to be ever-rising interest in "retro" computing. Today, thousands of people the world over trade stories, play old games, and use their now-"vintage" STs on a daily basis—including yours truly. It's a respite from the daily onslaught of the web and social media. And so much of the software still holds up. Power without the price indeed.

Acknowledgements

Plenty of people helped make this book possible. My tireless editor Matthew Murray, who once again helped me turn this book into something coherent. Dan Costa, for his continued support of my undying love for old computer hardware. Wendy Sheehan Donnell, for teaching me what good writing and editing really are. My parents, who bought me the Atari 520ST probably without a second thought the moment they learned it existed, given my thirst for knowing and playing all things Atari throughout my childhood. And of course, my wife Allison and daughter Siena, both of whom have been incredibly supportive of my, er, eccentric and introverted work habits.

In addition, I'd like to thank many members of the thriving Atari enthusiast community I've come to know either in person or online. They include Joe Decuir, Steve Fulton, Jeff Fulton, Josh Malone, Eric Nelson, Allan Bushman, Kevin Savetz, Curt Vendel, Benj Edwards, Darren Doyle, Peter Putnik, Gary Pinkett, Wasabim, Antoine Clerc-Renaud, Amiga Bill (I support the truce!), Lotharek, Wade Ripkowski, Marco A. Breddin, and Marko Latvanen. Special thanks to Bill Lange and Peter Fletcher, both of whom provided valuable insight and support for this book.

I'd also like to thank people I haven't met personally, but who helped infuse me with the enthusiasm and excitement I had growing up with this computer. They are Shiraz Shivji, Leonard Tramiel, Sam Tramiel, Richard Garriott, Eric Chahi, Jez San, Ron Gilbert, Doug Bell, Bill Dunlevy, Harry Lafnear, Winston Douglas Wood, and Michael Current. Finally, in memoriam, Atari ST designer Ira Velinsky, who died at the age of 46 in November 2000; Tim Conrardy, a beloved sound designer and ST enthusiast that passed away in 2009 at 51; Jack Tramiel, who died in 2012 at age 83; and veteran game programmer Steve Bak (of Goldrunner fame, plus much more beyond the ST), who passed away in February 2019 at the age of 66.

Bibliography

"A Brief History of Computer Music." MusicRadar.com, October 13, 2008. https://www.musicradar.com/news/tech/a-brief-history-of-computer-music-177299

Aaron, David. "Playing With Apocalypse." *The New York Times Magazine,* December 29, 1985, 22.

"About the Atari 16/32-Bit Computers (ST, STe, Mega, Mega STe, Falcon030, STacy, TT)." Atari SIG 16/32-Bit Computers Support Area transcript, maintained by Kevin Savetz. https://www.atariarchives.org/cfn/06/02.php

Anniss, Matt. "Instrumental Instruments: Atari ST." Red Bull Music Academy Daily, October 6, 2017. http://daily.redbullmusicacademy.com/2017/10/atari-st-instrumental-instruments

"Apple Said to Settle Suit," *The New York Times,* December 20, 1989, D7.

Armstrong, Elizabeth Metzger. "HyperCard 'Without the Hype.'" *STart,* Winter 1987, 63-64.

The Atari Book Second Edition: The Ultimate Collector's Guide to Atari. Bournemouth, U.K.: Imagine Publishing, 2015.

AtariAge Forum thread. "Is there a way to test in [sic] my DMA chip is defective in my STE?" http://atariage.com/forums/topic/264271-is-there-a-way-to-test-in-my-dma-chip-is-defective-in-my-ste/

AtariAge Forum thread. "Ultima III MIDI Magic." http://atariage.com/forums/topic/258022-ultima-iii-midi-magic/

Atari Forum thread. "How many TOS-clones [sic] were produced?" http://www.atari-forum.com/viewtopic.php?t=9238

AtariCrypt. "Megaroids." https://ataricrypt.blogspot.com/2016/02/1985.html

"Atari Jaguar Revived as Dental Camera." 1UP.com, February 2004, retrieved via Wayback Machine: https://web.ar-chive.org/web/20150430093923/http://www.1up.com/news/atari-jaguar-revived-dental-camera

"Atari TT030." Centre for Computing History. http://www.compu-tinghistory.org.uk/det/33710/Atari-TT030/

Bagnall, Brian. *Commodore: The Amiga Years.* Winnipeg, Manitoba: Variant Press, 2018.

Bagnall, Brian. *On the Edge: The Spectacular Rise and Fall of Commodore.* Winnipeg, Manitoba: Variant Press, 2005.

Battles, Hosea. "Terrorism in the 22nd Century." *Computer Gaming World*, October 1988, 22-23.

Bell, Jon A., and Bass, Patrick. "The Mega 4." *STart,* Winter 1987, 31.

Bishop, David. "Gauntlet," *Computer & Video* Games, August 1987, 101.

Bisson, Gigi. "The 1986 ST Buyer's Guide." *STart,* Winter 1986, 53.

Bisson, Gigi. "C.O.L.R. Object Editor." *Antic,* November 1985, 20.

Bisson, Giselle. "Getting Down to Business." *STart* Special Issue #3, Business Issue, 1988, 42.

"CGW Salutes the Games of the Year." *Computer Gaming World,* November 1992, 110.

Chabris, Christopher. "Atari's First-Rate Freeware." *Antic,* June 1986, 83.

Chabris, Christopher. "ChessBase: A Centuries-Old Pastime Comes of Age." *STart,* Special Issue #4, Games & Entertainment Issue, 1988, 35-37.

Chin, Kathy. "Bold Plans for 'New' Atari." *InfoWorld,* December 10, 1984, 16

Chira, Susan. "Amiga's High Tech Gamble." *The New York Times,* August 29, 1984.

Cohen, Frank. "GFA BASIC Training Reboot Camp." *ST-Log,* March 1989, 78.

The Computer Chronicles, "Commodore Amiga and Atari ST" (as titled on YouTube), December 1985 (the exact air date is unknown). Guests: Rick Geiger, Commodore; Tim Mott, Electronic Arts; Bryan Kerr, Atari; Jim Tittsler, Atari; Lewis Moore, Home Computing; George Morrow, Morrow Computing; Gary Kildall, Digital Research; Tim Bajarin, Creative Strategies. https://www.youtube.com/watch?v=uVAf4x_tuRY

The Computer Chronicles, "Atari ST" (as titled on YouTube), April 25, 1989. Special episode focusing on the Atari ST. Guests: Jim Kent, Author; Vincent de Phillippo, Winners; Andrew Reese, START Magazine; Nathan Potechin, ISD Mktg Inc; Eric Peterson, Cogswell College; Gary Kildall, DRI. https://www.youtube.com/watch?v=wgG7cQCAprs

"Computer Ports of Ultima II." Ultima Codex Wiki. http://wiki.ultimacodex.com/wiki/Computer_Ports_of_Ultima_II

Current, Michael. "A History of Tramiel Technology." https://mcurrent.name/atarihistory/tramel_technology.html

Daniels, Jeffrey. "Three Years With the ST." *STart,* Summer 1988, 22-28.

Doudoroff, Martin. "The Antic Cyber Graphics Software and the Pre-history of Autodesk 3D Studio and Discreet 3ds max." http://doudoroff.com/atari/history3.html

Doudoroff, Martin. "Cyber Paint." http://doudoroff.com/atari/cyber-paint.html

Doyle, Tom. "Classic Tracks: Fatboy Slim 'Praise You.'" *Sound on Sound,* January 2017, https://www.soundonsound.com/techniques/classic-tracks-fatboy-slim-praise-you

Dyer, Landon. "How the Atari ST almost had Real Unix." Dadhacker.com, January 17, 2011, http://www.dadhacker.com/blog/?p=1383

"Eagle – The Atari clone is up and running." *ST Computer,* December 1994, via Google Translate: http://www.stcarchiv.de/stc1994/12_eagle.php

Eddy, Andy. "Spectrum 512." *ST-Log,* August 1988, 96.

Edwards, Benj. "7 Forgotten Atari ST Gaming Classics." *PCMag.com.* https://www.pcmag.com/feature/355111/7-forgotten-atari-st-gaming-classics/1

Englisch, Lothar and Walkowiak, Joerg. *Presenting the Atari ST, Revised Edition.* Abacus Software. Grand Rapids, MI: Abacus Software, 1986.

Erickson, Jonathan. "The Real Deal." *Dr. Dobb's,* December 1, 1997. http://www.drdobbs.com/the-real-deal/184410352

Farquhar, David L. "Why Jack Tramiel Left Commodore." *The Silicon Underground.* https://dfarq.homeip.net/why-jack-tramiel-left-commodore/

Fasoldt, Al. "Who killed the Atari ST? A drama in three parts." The *Syracuse Post-Standard*, 1989. http://www.technofileonline.com/texts/stdoom89.html

"First Annual Antic ST Shoppers Guide." *Antic*, December 1985, 46.

Fleischman, Mike. "Megamax C." *Antic,* September 1986, 68.

Forbes, Jim. "Business Software Slated for Atari ST." *InfoWorld,* December 9, 1985, 19.

Friedel, Frederic. "Garry Kasparov on how it all started." *ChessBase Chess News*, December 24, 2017. https://en.chessbase.com/post/garry-kasparov-on-how-it-all-started

Garriott, Richard and Addams, Shay. *The Official Book of Ultima: Second Edition.* Greensboro, North Carolina: Compute Publications International, 1992.

Giovetti, Alfred C. "Gods." *Compute!,* December 1992, 104.

Goldberg, Marty, and Vendel, Curt. *Atari Inc. Business Is Fun.* Carmel, NY: Syzygy Company Press, 2012.

Hastings, Tony. "Thinking of Going 24-Track?" *Sound on Sound,* July 1986, 42-43.

Higham, Mark. "Midwinter." *ST Format,* April 1990, 45.

Holfhill, Tom R. "The Next Generation: New Computers at the Winter Consumer Electronics Show." *Compute!,* April 1985, 25.

Klaus, Gerits, Englisch, Lothar, and Bruckmann, Rolf. *Atari ST Internals, Third Edition.* Grand Rapids, MI: Abacus Software, 1988.

Leavens, Alex. "The New TOS ROMs." *STart,* Winter 1987, 31.

Leigh, Peter. "Atari Falcon 030." The Nostalgia Nerd. October 16, 2018. https://www.youtube.com/watch?v=cBTXGgb__y4

Leyenberger, Arthur. "Atari Gift Guide!" *ANALOG Computing,* November 1989, 74.

Mace, Scott. "AtariWriter Subs for GEM." *InfoWorld,* Sept. 23, 1985, 17.

Mackenzie, James. "Use Your PC to Create a Bootable Atari ST Game Disk." James Mackenzie's personal blog, September 22, 2015. https://www.jamesfmackenzie.com/2015/09/22/use-your-pc-to-create-a-bootable-atari-st-game-disk/

Mallinson, Paul. "Ultima Ascension." *PC Zone,* September 1999, 40.

Maremaa, Tom. "Atari Ships New 520 ST." *InfoWorld,* June 3, 1985, 23.

McCracken, Harry. "Amiga, Warhol, Debbie Harry: The ultimate 1980s tech keynote." *Fast Company,* July 20, 2018. https://www.fastcompany.com/90206266/amiga-warhol-debbie-harry-the-ultimate-1980s-tech-keynote

McGeever, Christine. "Atari Predicts ST Success Next Year." *InfoWorld,* October 28, 1985, 8.

Meenakshisundaram, Ram. "Transputer Home Page." http://www.classiccmp.org/transputer/rtu_atw800.htm

Merciez, Gil. "VIP Professional." *Antic,* May 1986, 59.

MMXI and Crooked Bee. "RPG Codex Retrospective Interview: Winston Douglas Wood on Phantasie and Star Command," RPG Codex, February 15, 2013. https://rpgcodex.net/content.php?id=8786

Miller, George. "For the Fun of It." *STart,* May 1989, 91-92.

Milmeister, Gérard. *The Rubato Composer Music Software: Component-Based Implementation of a Functorial Concept Architecture.* Berlin/Heidelberg, Germany: Springer, 2009, 71.

Mitchell, Peter W. "CES: The Shakeout Continues." *The Boston Phoenix: Home Electronics Supplement,* February 19, 1985, 30.

Miner, Jay. "The AUI Interview: Jay Miner, The Father of the Amiga." *Amiga User International,* June 1988, 20.

Mosher, Gene. "In the Beginning: Graphic Touchscreen Point of Sale." ViewTouch website, August 1, 2016. https://www.viewtouch.com/birthplace.html

Naman, Mard. "Rock 'n' Roll With Your Atari." STart Special Issue #2, Music and Graphics Issue, 1988, 68-73.

Needle, David. "From the News Desk." *InfoWorld,* July 13, 1984, 9.

Nelson, Bruce D. "Gemulator II/emulator/commercial." The Cleveland Free-Net Atari SIG Historical Archive, June 1, 1993. https://www.atarimax.com/freenet/freenet_material/6.16and32-BitComputersSupportArea/6.ProductSummaries/showarticle.php?22

Nicholson, Ron. "Thread: Elite – Amiga Version – Detail questions." Frontier forum post, https://forums.frontier.co.uk/showthread.php?t=3220&page=10&p=121682&viewfull=1#post121682

The Night Owl. "Checking out the Atari ST's Power Pack." The Late Night Session. https://thelatenightsession.com/2017/06/21/checking-out-the-atari-sts-power-pack/

Nohaj, Miroslav. "STE Problems." Jookie's Home Page. http://joo.kie.sk/?page_id=250

Noonan, Bruce D. "ST Writer Secrets." *STart,* Winter 1986, 86-88.

Oren, Tim. "Professional GEM Column #15: Coping With GEMDOS." Antic Publishing, 1986. http://cd.textfiles.com/crawlycrypt1/program/books/progem/gemdos.15

Palmer, Scott D. "Flat-File Database Programs." *InfoWorld,* November 23, 1987, 46.

Park, Xanth. "FujiBoink! Behind the Bit Planes." *STart*, Fall 1986, 110.

Peers, Nick. "Battle of the Birds." *ST Format*, March 1995, 11.

Personal Computer Museum, Brantford, Ontario, Canada. PS-3000 entry. https://pcmuseum.ca/details.asp?id=32

Plotkin, David. "E Is for Enhanced." *STart,* December 1990, 22-28.

Plotkin, David. "Getting Around ST BASIC." *STart,* Winter 1986, 133-136.

Plotkin, David. "GFA BASIC 3.0." *STart,* January 1989, 35.

Plotkin, David. "Plutos, Airball, Barbarian, and Sub Battle Simulator." *STart,* Winter 1987, 87.

Putnik, Peter. "Atari Mega STE ASCI port, internal SCSI adapter." http://www.atari.8bitchip.info/MegaSTEACSI.html

Putnik, Peter. "Modification of Atari Mega STE's internal ASCI-SCSI adapter." http://atari.8bitchip.info/modmste1.html

Reggie C. "From the Pages of the Past, Games of Yesteryear – Phantasie II," World 1-1, May 27, 2013. extralives.wordpress.com/2013/05/27/from-the-pages-of-the-past-games-of-yesteryear-phantasie-ii/

Reese, Andrew. "The Future of Atari Computing." *STart,* December 1989, 17.

Reunanen, Markku. "How Those Crackers Became Us Demosceners." Widerscreen, April 15, 2014. http://widerscreen.fi/numerot/2014-1-2/crackers-became-us-demosceners/

Robby "The C= Guy." "Commodore Legends: Dave Haynie." http://www.mos6502.com/commodore-legends/commodore-legends-dave-haynie-%E2%80%93-part-i/

Root, Howard. "Three Hard Disk Drives." *STart*, Fall 1987, 78.

Sagez, Frédéric. "Atari ST – History of the OS." September 13, 2018. https://www.slideshare.net/fredericsagez/atari-st-history-of-the-os

Schrage, Michael. "Atari's 'Jackintosh' Enters Fray." *The Washington Post,* January 8, 1985.

Schrage, Michael. "Big Price Cut Is Expected From Atari." *The Washington Post,* November 13, 1984.

Scorpia. "Computer Role-Playing Game Survey." *Computer Gaming World,* October 1991, 109.

Small, David, and Wheeler, Doug. "The SyQuest Revolution." *STart,* March 1990, 86.

Small, David. "TTeriffic!" *STart*, February 1991, 22.

The Tag Team. "Space Quest IV – Interview with the Two Guys from Andromeda," *The Adventure Gamer,* June 15, 2015. https://advgamer.blogspot.com/2015/06/space-quest-iv-interview-with-two-guys.html

Tim's Atari Midi World. "Presto." http://www.atari-music.fddvoron.name/presto.htm

Turner, Danny. "Gary Numan's Career in Gear." MusicRadar.com, September 25, 2017. https://www.musicradar.com/news/gary-numans-career-in-gear

Vendel, Curt. Atari Museum entry on the EST. http://www.atarimuseum.com/computers/16bits/est.html

Vendel, Curt. Atari Museum entry on Sierra. http://www.atari-museum.com/computers/16bits/stmenu/historicalfiles/hf-sierra.htm

Vendel, Curt. Atari Museum entry on Mickey. http://www.atarimuseum.com/articles/mickey.html

Vendel, Curt. Atari Museum entry on the STBook. http://www.atari-museum.com/computers/16bits/stbook.html

Vendel, Curt. Atari Museum entry on the STPad. http://www.atari-museum.com/computers/16bits/stpad.html

Wasabim. "Lethal Xcess: Wings of Death II – Atari STE (1991) playthrough." https://www.youtube.com/watch?v=1Vk2_MzMDOE

Waugh, Ian. "Dr. T's Tunesmith." *Music Technology*, January 1989, 88-90.

Waugh, Ian. "Intelligent Music M." *Music Technology,* March 1988, 88.

Willox, Mike. "Vintage: Atari 520ST/" *MusicTech,* May 29, 2014. https://www.musictech.net/2014/05/atari-520st/

Wilson, Johnny L. "What Do the 'Sim'ple Folk Do?" *Computer Gaming World,* May 1989, 16.

Yoshihara, Nancy. "Atari to Acquire Federated Group for $67.3 Million: Deal Would Give Video Pioneer Access to a Retail Network." *Los Angeles Times*, August 24, 1987. http://articles.latimes.com/1987-08-24/business/fi-2005_1_atari

Notes

Introduction

1 https://www.musicradar.com/news/tech/a-brief-history-of-computer-music-177299

Chapter 1

[1] http://www.atarimuseum.com/computers/16bits/stmenu/historicalfiles/hf-sierra.htm

[2] Brian Bagnall, *Commodore: The Amiga Years* (Winnipeg, Manitoba: Variant Press, 2017), 45.

[3] Ibid.

[4] "The AUI Interview: Jay Miner, The Father of the Amiga," *Amiga User International*, June 1988, 20.

[5] http://www.atarimuseum.com/articles/mickey.html

[6] *The Atari Book Second Edition: The Ultimate Collector's Guide to Atari* (Bournemouth, U.K.: Imagine Publishing, 2015), 44.

[7] *The Atari Book*, 44.

[8] Marty Goldberg and Curt Vendel, *Atari Inc. Business is Fun* (Carmel, NY: Syzygy Company Press, 2012), 743.

[9] David Needle, "From the News Desk," *InfoWorld*, July 13, 1984, 9.

[10] Jeffrey Daniels, "Three Years With the ST," *STart*, Summer 1988, 23.

[11] Goldberg and Vendel, 742.

[12] Bagnall, 170.

[13] Kathy Chin, "Bold Plans for 'New' Atari," *InfoWorld*, December 10, 1984, 16

[14] https://mcurrent.name/atarihistory/tramel_technology.html

[15] Bagnall, 160-161.

16 Bagnall, 161.

17 Brian Bagnall, *On the Edge: The Spectacular Rise and Fall of Commodore* (Winnipeg, Manitoba: Variant Press, 2005), 425.

18 https://dfarq.homeip.net/why-jack-tramiel-left-commodore/

19 Susan Chira, "Amiga's High Tech Gamble," *The New York Times,* August 29, 1984.

20 http://www.mos6502.com/commodore-legends/commodore-legends-dave-haynie-%e2%80%93-part-i/

21 *The Atari Book,* 47.

22 Jeffrey Daniels, "Three Years With the ST," *STart,* Summer 1988, 24.

23 Ibid.

24 Klaus Gerits, Lothar Englisch, and Rolf Bruckmann, *Atari ST Internals,* Third Edition Grand Rapids, MI: Abacus Software, 1988), 3.

25 Gerits, Englisch, and Bruckmann, 48.

26 *The Atari Book,* 46.

27 Gerits, Englisch, and Bruckmann, 13.

28 Gerits, Englisch, and Bruckmann, 15.

29 Jon A. Bell and Patrick Bass, "The Mega 4," *STart,* Winter 1987, 31.

30 Gerits, Englisch, and Bruckmann, 20.

31 Gerits, Englisch, and Bruckmann, 28.

32 Gerits, Englisch, and Bruckmann, 41.

33 Kathy Chin, "Bold Plans for 'New' Atari," *InfoWorld,* December 10, 1984, 15.

34 Jeffrey Daniels, "Three Years With the ST," *STart,* Summer 1988, 23-24.

35 Ibid.

36 Ibid.

37 http://cd.textfiles.com/crawlycrypt1/program/books/progem/gemdos.15

38 Jeffrey Daniels, "Three Years With the ST," *STart,* Summer 1988, 24.

39 Michael Schrage, "Big Price Cut Is Expected From Atari," *The Washington Post,* November 13, 1984.

40 Ibid.

41 Kathy Chin, "Bold Plans for 'New' Atari," *InfoWorld,* December 10, 1984, 15.

42 https://mcurrent.name/atarihistory/tramel_technology.html. Verified via several photos Atari historian Curt Vendel uploaded to AtariAge.

43 Michael Schrage, "Atari's 'Jackintosh' Enters Fray," *The Washington Post,* January 8, 1985.

44 Jeffrey Daniels, "Three Years With the ST," *STart,* Summer 1988, 24.

45 Michael Schrage, "Atari's 'Jackintosh' Enters Fray," *The Washington Post,* January 8, 1985.

46 Ibid.

47 Peter W. Mitchell, "CES: The Shakeout Continues," *The Boston Phoenix: Home Electronics Supplement,* February 19, 1985, 30.

48 Jeffrey Daniels, "Three Years With the ST," *STart,* Summer 1988, 24.

49 https://mcurrent.name/atarihistory/tramel_technology.html

50 Ibid.

51 Ibid.

52 Tom R. Holfhill, "The Next Generation: New Computers at the Winter Consumer Electronics Show," *Compute!,* April 1985, 25.

53 Jeffrey Daniels, "Three Years With the ST," *STart,* Summer 1988, 25.

54 https://mcurrent.name/atarihistory/tramel_technology.html

55 Jeffrey Daniels, "Three Years With the ST," *STart,* Summer 1988, ??.

56 Tom Maremaa, "Atari Ships New 520 ST," *InfoWorld,* June 3, 1985, 23.

57 Ibid.

58 *The New York Times,* "Atari Is Shipping 520 ST Computer," July 10, 1985, D5.

59 You can see a recording of the show on YouTube: "Amiga vs Atari ST - Computer Chronicles 1985," https://www.youtube.com/watch?v=FoNmsL74T7Y

60 Michael Schrage, "Personal Computers," *The Washington Post,* January 13. 1986.

61 *The Atari Book,* 47.

62 *The Atari Book,* 44.

Chapter 2

1 Mike Fleischman, "Megamax C," *Antic,* September 1986, 68.

2 Lothar Englisch and Joerg Walkowiak, *Presenting the Atari ST,* Revised Edition (Grand Rapids, MI: Abacus Software, 1986), 59.

3 Englisch and Walkowiak, 60.

4 Englisch and Walkowiak, 79.

5 David Plotkin, "Getting Around ST BASIC," *STart,* Winter 1986, 133-136.

6 Scott Mace, "AtariWriter Subs for GEM," *InfoWorld,* Sept. 23, 1985.

7 Bruce D. Noonan, "ST Writer Secrets," *STart,* Winter 1986, 86.

8 Christopher Chabris, "Atari's First-Rate Freeware," *Antic,* June 1986, 83.

9 Bruce D. Noonan, "ST Writer Secrets," *STart,* Winter 1986, 88.

10 Englisch and Walkowiak, 50.

11 https://ataricrypt.blogspot.com/2016/02/1985.html

12 Martin Doudoroff, "The Antic Cyber Graphics Software and the Pre-history of Autodesk 3D Studio and Discreet 3ds max," http://doudoroff.com/atari/history3.html

13 Harry McCracken, "Amiga, Warhol, Debbie Harry: The ultimate 1980s tech keynote," *Fast Company,* July 20, 2018. https://www.fastcompany.com/90206266/amiga-warhol-debbie-harry-the-ultimate-1980s-tech-keynote

14 Gigi Bisson, "C.O.L.R. Object Editor," *Antic,* November 1985, 20.

15 Bisson, *Antic,* November 1985, 21.

16 http://wiki.ultimacodex.com/wiki/Computer_Ports_of_Ultima_II

17 Richard "Lord British" Garriott and Shay Addams, *The Official Book of Ultima: Second Edition* (Greensboro, North Carolina: Compute Publications International, 1992), 25.

18 Paul Mallinson, "Ultima Ascension," *PC Zone,* September 1999, 40.

19 Benj Edwards, "7 Forgotten Atari ST Gaming Classics," *PCMag,* https://www.pcmag.com/feature/355111/7-forgotten-atari-st-gaming-classics/1

20 Gigi Bisson, "The 1986 ST Buyer's Guide," *STart,* Winter 1986, 53.

21 "First Annual Antic ST Shoppers Guide," *Antic,* December 1985, 46.

22 Jim Forbes, "Business Software Slated for Atari ST," *InfoWorld,* December 9, 1985, 19.

23 Christine McGeever, "Atari Predicts ST Success Next Year," *InfoWorld,* October 28, 1985, 8.

Chapter 3

1 *STart,* "The 1986 ST Buyer's Guide," Winter 1986, 53.

2 https://mcurrent.name/atarihistory/tramel_technology.html

3 Howard Root, "Three Hard Disk Drives," *STart,* Fall 1987, 78.

4 Gil Merciez, "VIP Professional," *Antic,* May 1986, 59.

5 David Plotkin, "GFA BASIC 3.0," *STart,* January 1989, 35.

6 Frank Cohen, "GFA BASIC Training Reboot Camp," *ST-Log,* March 1989, 78.

7 Xanth Park, "FujiBoink! Behind the Bit Planes," *STart,* Fall 1986, 110.

8 Tony Hastings, "Thinking of Going 24-Track?" *Sound on Sound,* July 1986, 42-43.

9 https://pcmuseum.ca/details.asp?id=32

10 Danny Turner, "Gary Numan's Career in Gear," MusicRadar.com, September 25, 2017. https://www.musicradar.com/news/gary-numans-career-in-gear

11 Mard Naman, "Rock 'n' Roll With Your Atari," *STart* Special Issue #2, Music and Graphics Issue, 1988, 68-73.

12 Ibid.

Chapter 4

1 David Bishop, "Gauntlet," *Computer & Video* Games, August 1987, 101.

2 https://advgamer.blogspot.com/2015/06/space-quest-iv-interview-with-two-guys.html

3 https://rpgcodex.net/content.php?id=8786

4 https://extralives.wordpress.com/2013/05/27/from-the-pages-of-the-past-games-of-yesteryear-phantasie-ii/

5 Scorpia, "Computer Role-Playing Game Survey," *Computer Gaming World,* October 1991, 109.

6 Jeffrey Daniels, "Three Years With the ST," *STart,* Summer 1988, 25.

7 Ibid.

Chapter 5

1 Alex Leavens, "The New TOS ROMs," *STart,* Winter 1987, 31.

2 Martin Doudoroff, "Cyber Paint," http://doudoroff.com/atari/cyber-paint.html

3 Andy Eddy, "Spectrum 512," *ST-Log,* August 1988, 96.

4 Ibid.

5 https://www.viewtouch.com/birthplace.html

[6] Giselle Bisson, "Getting Down to Business," *STart* Special Issue #3, Business Issue, 1988, 42.

[7] https://github.com/ViewTouch/viewtouch

[8] Jonathan Erickson, "The Real Deal," *Dr. Dobb's,* December 1, 1997. http://www.drdobbs.com/the-real-deal/184410352

[9] Scott D. Palmer, "Flat-File Database Programs," *InfoWorld,* November 23, 1987, 46.

[10] "Apple Said to Settle Suit," *The New York Times,* December 20, 1989, D7.

[11] Elizabeth Metzger Armstrong, "HyperCard 'Without the Hype,'" *STart,* Winter 1987, 63-64.

[12] Christopher Chabris, "ChessBase: A Centuries-Old Pastime Comes of Age," *STart,* Special Issue #4, Games & Entertainment Issue, 1988, 35-37.

[13] https://en.chessbase.com/post/garry-kasparov-on-how-it-all-started

[14] Ibid.

[15] Ibid.

[16] Ibid.

[17] David Aaron, "Playing With Apocalypse," *The New York Times Magazine,* December 29, 1985, 22.

[18] David Plotkin, "Plutos, Airball, Barbarian, and Sub Battle Simulator," *STart,* Winter 1987, 87.

Chapter 6

[1] David Bishop, "Gauntlet," *Computer & Video* Games, August 1987, 100.

[2] Ibid.

[3] Nancy Yoshihara, "Atari to Acquire Federated Group for $67.3 Million: Deal Would Give Video Pioneer Access to a Retail Network," *Los Angeles Times,* August 24, 1987. http://articles.latimes.com/1987-08-24/business/fi-2005_1_atari

[4] Ibid.

[5] Ibid.

Chapter 7

[1] Ian Waugh, "Dr. T's Tunesmith," *Music Technology,* January 1989, 88-90.

[2] Gérard Milmeister, *The Rubato Composer Music Software: Component-Based Implementation of a Functorial Concept Architecture* (Berlin/Heidelberg, Germany: Springer, 2009), 71

[3] http://www.atari-music.fddvoron.name/presto.htm

[4] Ian Waugh, "Intelligent Music M," *Music Technology,* March 1988, 88.

[5] An excellent AtariAge thread has plenty of MT-32-related details: http://atariage.com/forums/topic/258022-ultima-iii-midi-magic/

[6] *The Computer Chronicles,* April 25, 1989. https://www.youtube.com/watch?v=wgG7cQCAprs

[7] http://doudoroff.com/atari/cad3d.html

[8] Ibid.

[9] Arthur Leyenberger, "Atari Gift Guide!" *A.N.A.L.O.G. Computing,* November 1989, 74.

[10] Email exchange with Christophe Andréani, February 21, 2019.

[11] George Miller, "For the Fun of It," *STart,* May 1989, 91-92.

[12] "3-D Mantattack," *The Games Machine,* June 1988, 39-41.

[13] Hosea Battles, "Terrorism in the 22nd Century," *Computer Gaming World,* October 1988, 22-23.

[14] https://forums.frontier.co.uk/threads/elite-amiga-version-detail-questions.3220/page-7

[15] Jeffrey Daniels, "Three Years With the ST," *STart,* Summer 1988, 25.

[16] Ibid.

[17] Ibid.

[18] Ibid.

Chapter 8

[1] https://www.atariarchives.org/cfn/06/02.php

[2] https://mcurrent.name/atarihistory/tramel_technology.html

[3] https://demozoo.org/platforms/9/

[4] David Plotkin, "E Is for Enhanced," *STart,* December 1990, 28.

[5] http://atariage.com/forums/topic/264271-is-there-a-way-to-test-in-my-dma-chip-is-defective-in-my-ste/

[6] Andrew Reese, "The Future of Atari Computing," *STart,* December 1989, 17.

[7] https://mcurrent.name/atarihistory/tramel_technology.html

[8] David Small and Doug Wheeler, "The SyQuest Revolution," *STart,* March 1990, 86.

[9] http://www.classiccmp.org/transputer/rtu_atw800.htm

[10] https://thelatenightsession.com/2017/06/21/checking-out-the-atari-sts-power-pack/

[11] Mark Higham, "Midwinter," *ST Format,* April 1990, 45.

Chapter 9

[1] http://www.atarimuseum.com/computers/16bits/est.html

[2] Jeffrey Daniels, "Three Years With the ST," *STart,* Summer 1988, 28.

[3] Landon Dyer, "How the Atari ST almost had Real Unix," Dadhacker.com, January 17, 2011, http://www.dadhacker.com/blog/?p=1383

[4] Dave Small, "TTeriffic!" *STart,* February 1991, 22.

[5] http://www.computinghistory.org.uk/det/33710/Atari-TT030/

[6] Geoff Keighley, "Simply Divine: The Story of Maxis Software," GameSpot, January 10, 2010.

[7] Johnny L. Wilson, "What Do the 'Sim'ple Folk Do?" *Computer Gaming World,* May 1989, 16.

[8] Ibid.

[9] https://mcurrent.name/atarihistory/tramel_technology.html

[10] http://www.atarimuseum.com/computers/16bits/stbook.html

[11] Ibid.

12 http://www.atarimuseum.com/computers/16bits/stpad.html

13 Alfred C. Giovetti, "Gods," *Compute!,* December 1992, 104.

14 Ibid.

15 "CGW Salutes the Games of the Year," *Computer Gaming World,* November 1992, 110.

16 Wasabim, https://www.youtube.com/watch?v=1Vk2_MzMDOE

Chapter 10

1 http://www.atari-fo-rum.com/viewtopic.php?f=27&t=31106&sid=9c5a04e6992a810429fb066af475aba3

2 http://www.old-computers.com/museum/computer.asp?c=635&st=1

3 Peter Leigh, "Atari Falcon 030," The Nostalgia Nerd, October 16, 2018, https://www.youtube.com/watch?v=cBTXGgb__y4

4 Ibid.

5 https://www.atariarchives.org/cfn/06/02.php

6 Peter Leigh, "Atari Falcon 030," The Nostalgia Nerd, October 16, 2018, https://www.youtube.com/watch?v=cBTXGgb__y4

7 Ibid.

8 http://widerscreen.fi/numerot/2014-1-2/crackers-became-us-demosceners/

9 Matt Anniss, "Instrumental Instruments: Atari ST," *Red Bull Academy Music Daily*, October 6, 2017. http://daily.redbullmusicacademy.com/2017/10/atari-st-instrumental-instruments

10 Ibid.

11 Mike Willox, "Vintage: Atari 520ST," *MusicTech,* May 29, 2014. https://www.musictech.net/2014/05/atari-520st/

12 Matt Anniss, "Instrumental Instruments: Atari ST," *Red Bull Academy Music Daily*, October 6, 2017. http://daily.redbullmusicacademy.com/2017/10/atari-st-instrumental-instruments

13 Tom Doyle, "Classic Tracks: Fatboy Slim 'Praise You,'" *Sound on Sound,* January 2017, https://www.soundonsound.com/techniques/classic-tracks-fatboy-slim-praise-you

14 Matt Anniss, "Instrumental Instruments: Atari ST," *Red Bull Academy Music Daily*, October 6, 2017. http://daily.redbullmusicacademy.com/2017/10/atari-st-instrumental-instruments

15 http://www.atari-forum.com/viewtopic.php?t=9238

16 Ibid.

17 Nick Peers, "Battle of the Birds," *ST Format,* March 1995, 11.

18 *ST Computer,* December 1994, via Google Translate: http://www.stcarchiv.de/stc1994/12_eagle.php

19 http://www.atari-forum.com/viewtopic.php?t=27775

20 https://web.archive.org/web/20150430093923/http://www.1up.com/news/atari jaguar-revived-dental-camera

21 *The Atari Book,* 47.

²² Al Fasoldt, "Who killed the Atari ST? A drama in three parts," The *Syracuse Post-Standard*, 1989, via http://www.technofileonline.com/texts/stdoom89.html
²³ Ibid.

Chapter 11

¹ https://www.atarimax.com/freenet/freenet_material/6.16and32-BitComputersSupportArea/6.ProductSummaries/showarticle.php?22
² Ibid.

Chapter 12

¹ http://www.atari.8bitchip.info/MegaSTEACSI.html and http://atari.8bitchip.info/modmste1.html
² http://www.indieretronews.com/2018/07/micro-gotek-move-over-chunky-gotek.html
³ http://atari.sk/cosmosex-3-0/
⁴ http://www.atari-forum.com/viewtopic.php?t=11153
⁵ Frédéric Sagez, "Atari ST – History of the OS," September 13, 2018. https://www.slideshare.net/fredericsagez/atari-st-history-of-the-os

Chapter 13

¹ http://joo.kie.sk/?page_id=250
² http://www.atari-forum.com/viewtopic.php?t=33944

Index

1

1.44MB floppy disks, 233
1040ST, 11, 33, 68-70, 84-85, 169, 171, 174, 180, 187-189, 207, 221, 258, 261, 268, 270, 271
1040STE, 189-191, 210, 218-219, 231-232, 246, 250, 256, 261, 267-271, 274
10th Frame, 145-146
130ST, 25
130XE, 27-28, 33, 139
1850XLD (prototype), 17
1st Word, 45-46, 63, 72-74
1st Word Plus, 72-73

2

2001: A Space Odyssey, 175
260ST, 31, 70, 261

3

3.5-inch floppy disks, 10, 16, 28, 31, 37, 59, 63, 68, 70, 84, 111, 187, 257
3-D Galax, 194
3D Studio Max, 167
3D-Calc, 76

5

5200 SuperSystem, 139
520ST, 11, 25-26, 28-29, 31-32, 34-36, 38-39, 45, 48, 63, 68-69, 72, 77, 84, 116, 174, 188, 219, 237, 259, 261, 267-268, 270-271

6

65XE, 28, 33, 139
65XEP, 187

A

A Mind Forever Voyaging, 58-59
A.N.A.L.O.G. Computing, 302
A&R Computer World, 185
Access Software, 102, 145
Accolade, 53, 101-102, 146, 171, 178, 179, 240
Acorn Archimedes, 154, 176, 224, 280
Activision, 17, 81, 106, 108, 151
Adlib, 195
Advanced Dungeons & Dragons (AD&D), 125, 178
Adventure Game Interpreter 2 (Sierra), 92
Aegis Animator, 78, 115

Aegis Development, 78
AES 3.40, 233
After Burner, 194
Afterburner, 153, 245
Afterburner 040, 245
Airball, 130-132, 252
Akai, 274
Alda, Alan, 19
Aldus PageMaker, 165-166, 193
Alesis ADAT, 274
algorithmic music composition, 163, 273
Alternate Reality: The City, 98-100
Alternate Reality: The Dungeon, 100
Amiga 1000, 20, 31, 52
Amiga 1200, 234
Amiga 500, 154, 186, 190-191
Amstrad CPC, 15
AMY, 16, 21
Anarchy, 195
Andréani, Christophe, 171, 302
Android, 45, 117, 253
Andromeda Software, 148
Another World, 77, 223-224
    Antic: The Atari Resource, 28, 42, 46, 49, 52, 55-56, 60, 63-64, 71, 75, 78, 80, 82-83, 90-91, 98, 101, 109, 114-115, 183, 185, 279
Antic Software, 52
Apple, 9, 15-16, 20, 22, 24, 33, 43, 57, 59, 69, 75, 94, 110-111, 113, 116-117, 124, 159, 165, 183, 188, 193, 204, 207, 221, 234, 246, 274, 282-283
Apple ClarisWorks, 235
Apple II, 15-16, 22, 33, 57, 59, 69, 75, 94, 116, 124, 159, 165, 204, 282
Apple IIc, 69
Apple IIGS, 33, 53
Apple LaserWriter, 113
Apple Lisa, 15, 24
Apple Macintosh, 9-10, 16, 21, 24, 26, 30, 33, 37, 40, 45-46, 53, 69, 70-72, 110, 133, 143, 162, 165, 166, 188, 190, 192-193, 208-209

Apple Mockingboard, 22
Apple PowerBook, 193
AppleTalk, 209, 219
ARAnyM, 253
Arcadia Software, 182
Architecture, ST, 21-23
Archon, 132, 196
Argonaut Software, 179
Arkanoid, 150-151, 194, 228
Arkanoid: Revenge of Doh, 151, 194
ARP, 164
artificial intelligence, 67, 132, 193
ASCI, 36, 209, 233, 256
ASCII, 46, 72, 96-97
Ashton-Tate, 73, 235
assembler, 21
assembly, 11, 24, 41, 44, 52, 57, 77, 89, 91, 171, 180, 224, 236, 238
Asteroids, 49, 53, 143, 154
Atari 400, 53, 88, 139, 175
Atari 7800, 20, 139
Atari 800, 10-11, 15-16, 35-36, 38, 41, 44-45, 47, 53-54, 59, 63, 67, 82, 86, 88, 139, 142, 165, 175, 233, 246, 268, 272
Atari Age, 166
Atari Corporation, 9, 19-21, 23-25, 34, 64, 67, 110, 139, 183, 228
Atari EST (prototype), 207-208
Atari Explorer, 47, 166
Atari Games, 13, 147, 148
Atari Gaza (prototype), 16
Atari Jaguar, 210, 227, 243, 245-246,
Atari Legend, 279
Atari Lynx, 11, 205, 246
Atari Lynx II, 205
Atari Panther (concept), 245
Atari Portfolio, 183, 228
Atari Sierra (prototype), 16
Atari ST User, 82
Atari Teenage Riot, 238
AtariAge, 107, 278
Atarian Computing, 281
AtariCrypt, 274, 279
Atari-Forum, 244, 278
Atarimania, 13, 44, 175, 278
Atarimuseum.com, 208, 220-221

AtariWorks, 235
ATASCII mode, 50
Autodesk, 167
Autodesk 3D Studio, 167

B

B.A.T., 197
B&C ComputerVisions, 49, 205, 281
Baal, 170, 198, 224
Bajarin, Tim, 32
Balance of Power, 132-133
Ballblazer, 199
Barbarian, 133-134, 224
Bard's Tale, The, 95, 123-125, 178
Batteries Included, 51-53, 74-75, 77
Battle Chess, 195-196
BattleZone, 86
BBC Micro, 15, 22, 175
Bell, Doug, 53, 59, 120
Bell, Ian, 175
Bell, John, 52
Berners-Lee, Tim, 117
Best Electronics, 265, 268, 281
Beyond the Ice Palace, 194
Bisson, Gigi, 55, 299
bit block transfer (BitBlt), 56
Bitmap Brothers, 182, 214, 224
bitmapped graphics, 51, 56, 116
Black Lamp, 194
Blitter chip, 48, 84, 112-113, 141,
    150, 188-190, 198, 205, 208, 219,
    221, 226, 232-234, 250, 252, 254,
    265, 270, 279
Blood Money, 195, 197-198
Bloom County Software, 109
Bomb Jack, 194
Bombuzal, 194
Braben, David, 53, 175-176
Brataccas, 89, 90, 134
Braun, Jeff, 217
Breakthru, 273
Breddin, Marco A., 237
Broderbund, 169
Brøderbund, 79, 180, 203, 216-217
Bubble Bobble, 153
Bubble Ghost, 171-172

Bueche, Chuck (Chuckles), 100
Buggy Boy, 194
Bulletin Board Systems (BBSes), 50,
    71, 114, 274
Bushnell, Nolan, 19
Byte, 63, 68, 84

C

C.O.L.R. Object Editor, 55-56
CAD-3D, 144, 167-168
Calamus, 165-166, 168, 209, 244
California Games, 205
Cannon Fodder, 241-242
Captain Blood, 172-174
Carebears, The (TCB), 236
Carrier Command, 174, 176
Carter Graphics SQ-44, 192
cartridge port, 36, 81, 112, 168, 192,
    197, 209, 264
Caruso, Bruce, 49
Casio CZ-101, 162
Casio CZ-5000, 142
CD-ROM drives, 64
CeBIT, 210
Centek CenTurbo II, 245
Centipede, 154
CENTscreen, 262
Chahi, Eric, 53, 77, 224
Championship Basketball Two-on-
    Two, 101
Championship Wrestling, 105
Charles, Cliff, 237
Cheifet, Stewart, 205
ChessBase, 118-119, 135
Chessmaster 2000, The, 134-135
Chop Suey, 104
Choplifter, 143, 180
Chopper X, 194
Cinematronics, 153
Cinemaware, 53, 128
Civilization, 137, 202, 239
C-Lab, 158-160, 210, 237-238, 243
C-Lab Falcons, 243
Coldfire Project, 265
ColecoVision, 16-17, 22, 154
collecting, 267-275

Colley, Nick, 116

Commodore, 9, 15-16, 18-20, 23-25, 29, 31-33, 43, 51, 59, 67, 80, 106, 124, 154-155, 158-159, 162, 182, 202, 217, 246-247, 250, 272, 279, 283

Commodore 64, 15, 18, 25, 33, 80, 106, 124, 158-159, 162, 182, 202, 217, 227, 237, 250, 272, 279

Commodore 900 (Z-8000), 18-20

Commodore Amiga, 9,-10, 13, 17, 20-21, 26, 31-32, 34, 52-53, 57, 59, 69, 77-79, 82, 110, 113, 115-116, 139, 153-154, 162, 166-167, 173, 175, 179-180, 182, 185-186, 189-191, 197-200, 205, 210, 212-217, 222, 224, 226-227, 231-232, 234, 236, 247, 264, 280, 284

Commodore GEOS, 34

Commodore PET 2001, 18

Commodore Plus/4, 23

Commodore SX-64, 23

Commodore VIC-20, 15, 18

Compaq, 207, 255

CompuServe, 47, 50

Compute!, 29, 43, 86, 102, 107, 185

Computer + Video Games, 106, 132, 150

Computer Chronicles, 32, 83, 115, 166, 205, 280

Computer Gaming World, 128, 174, 180, 185, 197, 224

computer role-playing games (CRPGs), 58, 93, 95, 97, 120, 123, 125, 178

Computer Shopper, 207

Computer-Aided Design, 10, 12, 14, 144, 167-168, 183-184, 189, 193, 210, 284

Consumer Electronics Show (CES), 19, 22, 25, 27, 29, 42, 68, 111, 187

Copland, James, 20

Copyist, The 162

CosmosEX, 260, 264

CP/M-68K, 16, 24, 26, 29

CPU, 10, 16, 19, 21, 33, 69, 88, 111, 112, 208, 232-233, 251, 273

Crane, David, 106

Cranford, Michael, 123

Crawford, Chris, 132

Crazy Cars, 241

Creator, 119-120, 158, 159, 160, 243, 282

Crystal, 24, 148, 264

Crystal Atari Browser (CAB), 264, 273

Crystal Castles, 148

Cubase, 80, 160-161, 210, 238, 243, 250, 263, 273

Cubase Audio, 243

Cubase Lite, 273

Current, Michael, 13

Cyber Paint, 115, 212

Cycling 74, 163

D

D&D, 94

Dahlman, Troy, 55

Dailly, Mike, 225

Daleks, 109-110

Dandy, 63

Das Boot, 109

Data Welt (magazine), 208

DB Master One, 48-49, 63

Dean, Roger, 133, 170

Debbie Harry, 52

Decuir, Joe, 17, 287

Defender, 128-130, 176, 194

Defender of the Crown, 128-130, 194

Degas, 51, 77, 115-116, 120, 167-168, 171, 212, 282

Degas Elite, 77-78, 115, 167-168, 171, 212

Del Nero, Jean-François, 259

Dell, 207

Delphine Software, 223

Deluxe Paint ST, 212

Demozoo, 274

Desktop publishing, 165

Diablo, 97, 123, 178

diagnostic software, 265

dialog boxes, 38, 52, 233

Digital Research, 9, 24-25, 29, 40, 42, 43, 72, 142, 291
Discovery Pack, 195
Discovery Pack Plus, 195
display upgrades, 262-263
Ditek International, 165
DMA, 22, 70, 113, 188, 191-192, 209, 219, 256, 271
Doctor Who, 110
Domurat, Jerome, 88
Double Dragon, 194
Doyle, Darren, 280
Dr. T's, 161-162
Dragon (magazine), 94, 132, 153, 178, 185
Dragon 32/64, 132
Dragon Age, 178
Dragonlance Chronicles, 178
Driving controllers, 152
Dual TOS, 261
Dungeon Master, 60, 120-123, 139, 268, 279
Dungeons & Dragons, 93, 97-98, 123-124, 178
Dunlevy, Bill, 63
Dyer, Landon, 208
DynaCADD, 167, 209, 282

E

Eclipse Software, 215, 225
Eddie Edwards Super Ski, 194
EGA, 195, 228, 239
Eidolon, The 199
Eidersoft, 104
Electric Dreams Software, 152
ElectroCop, 205
Electronic Arts (EA), 132, 135, 202, 212, 291
Eliminator, 194
Elite, 77, 175
Emagic, 159
Empire, Alec, 238
Emu, 164
EmuTOS, 251-252
emulation, 250-254
Enchanter, 58

Enduro Racer, 194
Ensoniq, 33, 162, 164
Epyx, 53, 96-97, 102, 105, 205
Epyx Handy, 205
ET4000, 263
EtherNEC, 264
Excellence in Art, 274
Exceptions, The (TEX), 236
Exxos, 261-262, 281
Exxos Store, 261, 281

F

Falcon030, 231-232, 235, 238, 243-244
Falstein, Noah, 199
Fatboy Slim, 238
Feagans, John, 24, 44
Federated Group, 154, 183
fenarinarsa, 274
Field Service Diagnostic cartridges, 265
files, 30, 38, 40, 44, 49-50, 56, 71-72, 82, 114, 117, 120, 158, 212-222, 250, 252, 256-260, 264, 273-274, 282
FireBee, 265
FirST BASIC, 194
First Row Software, 135
Flash Floppy, 258
Fleet Street Publisher, 166
Fleetwood, Mick, 84, 211
Fleischman, Mike, 52
Fletcher, Peter, 145, 281
floating-point unit (FPU), 189, 244, 253, 265
folders, 38, 71, 212, 253
Formula One Grand Prix, 240
forums, ST, 278
Fox, David, 199
Freitas, Jean-Francois, 224
Friedel, Frederic, 118
Frontier Software, 261
FTL Games, 53, 59
FujiBoink, 79
Future Crew, 236

G

Gabriel, Peter, 237
Gadgets by Small, 192-193
Galaga, 141
Galaxian, 154
Games Machine, The 174
Gamestar, 101
Garriott, Richard, 57, 60, 100, 127, 204
Gates of Zendocon, 205
Gateway 2000, 207
Gauntlet, 13, 61-63, 89, 148-150, 252, 279
GEM, 23-24
GEMBENCH, 265
GEMDOS, 24, 29-30, 252
Gemulator, 254, 294
General Instrument AY-3-8910, 22
General MIDI, 165
Geneva, 262
GEnie, 50
GeSoft Eagle, 194, 244
Get Fresh (TV show), 182
GFA BASIC, 76-77
Ghosts 'n' Goblins, 153
Gilbert, Ron, 199, 287
GLU, 22
Gods, 224
Going online, 50-51
Gold, Rich, 106-107
Golden Axe, 153
Goldrunner, 141-142, 177, 182, 216
Goldrunner II, 177, 182
GoldStar, 28
Gorlin, Dan, 180
Gotek, 257-260, 281
Gould, Irving, 18
Gran Trak 10, 152
Graphical Environment Manager (GEM), 9, 23-26, 29, 37-40, 42-44, 49, 52, 56-57, 72-77, 80, 84, 98-99, 142, 159, 166, 186, 217, 220, 233, 235, 253, 262-263
Graphical User Interface (GUI), 12, 15, 16, 24, 26, 34, 37, 41, 45-46, 73, 94, 116, 125-126, 135, 182, 190, 237

GraphicConverter (Mac), 282
Gribnif Software, 211-212, 262
GST Holdings, 45

H

Habawriter, 72
Hardball!, 101
Harris, Neil, 155
Hatari, 250-253, 255, 278
Hataroid, 253
Hayes Smartmodem, 114, 268
HDMI, 262
Heckel, Paul, 117
Heitman, Eric, 57
Helios, 193
Heroes of the Lance, 177-178, 185
Hewlett-Packard (HP), 20
Hickman, Tracy, 178
High resolution, 263, 269
HiSoft, 235
Hitachi, 28
Hotz MIDI Translator, 211
Hotz, Jimmy, 84, 211
Hubbard, Rob, 142
Hudson, Tom, 51, 144, 167-168
Huelsbeck, Chris, 228
Hunt for Red October, The 109
HxC firmware, 258-259
HxC Floppy Emulator, 257
Hybrid Arts, 144, 162
HyperCard, 117, 193

I

IBM, 15-16, 20, 22, 24, 30, 33, 40, 43, 92, 111, 113, 117, 183, 208, 231, 234, 283
IBM PCjr, 15, 22, 33, 91-92
IBM PS/2, 111
ICBMs, 85
icons, 9, 29, 35, 38-39, 52, 80, 97, 134, 173-174, 202, 212, 219, 233, 262
Ikari Warriors, 194
Imagin Systems, 246
Indiana Jones and the Last Crusade The Graphic Adventure, 199, 228

Indy 500, 152
Infocom, 12, 58-59, 91, 93, 120
Infogrames, 172, 174
InfoWorld, 20, 25, 31, 43, 65, 117
Intelligent Music M, 163
Intellivision, 22, 182
International Karate, 102, 194
Internet Archive, 265, 279
Interplay, 123, 195
Into the Vertical Blank (podcast),
  280
Iomega, 192
Irem, 153
ISD Marketing, 75, 165

J

Jaguar CD, 245
Jarre, Jean-Michel, 172-173
Jinnee 2, 262
Jobs, Steve, 20
Jones, David, 198-225
Jookie, 256-257, 260
Joust, 54-56, 147
JTS, 247
Jungen, Chris, 242
JVC, 28

K

Karate Champ, 102
Karate Kid Part II: The Computer
  Game, The, 103
Karateka, 216
Kasparov, Garry, 118-119
Kent, Jim, 78, 115, 291
K-Mart, 31
Korg, 158, 164
Koronis Rift, 138, 199

L

Lafnear, Harry, 63
LairWare, 101
Laser C, 53
Lattice, 53
Latvanen, Marko, 278
LC Technologies, 168

LDW Calc, 76
Lech, Robert, 55
Leigh, Peter (The Nostalgia Nerd),
  280
Lemmings, 89, 225
Lemmings 2
  The Tribes, 225
Lesser, Hartley, 94
Lesser, Patrick, 94
Lethal Xcess, 225-226
Lightning VME, 260
Links, 102
Linux, 166, 210, 250, 251, 253, 255
Lisp, 193
Little Computer People, 106-107
Livewire, 51
Llamasoft, 226-227
Llamatron, 226-227
Logic Audio, 243
Logic Pro X, 159, 161
Loom, 199, 228
Lorraine, 17, 20-21
Lotharek (Krawczyk, Przemyslaw),
  256, 259, 264, 268, 281
Lotus 1-2-3, 75, 273
Lotus III
  The Ultimate Challenge, 213
Lotus Symphony, 235
Lotus Turbo Challenge 2, 213
Lotus Turbo Esprit Challenge, 213
LucasArts, 53, 92, 120, 199

M

M.U.L.E., 132, 136
Mac OS X, 210
Macadam Bumper, 178
Mackenzie, James, 280
MacPaint, 47
Mad Max, 136
Madonna, 237-238
Maelstrom Games, 200
MagiC, 253, 257, 260, 262
MagiCDesk, 262
Magnavox 1CM135, 191
Magnetic Scrolls, 91
Magnum, 261

Mahjong, 108
Major Motion, 86-87, 142, 147
Maniac Mansion, 199
Marble Madness, 153, 164, 194
Mark Williams C, 53
Martens, Maarten, 279
Martin Doudoroff, 167
Martinsen, Per, 237
Master Tracks Junior, 159
Master Tracks Pro, 159-160, 273
Mastertronic, 182
Maxis, 217, 302
McClendon, Brian, 110
Mean 18, 102
Mechner, Jordan, 216
Medium resolution, 90
Medusa Computer Systems, 244
Medusa Hades, 244, 253
Medusa T40, 244
Mega STs, 11, 111-113, 166, 188-
189, 235, 268
Mega STE, 218-219, 252, 257, 260,
263, 270, 272
Megafile, 113, 192, 210, 255
Megamax, 49, 52-53, 171
Megamax C, 52-53, 171
Megaroids, 49, 53, 63
Meier, Sid, 201-202
memory upgrades, 260-261
menus, 9, 29, 38, 46, 52, 57, 71, 73,
75, 120, 137, 162, 233
Merciez, Gil, 75
Meretzky, Steve, 58
MichTron, 53, 61, 63, 76, 86, 120
Mickey (prototype), 18
Microdeal, 53, 103, 120, 130, 141,
142, 177, 179
MicroProse, 53, 108, 201-203, 239
Microsoft, 15, 24, 33, 64, 72, 74-75,
108, 186, 207, 235, 274
Excel, 75
Office, 72, 235
Windows, 15, 24, 33, 37, 38, 71,
77, 94, 108, 166, 186, 207, 211,
250, 253-255
Word, 74, 186, 274
Write, 186

MIDI, 10, 22-23, 27, 29, 34, 36, 68,
80-82, 127, 144-145, 157-164, 173,
182, 186, 188, 190, 195, 201-202,
209, 211, 221-223, 237-238, 243,
273-274
MIDI Maze, 144-145
MIDI Music bundle, 195
MIDI ports, 10, 22, 34, 68, 80, 144,
162, 164, 190, 221
MIDI sequencer, 81-82, 84, 157-162,
182, 211, 274
MIDI System Exclusive (SySex)
messages, 81, 159
Midwinter, 200
Milan Computer, 244
Mindscape, 53, 128
Miner, Jay, 16, 34
Minimoog, 164
Minnie (prototype memory
expansion), 18
MiNT, 233, 257, 260-262
Minter, Jeff, 53, 226, 227, 245
Missile Command, 153
MMU, 22, 100, 115, 253
mods (upgrading your ST), 255-265
Molyneux, Peter, 53, 202
Monitor Master, 169, 263
MonSTer, 260
Moody Blues, The 237
Moog, 164
Morris, Gareth, 263
MOS 6502, 57
Mosher, Gene, 116
Motorola, 9, 17, 21-22, 208, 231,
232, 246
Motorola 56000 DSP, 232-233, 236
Motorola 68000, 9, 16-17, 19, 21, 24,
26, 43, 52, 56, 63, 77, 91, 112, 167,
171, 188, 193, 221, 224, 245-246
68030, 208-209, 232, 234, 244, 246
68881, 189, 208
68882, 208, 232, 244, 253
MC6850, 23
MC68901, 23
mouse upgrades, 264
Mouse Master, 169, 263
Mouse Trap, 194

MS-DOS, 30, 38, 59, 76-77, 101, 127, 162, 167, 179, 182, 186, 193, 209, 211-213, 224, 226, 234, 236
MSX, 175
MultiTOS, 233, 261
Music Maker, 194
Music Production, 237
Music Studio, The (Activision) 81-82
Myst, 91

N

National Semiconductor, 21
Nebulus, 194
Nemesis Falcon System Accelerator, 245
NEOchrome, 46-48, 51, 63, 69, 78, 115-117, 120, 212, 282
NeoDesk, 211-212, 262
networking upgrades, 264
Netusbee, 264
Neubauer, Doug, 88
Newsie, 264, 273
NeXT, 210
NeXTSTEP, 210
Nicholson, Ron, 17
Nilford Labs, 162
Nintendo Entertainment System (NES), 87, 105, 139, 154, 170, 178, 205, 224, 227
Nintendo Game Boy, 205
No Second Prize, 242
Nohaj, Miroslav, 256
Noisetracker, 223
Noonan, Bruce, 45
Norton, 211
Notator Logic, 159
Nova, 263
NTSC, 84, 262

O

Obliterator, 134
Oh No! More Lemmings, 225
Oids, 143, 279
Oingo Boingo, 78
Oliver, Dan, 44
One, The (magazine), 175, 214

OpenGL, 253
OS alternatives, 261-262
Oren, Tim, 71
Organiser, 194
Origin Systems, 57, 93, 100
Out of This World, 223
Out Run, 153, 194-195, 213, 241
Overlander, 194

P

Pacific Software, 72
Pac-Mania, 194
PAL, 84, 262
Panak, Steve, 137
Papyrus, 72
Park, Xanth, 79
Parliament, 78
Pascal, 76
Passport Software, 159, 160, 238
Pawn, The 90-91, 120
PC Zone, 60
PC-Ditto, 193
Pearlman, Gregg, 98
Peck, Kevin, 126
Phantasie, 93-95, 125, 126, 139, 178
Phantasie II, 95, 125
Phantasie III: The Wrath of Nikademus, 125
Philips, 20
Pinball Factory, 179
Pinball Wizard, 178-179
Pixel Twins, The, 274
Pirates!, 164, 201-202
Planetfall, 93
PLCC socket, 112, 271
Plotkin, David, 60, 191
POKEY, 22, 99, 104
Pole Position, 240
Populous, 202, 228
Populous II: Trials of the Olympian Gods, 203
Power Pack, 12, 194, 195, 282
Powermonger, 203
PowerPhenix CT60/CT63, 244
PP driver, 257
Practical Solutions, 168, 169, 263

Predator, 194, 245
Presto, 163, 273
Price, Philip, 98
Prime Time, 135
Prince of Persia, 216, 217, 223, 228
Print Shop, The, 79, 80
PrintMaster, 79-80
Pro Tools, 161, 274
Pro-24, Steinberg, 80-81, 158, 263
processor upgrades, 262
Prolog, 193
ProTracker, 223
PS-3000, 83
Psygnosis, 53, 89, 133-134, 170, 197,
    224-225
Publishing Partner, 165, 166
Putnik, Peter, 257, 261, 279

Q

Q-Ball, 194
Quadralien, 194

R

Radio Shack TRS-80, 63, 132
Raid on Bungeling Bay, 217
Rainbird, 53, 85, 90-91, 174-176,
    179, 200
Rainbow Arts, 227
Rampage, 151, 194
Rana Rama, 194
Read-Only Memory (ROM), 11, 27,
    30, 34, 36, 38-39, 43, 63-64, 69,
    71, 80, 99, 108, 113, 188, 190, 223,
    233, 244-245, 250-252, 261-262,
    268
Reese, Andrew, 206
Rescue on Fractalus, 86, 138, 199
retrobrighting, 269-270
Retronic Design, 281
Return to Genesis, 194
Rhayader Computers, 281
Rings of Zilfin, 125-126
Road Runner, 153
Road Wars, 194
Roadwar 2000, 136, 137
Roadwar Europa, 138

Robotron: 2084, 153, 226-227
Rogue, 96-97, 279
Roland, 162, 164-165, 168
    CM-32L, 165
    D-50, 164
    DG DXY-990, 168
    JUNO-106, 164
    LAPC-1, 165
    MPU-401, 164
    MPU-IPC-T, 164
    MT-32, 162, 164-165, 228
    Roland SC-55, 165
    Sound Canvas/SCC-1, 165
role-playing games (RPGs), 56, 95,
    125-126, 137, 178, 197
Ross, Steve, 19
R-Type, 153, 194, 197
R-Type II, 153
Rugby Circle, The 55
RuneQuest, 94

S

SainT, 254
Saitek, 118
Samsung, 28
San, Jez, 53, 86, 167, 176
Savetz, Kevin, 279
SC1224, 27, 28, 31, 268
SC1425, 191
SC1435, 191, 219
SCART, 262
Scio, Ed, 132
Scott, D.F., 141
Scott, Pete, 132
SCSI, 36, 209, 218, 233, 243, 250,
    257, 260
SDM124, 28
Seconds Out, 194
Secret of Monkey Island, The 199
Sega, 12, 86, 139, 142, 153-154, 170,
    195, 198, 205, 213-214, 216, 224-
    245
    Game Gear, 205
    Genesis, 139, 154, 170, 195, 198,
        214, 216, 224, 245
    Master System, 142

Mega Drive, 195
Sensible Software, 241
Sequential Circuits, 164
    Prophet 5, 164
Seven Cities of Gold, 132
SF314, 70, 174, 180, 253, 268
SF354, 28, 31, 37, 70, 253, 267-268
SH204, 70, 112
SH205, 113
Shanghai, 108
Sharp Wizard, 234
Shields, Paul, 132
Shifter, 22, 115, 189, 208
Shivji, Shiraz, 18-23, 27, 34, 84, 154, 246
Sierra, 16, 21, 53, 56-57, 91-93, 126, 164, 296
Silent Service, 108-109
Silicon Graphics, 20
Silver & Gold, 16
SimCity, 106, 217
SIMM modules, 189, 260
Simon & Schuster Interactive, 138
Simple Sequencer, 80
Singleton, Mike, 200
Sinister Developments, 154
Slap Fight, 194
SLM804, 113, 166
SLMC804 interface, 113
SM124, 27, 31, 40, 113, 147, 188, 191, 210, 267, 269
SM125, 191
SM147, 210
SM195, 210
SMM804, 28
Software Development Kit (SDK), 52, 67
Software packs (UK), 194-195
software piracy, 31, 146, 175, 246
Software Toolworks, The, 134, 135
Sonic the Hedgehog, 228
Sony Computer Entertainment Europe, 89
Sony PlayStation, 89, 178, 245
sound upgrades (internal), 263
Space Ace, 153
Space Harrier, 153, 194

Space Invaders, 154
Space Quest: The Sarien Encounter, 92-93, 164
Space Quest II: Vohaul's Revenge, 93
Spectre GCR, 192-193, 209, 254
Spectrum 512, 115-116
Speedball II
    Brutal Deluxe, 214
spreadsheets, 75-76, 274
Sprint 2, 152
Spy Hunter, 86-87, 147
ST Action, 82, 142, 176, 182
ST Adventure Creator, 120
ST BASIC, 27, 41-42, 63, 69, 76
ST Format, 82, 160, 197-198, 200, 214
ST Karate, 104, 164
ST Writer, 43-46, 72, 74, 80, 186
STacy, 187-188, 191, 193, 195, 211, 220, 246
Star Goose!, 194
Star Raiders, 88-89, 175
Star Trek, 88, 92, 138
Star Trek: The Rebel Universe, 138
Star Wars, 85-86, 88, 92, 153, 179-180
Star Wars: The Arcade Game, 153, 180
Starglider, 85-86, 138, 167, 173-174, 176, 179-180, 194, 268
Starglider II, 179-180
Starquake, 194
StarRay, 194
STart, 30, 43, 45, 64, 71-72, 74, 79, 80, 82-84, 117, 120, 134, 162, 166, 169, 175, 185, 188, 191-192, 202, 206, 208, 210, 228, 246, 279
Staugas, Dave, 24, 47-48
ST Architecture, 21-23
STBook, 220-221
STC504, 28
Steam, 11, 97
Steem, 253, 255, 278
Steem SSE, 253, 255
Steinberg Research, 80-81, 160, 210, 238, 243, 263
StereoTek 3D Glasses, 168

STf, 69, 263
STfm, 69, 84, 262-263
ST-Log, 62, 82-83, 87, 116, 126, 137,
    141-142, 155, 206, 279
STm, 69
STM1, 31, 264
storage mods, 255-260
STOS Game Creator, 119-120, 282
STPad, 221, 222
ST upgrades (mods), 255-265
Strategic Simulations, Inc. (SSI), 53,
    93-95, 123, 125, 136-137, 177-178
Street Fighter II, 103
Strike Force Harrier, 194
Stunts, 203
Summer Olympiad, 194
Summer Pack, 194
SunDog: Frozen Legacy, 59-61, 83,
    85, 120
Super Cars, 241
Super Cycle, 195
Super Hang-on, 194
Super Huey, 195
Super Monaco GP, 154, 241
Super Nintendo (SNES), 86, 198, 245
Super Pack, 194
Super Sprint, 152, 194, 241
Supra Corporation, 53, 70, 113
SupraDrive, 71
SVGA, 263
SX212, 114, 144
SyQuest, 192
SYSINFO, 265

T

T800 processor, 193-194
Taito, 150
TaleSpin, 120
Tangerine Dream, 237
Tascam DA-88, 274
TCB Tracker, 223
Tempest, 51, 227, 245
Tempest 2000, 227, 245
Temple of Apshai Trilogy, 97-98
Teoman Irmak, 148
TeraDesk, 261

Terrific Software, 119
Test Drive, 146-147, 194
Tetris, 194
Teverbaugh, Rick, 109
Texas Instruments SN76489, 22
Texas Instruments TI-99/4A, 22
Texel (spreadsheet), 273
Thalion Software, 215, 242
Their Finest Hour: The Battle of
    Britain, 200
Thrust, 194
Thunder! The Writer's Assistant, 74
Thundercats, 194
Tilley, Graham, 89
Time Bandit, 61-63, 83, 85, 142
Timeworks, 73, 76, 166
    Desktop Publisher, 166
    SwiftCalc, 73, 76
Toad Computers Toadfile 44, 192
Torchlight, 97, 123
TOS, 37-40
TOS 1.0, 39, 100, 113, 188, 189, 251,
    252, 261
TOS 1.02, 113
TOS 1.04, 188, 251
TOS 1.6, 189, 251
TOS 1.62, 189, 251
TOS 2.05, 219
TOS 2.06, 219, 221, 252, 254, 260-
    261, 268
TOS 3, 209
TOS 4, 233, 243-244
TOS 4.00, 233
TOS 4.04, 243-244
TOS switcher, 261
Trailblazer, 194
Tramiel, Jack, 18-20, 24, 26, 29, 31,
    34, 67, 194, 231
Tramiel, Leonard, 20, 24, 30, 183,
Tramiel, Sam, 25, 67, 232
Tramiel Technology, 18-19
Transputer Workstation (ATW800),
    193
Trash, 38
Trio Engineering, 115
TRS-80 Color Computer, 132
Tseng Labs, 263

Tsikanovsky, Boris, 115

TT030, 11, 205, 207-210, 212, 218-219, 228, 232, 244, 246, 249-254, 260, 263-264, 267, 269-273, 282, 284

Tumlin, Scott, 174

Tunesmith, 162

Turrican II: The Final Fight, 227

Typhoon Thompson, 169, 180

U

Ubisoft MV16, 197

ULM, 236

Ulrich, Philippe, 172

Ultima II: The Revenge of the Enchantress, 56-57, 100, 124, 127, 227

Ultima III: Exodus, 100, 124, 127

Ultima IV: Quest of the Avatar, 93, 95, 126-128, 203-204, 228

Ultima V: Warriors of Destiny, 203-204, 228

UltraSatan, 256-260, 268-269, 271, 274, 280-281

Unison World, 79-80

USB upgrades, 264

US Gold, 148, 153-154

V

Velinsky, Ira, 23, 187, 287

Vendel, Curt, 13, 16, 208, 221

Ventura Publisher, 165-166

VGA, 102, 195, 208, 216, 228, 241, 262

VIDEL chip, 233

Video Computer System (2600), 15-17, 31, 54, 139, 145, 152, 154, 182, 278

VideoKey, 169

ViewTouch, 116-117

VIP Professional, 75-76

Virgin, 241

Virus, 176

VisiCalc, 75

VME bus, 209-210, 219, 260, 263

VT52, 50, 69

W

Walker, Dennis, 120

Walnum, Clayton, 155

Warlock, 194

Warner Communications, 19

Wasabim, 280

websites, ST, 278-280

Weis, Margaret, 178

Western Digital 1772, 23

Westwood, 125, 136

Whitehead, Dan, 200

Whittaker, David, 134, 182

Williams, 54

Williams, Roberta, 91

Wings of Death, 215, 224-226

Wings of Death 2, 225

Wipeout/Wipeout XL, 89

Wizardry (series), 93, 95, 124

Wizball, 194

Wood, Winston Douglas, 94

Word Writer ST, 73-74, 186

WordPerfect, 186

World Karate Championship, 102

WPIX, 182

Wright, Will, 107, 217

Wüllenweber, Matthias, 118

WYSIWYG, 46, 166, 235

X

XaAES, 261

XE Game System, 139, 204

Xenon, 182, 194-195, 279

Xenon 2: Megablast, 182

Xerox Palo Alto Research Center (PARC), 9

XM301, 144

Xtra-RAM, 261

Xtree, 211

X-Windows, 193

Y

Yamaha DX7, 162, 164

Yamaha YM2149, 22, 147, 180, 189, 215, 263

ymVST, 263

Yost, Gary, 52, 71, 167

Z

Zak McCracken and the Alien
   Mindbenders, 199
Zarch, 176

Zdybel, Robert, 88
Zilog Z8000, 19
Z-Machine interpreter, 59
Zoomracks II, 117
Zork (series), 58
ZX Spectrum, 15, 22, 179
Zynaps, 194

About the Author

Jamie Lendino is an editor, mixing engineer, and vintage tech enthusiast. He is the author of *Breakout: How Atari 8-Bit Computers Defined a Generation* and *Adventure: The Atari 2600 at the Dawn of Console Gaming*. Jamie has written for ExtremeTech, *PC Magazine*, *Popular Science*, *Electronic Musician*, *Consumer Reports*, *Sound and Vision*, and CNET. He has also appeared on NPR's *All Things Considered*, CNBC, WCVB Channel 5 Boston, Reuters TV, and many terrestrial radio stations across the United States. Jamie lives with his wife and daughter in Collingswood, NJ.

Printed in Great Britain
by Amazon